GOOD OWNERS, GREAT CATS

GOOD OWNERS, GREAT CATS

Brian Kilcommons
and Sarah Wilson

WARNER BOOKS

A Time Warner Company

Warner Books Inc., 1271 Avenue of the Americas, New York, NY 10020

 A Time Warner Company

Printed in the United States of America

First Printing: November 1995

10 9 8 7 6 5 4 3 2 1

LIBRARY OF CONGRESS CATALOGING-IN-PUBLICATION DATA
Kilcommons, Brian.
Good owners, great cats/Brain Kilcommons and Sarah Wilson.
    p.   cm.
Includes bibliographical references and index.
ISBN 0-446-51807-7 (hc)
1. Cats.   2. Cats—Behavior.   3. Cats—Training.
I. Wilson, Sarah 1960–   . II. Title.
SF447.K55   1995
636.8—dc20   95–10556
CIP

Book design by Kathryn Parise

To Walter and Jane

We can never say thank-you enough.

Contents

Preface 🐾

"The thing about cats as you might find,
Is that no one knows what they have in mind."
—John Ciardi,
My Cat, Mrs. Lick-a-chin

That's still true. But if anyone comes close, it's Brian Kilcommons and Sarah Wilson in this book.

From behavior to toys to feeding to air travel, the questions most human cat companions want answered are here. And if you've ever wondered about those F.R.A.P.s (Frenetic Random Activity Periods), turn to page 77.

I've read most books on cats and have shared my house with four of them over the past thirty years, and the observations, advice and humor in *Good Owners, Great Cats* echo my own experience.

If you can only buy one cat book, make it this one.

Franklin M. Loew, D.V.M.
Dean, Tufts University
School of Veterinary Medicine

Introduction

Brian's Cats

My introduction to cat society came at a farm in Pennsylvania where my family went for summer vacations. The barn cats were many, the kittens adorable. I fed the cats as I hand-milked the cows: one squirt for the bucket, one squirt for a cat. I watched mothers teaching their young to hunt, numerous females nursing and protecting all the kittens communally, and toms establishing their territories.

What amazed and shocked me as a child was seeing a newly reigning tom cat routinely kill the kittens fathered by the previous top male. Doing so brought the queens (females) into heat quicker, allowing the new tom to breed. This cycle put his genetic material into play as quickly as possible. Lions practice this same bloody behavior.

Through the years, I've learned that just about the only differences between our cats Ben and Emily and the lions on the plains of Africa are size and color. The same primitive beauty, grace, familial devotion, and predatory feline focus found in the lion graces millions of homes in miniature.

I was lucky enough to briefly work with big cats. This incredible experience taught me a great deal about our smaller domestic companions. Cats rarely betray their dignity, have unique, individual likes and dislikes, and love to interact. Interaction is what *Good Owners, Great Cats* is all about: improving and understanding the interaction between you and your cat(s) and vice versa.

Sarah's Cats

Some of my earliest memories are of cats—Mr. Cat, Thorny, Peppermint, Licorice—can you tell that children named these friends? But my soul mate was Captain. As a child, Captain always walked with me. The hours I spent in the woods in back of our Massachusetts home were hours spent with Captain. Together we

caught frogs, climbed trees, hid from my brothers—we were a team. No one had ever told us the well-established lie that cats are aloof, independent, or uncaring. Captain certainly never was.

I raised him from a tiny kitten after his mother was killed. I nursed him back to health against all odds after a nearly fatal accident. He brought me his kills, I combed out his mats. He comforted me when I was lonely, I cuddled him when he was. He was an incorruptibly fine soul, and I am the richer to have known him.

Few things bring out the passion in people like cats. Many humans adore felines as they adore no other creature. Others have no use for them, not understanding the attraction at all—but this book is not for them.

Good Owners, Great Cats is for all of us who find something special in our cats. Whether it be the wonder of looking into the eyes of a tiny lion who shares our life, or the joy of watching a kitten chase a bit of fluff across the floor. Or maybe it's the beauty of your friend stretched full length in the sun sleeping peacefully,

or the inner joy you feel when your cat jogs to meet you when he hears your keys in the door. I personally like the peace a cat curled sleeping on my lap, his head nestled close against my body, gives me and the kinship of exchanging head rubs with Emily. It is the feeling that I am a trusted and special friend, fully sanctioned to enter a private world.

There is an intimacy to cats—a club only they can invite you to join. Their souls cannot be bought for money, they are not impressed by possessions or who you know. They will choose your company over all others in the world and they will make that choice every time till the day they die. What other relationship in our lives offers us this surety, faith, and acceptance?

The reasons we all share our lives with our cats may be different, and yet somehow they are tied by a common thread. It is love that links us together: love of the animals—their grace, simplicity, honesty, beauty, devotion, affection, spontaneity, playfulness—and their love for us, for reasons known only to them, but it's all the same. It's all love.

GOOD OWNERS, GREAT CATS

1 🐾
Required Reading

Cats grace us with their affection. They are rarely angling for anything—unless it is around dinnertime. When they curl up on your lap, it's because they think you're worth spending time with. When they climb onto your shoulder, it's because they trust that you will carry them safely. When they lie across your magazine, it's because they can't believe their best friend would rather look at this flat, boring thing than their sleek, gorgeous, purring selves.

Most of this book was written with Emily curled on Sarah's lap keeping her company at the computer. At this moment, Emily hops to the floor with a parting squeak. She proceeds to drink a little water, then jumps back up on the desk. She starts grooming herself, one leg pointed skyward as she cleans her sweet, soft belly. Then she lounges back coyly with a small meow—asking for a bit of attention. When it is not forthcoming, she leaps to the printer, continues her toilette, and prepares, we are sure, to curl into the top for a well-deserved nap.

She is ever close, ever present, ever observing but she rarely intrudes. Her world is linked to ours but does not revolve around it. To share your life with a cat is to see grace of body and spirit on a daily basis, if you pay attention, if you know what to look for.

Understanding Your Cat

As usual, Emily is curled on my lap. An occasional paw gently touches my fingers as they fly across the keyboard. Her tail drapes slackly across my left arm. Her head is pressed against the inside of my right arm. Her warmth fills my lap and her purrs lull us both.

Cats have the mistaken label of being aloof—uninterested in human companionship. This is not true. They just don't worry about what you want from them.

Cats have a natural elegance, as Winny shows us here.

Anyone who has lived with a well-socialized cat who is carefully cherished knows that strong bonds can be formed between humans and felines. Cats are affectionate, playful, charming, and sweet companions. In the same breath, anyone who has ever cohabited with a cat who was not socialized with people at an early age knows that such a cat is quite content to live his life quietly separate from any human companion. That ability to adapt and thrive in very different scenarios is part of the mystery of cats.

To gain insight into this species, you first need to understand some basics about their social structure. Let's start by looking at cats as individuals. Each cat has four basic areas that he is quite aware of. You, as a human, have similar zones, so to illustrate we'll draw comparisons for you.

The first, and smallest, zone is your personal space. This space is reserved for intimates. This is the sit-right-down-next-to-you space. If you were in an empty room and some stranger came in and sat down so close he was touching you, you would think this odd. You probably would glare at him, ask him to move, or move yourself. Your cat has this same range. He allows his close friends and family into it. He'll sit on your lap fine. But many cats won't sit on a stranger's lap for a second. He'll allow his best buddy to groom him, but if a strange cat walked into the house—look out!

The next zone is his social zone. This correlates to your general friend zone. Depending on who is in the zone, he'll allow them quite close or keep a few feet distance. But he won't happily allow touching. Ben and Emily stay within this comfort zone with each other. They'll share a bowl, sleep in the same area of a room, but they are not buddies and probably never will be. Ben is up for some closeness but not Emily. She either threatens him or retreats when Ben tries to touch her. This is the zone your cat shares when he allows a guest to sit on the couch near him.

Next is his home zone. This correlates to your house and yard. This is the area he considers his and his alone. He'll chase off any intruders, patrol his property, and generally keep it private. The size of this zone varies widely depending on the cat population within the area and how much food is available. Cats can learn to tolerate close quarters with

one another, *if* there is plenty of food. Not enough food means more struggle for larger territories. Not so very different from us, are they?

The last zone, and the largest, is his neighborhood zone. This is the area he knows well, but shares with other cats. Just as you have no problem with your neighbors being in their yards, cats have little problem with the neighboring cats being in their territories. The whole group watches over the area together. They know one another, accepting one another's comings and goings, but they do not accept strangers wandering around.

Most cats live as individuals within a private, relatively spacious territory. But if there is a plentiful food supply, cats will congregate. Cats living in large numbers together form a social system—often a complex one. Within this system there are three basic levels of status.

On the top of the heap you have the king of all he surveys; the one for whom the sea parts. This is normally an intact male. He is respected by all.

The next layer are the masses. Most of the cats fall into this grouping. Their main similarity is that they all understand that the king is the king. Other than that, they are of equal status to one another.

Within this group are matriarchal family units containing mothers, daughters, aunts, nieces, all of whom work together to care for their young. Females within these groups will suckle one another's young, hunt for all, and defend one another's kittens fiercely.

Below them are the unlucky few with the "kick me" signs pasted on their backs. They are the feline version of the kids who always get beat up on the playground. These cats stay on the perimeter of the group, trying to stay out of the line of fire.

Understanding this basic feline social structure allows you to better understand your cat's behaviors. If you live with a group of cats, as many cat lovers do, you will see much of this social network in action. But understanding the larger social system is not all that helpful unless you understand the language of cats.

Feline Communication

Cats communicate using body posture, movement, voice, and scent. Their language is universal. A cat from Greece will understand a cat from Canada perfectly. Seemingly, no cat speaks with an accent.

BODY LANGUAGE

Limber, agile, muscular, flexible, athletic—all these words describe a fit cat. Cats use their bodies eloquently. Cats can be the masters of understatement. If a cat sits with his back to you, he is saying just what you think he is saying. Not now, not here, not you. If a cat lounges in front of you, he is feeling confident and relaxed. If he rolls on his back, he may be feeling relaxed, trusting, and playful. Don't count on that though. A cat on his back is also in a defensive position. Even a mellow cat may react

Sarah Wilson

Ben greets Sarah by rubbing against her legs, marking her with his scent.

with a scratch or bite if you pet his belly. It is an instinctive response for many cats.

In general, any cat who is trying to appear larger than he is by arching his back and puffing out his hair is on the defensive. Cats tend to turn sideways to the aggressor in order to appear as large as possible. He is frightened, trying to look intimidating, and will fight if pressed.

A cat attempting to appear smaller than nature intended, by lying down, lowering her head, flattening back her ears, whiskers held close to the face, fur not raised up, tail held close to the body, possibly wagging against the ground, is frightened and hoping no one notices her. She will defend herself intensely if pressed but would prefer to be left alone.

A semi-flattened, crouching cat, usually emitting a long, low growl, with tail held near to the body, prob-

ably wagging back and forth, is on the aggressive. Ears are mostly forward and up, whiskers are bristling. He is ready and able to stand his ground, so don't press him.

EYES

Eyes are indeed the window to the soul, especially with cats. Cats, not being a deceiving group, will let you know precisely what they think of you with a glance.

If a cat looks at you for a few seconds, blinks, then turns away, you have been acknowledged but not invited. Sort of the feline version of the curt nod you might make to someone on the street. Hardly an invitation to a long conversation, but not rude either.

A long, hard stare is more likely than not a threat. It has a universal meaning whether it is some stranger on the street glaring at you or a cat doing it—proceed with caution.

A cat who is your friend may make extended eye contact in a soft way, and mean nothing but nice things by it. The whole body must be read in certain situations to understand what the cat's motivation is.

The pupils of the eyes tell you much. Dilated wide, they scream fear at you. If you are not sure your cat is frightened or not, look at those pupils. Wide eyes with wide pupils means something scary is afoot. An aggressive cat's pupils may be slits, as contracted as possible.

EARS

A cat's ears are wildly more mobile than ours, cupped to catch the tiniest sound. Cats hear much more than we do. Because the ears are so visible and mobile, cats use them to communicate with one another. Some cats even have tufts of hair on the tips of their ears, which act as flags, making the language of the ear even more clear.

Ears held up may be curious, happy, playful, relaxed, but whatever they are, they are usually a positive sign. The exception to this is some aggressive cats, whose ears are up due to confidence, not friendliness.

Ears held to the side show fear, distrust, or defense, depending on the cat and the situation. If the cat is upset, respect these signs and steer clear.

Ears flattened back against the head indicate panic, aggression, full attack, and are a huge, red blinking behavioral light for you. Warning! Retreat if at all possible, or pay the consequences.

TAIL

If you can read a cat's tail, you'll know pretty much what your cat is thinking.

There is the straight-up parade tail used to display confidence and pride. Cats holding their tail like this tend to strut.

There is the bottlebrush tail of fear. Puffed up and trying to look larger than life, this tail is bravado and fear all rolled up into one. Never try to pick up a frightened cat, he won't appreciate it and neither will you.

There is the slow wag of mild annoyance. This comes from a good sleep being interrupted or an uninvited pat. Many cats want to be near you but not have you stroking them all the time. Watch for that slow wag, it's telling you—enough.

Sienna is showing classic play posture. Her tail is slightly puffed, her toes are spread wide with claws out ready to grab, ears and whiskers are forward—she's playing Queen of the Jungle very well here.

EXPRESSIONS NO ONE TELLS YOU ABOUT

WHO ME?
Captain, my beloved longhaired cat, periodically fell into the toilet. When discovered, soaking wet, he looked at me with a slow blink. "I did it on purpose," he seemed to say. Then turning slowly, he strolled away, holding his soaking tail aloft.

HOW DARE YOU?
A withering glance best describes this feline facial expression. I've seen it directed at a friend who laughed at Ben. Ben gave her a long, cold look, then turned away. He made his point quite clearly.

YOU CAN'T GET ME!
Cats love to sit just out of reach from dogs. When they do glance at the frothing canine they seem to say, "Oh, calm yourself." Then they stretch tauntingly slowly, head to a slightly sunnier spot.

Kathryn Parise

There is the fast, erect tail wag of a happy greeting that accompanies the rubbing, chirping, and purring of your welcome home.

There is the end of the tail twitch, which she'll use when staring out the window at a bird or preparing to pounce on a toy. The longer she stares, the faster the twitching until the whole tail is swinging back and forth vigorously.

SCENT GLANDS

Your cat uses scent to mark off his territory. Luckily for us, besides the urine spray, the markers are undetectable to the relatively primitive human nose.

You are probably marked daily by your cat, although you may not know it. Cats have scent glands in their lips, chin, and forehead areas. This being the case, cats mark by rubbing their lips and face against things. That blissful greeting by your cat when you walk through the front door, with him entwined in your legs rubbing and purring against you, is actually him marking you for all to smell: Mine, this person is mine, mine, mine! Which is why they do this when they see us after a long day, or when we come out of a room or in from outside. Our cats mark us with happy head rubs every morning as part of their greeting routine. We love it. Maybe our cats think we're marking them when we stroke them.

Scratching is another common way cats mark. They have scent glands in the pads of their feet and by dragging their feet over objects they effectively mark them. This is

why declawed cats will still go through the motion of scratching.

The other way cats mark, the more memorable and unpleasant way for us humans, is with their urine. Adult, unneutered male cat urine is about as bad a smell as you can get in this world. It has an amazing shelf life. You can scrub down an area thoroughly and still, on a warm humid day, that musty smell will haunt you.

Cats urine-mark by backing up to an object and spraying urine on it. Most commonly, the tail is held stiff and erect, vibrating rapidly, and the cat treads up and down with his hind feet. A few favorite places to spray are doorways, objects near windows (especially if that window gives your cat a view of a feline intruder), and new objects in the home.

PURRING

Purring is a more mysterious process than you might think. We always thought it was a sound that was made in a cat's vocal cords. Turns out it might be, or it might not be; no one has come to any real conclusions yet. And, it's generally thought that cats purr when they are content. That's true, but it's not the only time they purr. Emily purrs like a little motorboat at the vet's. She's not content there, but she purrs nonetheless. I've seen other cats purr when they must be in horrible pain. The cat that springs to mind was an automobile victim that had been struck in the head. His eyes were half-swollen shut, his jaw was wired, he could barely move, but purr he did.

Purring is like the common cold—

almost everyone has experienced it yet it is not well understood by science. But perhaps that doesn't matter; cats and owners know precisely what purring means. It is sharing moments together in quiet harmony. It is reaching out in the night for a best friend who is always there. It is a loving head butt against a life-saddened human chin. Whatever else it means, it surely is a cat's rendition of bliss.

KNEADING AND DROOLING

Kneading harks back to nursing, where the kitten kneads the mother's teats to bring down her milk. It is an extremely contented behavior, often accompanied by purring and frequently by drooling. The drooling is a Pavlovian leftover of nursing. Just like your mouth waters when you smell your favorite meal cooking, your cat's mouth waters when he goes through the motions of nursing.

Some kittens, who were separated from their mothers too early, will go as far as to nurse on you, or on a blanket or another animal. This generally harmless, if damp, behavior seems to be a comforting one. If you try to stop it, the animal's stress level will rise, causing it to comfort itself with—you guessed it—more nursing. It's best to simply allow it. Work on viewing it as sweet, adorable, charming, unique—that will make it easier on you in the long run. It's already easy for your cat, he's having a fine time.

SOUNDS

Cats vocalize for all kinds of reasons, some more than others. The Oriental breeds, like the Siamese and Abyssinian, are notorious talkers. Ben, of no visible Oriental breed heritage, is a major talker. He comments to me as he walks my way. He chats to himself as he goes about his day. He requests to go out, come in, to eat, get up, jump down, for water, and for anything else he desires. He complains about the puppy romping on him. Yet, for all his bellowing and wailing, he never harms the pup. He is a good soul, Ben.

Typical cat sounds are the greeting meow, that happy little chirp cats do when they see you come in. Ben does it as he trots across the floor to say hello. It's a happy sound.

Then there's the "I want something" meow. This is more demanding, louder and longer than the greeting chirp. Most owners hear this around mealtimes, when the cat is at the door, or a cat is shut somewhere he no longer wants to be.

The longest sound is the "I hate you" growl-scream that cats make when they are frightened or angry. It is usually directed at another cat who is an uninvited guest or a feared dog. It is an in-the-throat, tight sound, high-pitched and almost sirenlike. You'll know it when you hear it.

A wonderful cat sound is the chortle-purr that my cats give me when I wake them with a pat. The happy, high-pitched "Hi there! Glad to see you!" that is saved for only very special friends.

The rapid "keh-keh-keh" sound

HOW TO GREET A STRANGE CAT

When making friends with a strange cat, be polite. Make brief eye contact if he will. Squat down or bend over, offer out a hand, speak warmly, and wait. If he approaches you, great. Allow for him to sniff your hand if he wants to, then, reaching under his chin, give him a gentle stroke. He'll stay there if he enjoys it. He'll move closer if he wants more than that. He'll retreat if he's had enough. If you are respectful of these signals, you won't go wrong.

is one some cats make when they are looking at prey they can't have. Normally a human wouldn't hear this but if you have a window bird feeder where the cat sits and watches the birds but cannot get to them, you may get a chance to experience it. The cat will be riveted on the bird, the end of his tail will be twitching, and his jaw will move rapidly back and forth.

How to Handle a Cat

The best way to handle a cat is respectfully. If you respect your cat, you will both get along just fine. Part of respecting a cat is to pet them when they want petting and then let them alone when they want that.

When you touch them, touch them as they present themselves. Head to you, stroke the head. Rear to you, run your hand up the tail. Touch them gently. Slide your hand along with the lay of the fur. Must cats do not like rough petting.

If you are not sure what to do, allow the cat to tell you. Reach out toward the cat but do not touch him. If he stays still or retreats, leave him alone. If he reaches out and nuzzles you, run a hand along his cheek or the top of his head. If he rolls on his back—*beware*! Many cats will play the bite-and-kick game if you scratch their belly. And since *they* enjoy that game, they'll ask you to play it quite a lot. I rarely do since I don't enjoy it at all.

Many cats dislike constant strok-

ing. This is why they will purr happily along for a minute or two, then turn and bite you, seemingly out of the blue. Watch for subtle changes in your cat's body position. A wagging of the tail, a slight stiffening, can all be signs that the cat has had enough. Stroke them for less than a minute, then stop. Many cats will sit on your lap for a long time but can't tolerate the petting for more than a short time.

Don't betray your cat. Any relationship, animal or human, is based on trust. Break that trust and immeasurable things are lost. In few areas is this as clear as with a cat. Cats who have been raised with love and care, never teased or tossed, hurt or harassed are usually relaxed in your arms. They do not know that humans can cause harm. They have never experienced it and cannot imagine it.

Once they learn that hurt can happen, then all is different. Betrayal can be harassing them when they are asleep, holding too tight for too long, teasing the animal—often these acts are dressed up as human humor. People do exist who seem to think this sort of thing is funny—it isn't. The more obvious types of betrayal are hitting, throwing or in any other way hurting the cat. There is never any reason for this.

The good news is that betrayed cats can usually learn to trust again, given some time, patience, love, and an absolute cessation of all abuse. Ben is a good example of a cat who has recovered. When he first got home from the shelter, he'd tense every time we picked him up, imme-

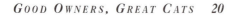

diately struggling to get down when held. He wanted to be near us, and would climb on a lap by his own power, but pick him up and he would struggle. We could feel his heart racing. Over time, though, he has come to learn that we will not harm him. He'll still tense if he is scooped up too suddenly, but then he relaxes again. He is home. He knows he is safe.

HOW TO PICK UP A CAT

Most cats have long memories and little sense of humor about being mishandled. A few are exceptions, our Spot was one. She loved the awkward attempts of children to pick her up, even if it was upside down by the haunches. If a cat can smile, Spot did so at those moments. When rescued from this by us, she would hop right down and go directly back to the child. But Spot, as we said, was an exception.

HOW TO AVOID GETTING SCRATCHED

DO *NOT* ENCOURAGE YOUR CAT TO USE HIS CLAWS
Do not play lots of pounce-on-the-hand games. This encourages aggressive play toward humans.

DO *NOT* BETRAY YOUR CAT'S TRUST
Don't turn petting into a wrestling match, and don't hit or yell at your cat—these things raise his distrust.

DO EXERCISE YOUR CAT
Cats, especially young ones, need appropriate outlets for their abundant energy and predatory urges.

DO TEACH YOUR CAT
Teaching basic behaviors and tricks not only builds communication between the two of you, increasing your bond, but also gives him the mental stimulation.

How Not to Pick Up a Cat

DON'T PICK HER UP BY THE NECK

Mother cats do carry their kittens around by the scruff but that is a tiny kitten and mainly, I am sure, because the mother does not have any thumbs and has to walk on all fours. But what is right for a tiny kitten is not correct or kind for an older animal. As the cat matures, their body gets heavier. Adult cats were never intended to be picked up that way and it is neither comfortable nor kind to do so.

DON'T PICK HER UP BY THE FRONT LEGS

As conveniently located as front legs are, they were never intended to be handles with which to hoist a cat. Picking a cat up by grabbing its front legs can injure it as well as frighten it. A frightened cat may well react poorly to this handling, which I am sure will make more of an impression on you than reading this will.

DON'T GRAB HER BY THE MIDDLE

Children are particularly prone to this type of pickup due to a combination of a large desire and small hands. But some adults will do it as well. Few cats enjoy this.

The key to picking up a cat is support. Support the whole body and you can't go too wrong. The easiest way to do this is to scoop the haunches up with one hand, and the chest, just behind the front legs, with the other. This supports the cat securely from both ends and is acceptable to most felines. A secure cat is less likely to try to free himself from a bad situation claws first.

Some cats like being held against your shoulder as if you were about to burp them like an infant. Ben likes this. This was not as good for Spot because she was a natural shoulder sitter and would inevitably attempt to climb your shoulder into her favored position. Shoulder riding is great fun but something I always do cautiously, as a quick movement can lead to claws digging in for balance. Some cats are masters of balancing without claws, but you'll have to ask your cat about that.

And lastly, some cats accept and even like being cradled in your arms like an infant. This vulnerable position is not every cat's favorite but the trusting cat will delight in it.

What Kind of Cat to Get

Here's the fun question. What kind of cat do you want? Let's start with some of the obvious criteria:

MALE OR FEMALE?

All pet cats need to be neutered. Once neutered, the differences between the two sexes lessen. Both males and females make wonderfully affectionate, devoted companions.

LONGHAIRED, SHORT-HAIRED, OR NO HAIR?

Hairless cats are their own unique selves, beautiful to those who love them. They love to cuddle and are quite a toasty nap companion because their body temperature, like that of all cats, is warmer than ours. Without the fur to insulate you from the skin, hairless cats feel like little purring hot water bottles. Of course, they don't shed and fleas find little sanctuary on a hairless cat. Often these are the perfect choice for people with allergies. These genetic creation of man's must stay under our

What's so hard about selection? All cats are perfect!

Wells Wilson

protection at all times. These are strictly indoor animals.

Longhaired cats vary. On the Persian end of things is the profuse soft coat that tangles virtually while they nap. These cats need *daily* attention to their fur. Maine Coon Cats and others like them have a harsher coat, that requires less grooming to stay beautiful. If you're considering a purebred cat, ask some breeders what will be required in the way of upkeep. If you are getting a longhaired, mixed-breed cat, expect to do daily combing, then be happy if it turns out you don't have to.

Shorthaired cats are the norm and easy animals to maintain. Brushing them is a weekly exercise except during the shedding season where you'll want to do it more often. Also, if your cat is prone to hairballs, groom more frequently. But all in all, these felines require little daily coat maintenance to live long, happy, and healthy lives.

PUREBRED OR MIXED BREED?

The majority of cat owners in this country have mixed-breed cats, and with the millions of cats who need homes every year, that is a very good thing.

Many cat owners know little about cat breeds past the Siamese and the Persian, but in fact there are many breeds with a wide variety of physical, mental, and structural features.

In general, the more of any of the Oriental breeds your cat is, the more active he is likely to be. Along with that activity comes a high intelligence, a desire to interact with you, and a penchant for getting into trouble. Expect Siamese and Siamese mixes to be pretty chatty as well.

KITTEN OR ADULT?

Kittens are adorable. They have to be, or no one would put up with their antics for the first year or so! They charm you with their big purr, right after they have knocked over the vase left to you from dear old Uncle Bob. They leap to your shoulder from the top of the draperies to nuzzle your ear. It's the best of times. It's the worst of times. It's kittenhood.

Adult cats, like a fine wine, just seem to get better with age. Dignity and decorum have, to a certain extent, caught up with curiosity and impulsiveness. They sleep a great deal, often over fifteen hours a day. They are who they are. The friendly cat you selected will no doubt be the friendly cat you live with for many years. Cats live a long time, well into their teens and occasionally into their twenties. An older cat—even one five or six or older—can give you a decade, probably more, of companionship.

COLOR?

We have had cats of all colors and are here to say that it doesn't make a bit of difference. The only thing I would stay away from is pure white cats with blue eyes, as they have a tendency to be deaf. Beyond that, fall in love with the unique personality of the cat and you will surely fall for his coloring.

There is a price to be
paid for popularity
and in the animal
world that price is
usually paid by the
animals themselves.
When a cat breed
becomes popular,
people who have no
business breeding
cats start breeding
the popular cats.
What does this mean
to you? It means that
you have to be
careful. Breeding just
for breeding's sake
can cause any
number of problems
genetically and
temperamentally. If a
purebred cat is what
you seek, look care-
fully. Take your time.
Always remember
you are purchasing a
friend who'll be with
you for close to two
decades. You are
about to invest a
serious amount of
emotion, time, and
money into this
companion; such a
friend deserves
careful consideration.

When we first got Emily, I
thought she was a rather ugly color,
what I called a faded tabby, kind of
murky and indistinct. Of course, now
that we know her and love her as we
do I see her coloring as subtle and
unique. Ah, through the eyes of love,
everyone is beautiful.

The Most Popular
Purebred Cats

Let it be said, up front, that the single most popular type of cat, by far, is
the combo-cat. The "I don't know
her history but this is the best cat in
the world" cat. Purebred cats are in a
minority, but it is still fun to see
which are the most popular and why.
It is in that spirit that this section
is written, for fun and for general
information. Maybe you'll see a bit
of one of these great breeds in your
heritage-unknown feline curled on
your lap right now.

PERSIAN AND
HIMALAYAN

Persian cats come in a wide range of
colors, including a type marked like
a Siamese, which is called a Him-
alayan. These are dream cats. Stun-
ning in full, groomed coat, elegant,
calm, dignified—many people can just
picture them lounging on their couch,
adding glamour to their lives. Well,
they do add that glamour, but they
also add hair. Lots of hair. Hair on the
cat to comb out daily and we do mean
daily. And hair everywhere else to vacuum up as you see fit.

As with other man-made animals,
Persians need your constant care and
protection. They are not outdoor animals for a variety of reasons. And
their extreme facial features, a very
short nose in particular, can lead to
health difficulties. Go carefully here.
Contact the national club and get as
much information as you can, *before*
you buy! There are many possible
pitfalls on the road to finding a wonderful, healthy Persian cat.

Known health problems in these
breeds: Chediak-Higashi syndrome (a
complex syndrome, noted for the animal's tendency to bleed and a possible
increased risk of infections), entropion
(inverted eyelids), excessive tearing,
glaucoma, tendency for FUS (feline urologic syndrome), seborrhea,
wheezing, snorting, and patellar luxation (slipping kneecaps). None of this
is the animal's fault, but rather the
fault of purebred fashions that encourage the creation of physical extremes
over and above the health and welfare
of the animals involved.

MAINE COON CAT

More active than a Persian (although
to be honest that isn't really saying
much, as most adult Persians are
pretty inactive), easy to maintain,
fewer health problems, and a charming personality have given the Maine
Coon Cat a steadily growing fan club.
They come in a wide range of colors
although tabby is the most common.
These large, sweet animals well
deserve the popularity they are
receiving.

Since this is not a breed that lends
itself to physical extremes, there is a

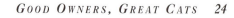

chance that their health will stay pretty good through the years, but tread warily here. Popularity has destroyed many pure breeds of animal. So far so good, but be cautious.

The health problems to keep an eye out for are patellar luxation (slipping kneecaps) and hip dysplasia—but frankly, both these problems are still pretty rare in the breed so we needn't worry about them too much.

SIAMESE

Slim, elegant, beautiful, agile, lithe—all these words and more describe the Siamese cat. Popular for many years, these are interactive animals. They tend to be talkative—a trait Siamese lovers find charming and Siamese haters rank up there with fingernails on a blackboard. This is not a breed to leave alone for long hours every day, as they will inevitably get into mischief looking for outlets for their intelligence and energy. Gregarious cats, they like the company of other animals.

The downside to these beauties is the many health problems that have come as a result of their popularity and thus of years of poor breeding done by profit-hungry people. These problems include hormone-related balding, rolling skin disease, malignant breast tumors, congenital heart defects, cross eyes, bronchial disease, mast cell tumors, esophagus problems, glaucoma, and hip dysplasia, all of which are seen more frequently in this breed than in most others.

ABYSSINIAN

When you think of Abyssinians, think active, agile, and athletic. Don't expect to watch TV by yourself, or stroll unaccompanied to the restroom if you have an Aby in your life. These cats want to be in the thick of it, no matter what. If you aren't willing or able to entertain them, then they will certainly entertain themselves. Chasing breakables across the floor, playing ankle hockey from under the bed, and generally making you notice them if you are shortsighted enough to have missed their charm in the first place.

If you want a pet to observe, this isn't the right choice. If you want a pet to interact with and who craves interaction with you, then by all means. Enjoy!

Kidney problems, eye problems, patellar luxation (slipping kneecaps), excessive licking and self-grooming can be problems.

WHAT IS PET QUALITY?

Unless you want to show your cat, pet quality is what you need. A pet-quality kitten is a healthy, happy normal cat who for one reason or another doesn't quite fit into the breeder's idea of a perfect show kitten. Maybe her coloring is a bit too dark, or her ears are a little wide apart. Who cares? Truth be told, how many of *us* would be show quality? Does that mean we aren't nice people? Loving family members? Devoted friends?

There is absolutely nothing wrong with a pet-quality kitten and tons of things that are right. Enjoy!

Cat Clubs

Cat clubs are wonderful resources of information on cat ownership in general as well as on many specific breeds of cat. Some support the beauty of the common combo-cat and others strive for the perfection of a pure-bred, while some do both; they all have lots to offer. When writing for information be sure to include a self-addressed, stamped envelope.

American Association of Cat
Enthusiasts
P.O. Box 213
Pine Brook, NJ 07058

American Cat Association
8101 Katherine Avenue
Panorama City, CA 91402

American Cat Fanciers Association
P.O. Box 203
Point Lookout, MO 65726

Canadian Cat Association
83 Kennedy Road
Unit 1806
Brampton, Ontario
Canada L6W 3P3

Cat Fanciers' Association
1805 Atlantic Avenue
P.O. Box 1005
Manasquan, NJ 08736-0805

Cat Fanciers' Federation
9509 Montgomery Road
Cincinnati, OH 45242

Happy Household Pet Cat Club
Lois Evers

P.O. Box 334
Rome, NY 13440

The International Cat Association
P.O. Box 2684
Harlingen, TX 78551

National Cat Fanciers' Association
20305 West Burt Road
Brant, MI 48164

Traditional Cat Association
1000 Pegasus Farms Lane
Alpharetta, GA 30201

Where to Get Your Cat

SHELTERS

Who says the best things in life aren't free? Or almost free? Shelters all over the country are filled with delightful cats and kittens all eagerly awaiting your caring home.

Every possible combination of age, personality, and coat length can be found. Best of all, these cats really need your love; without it most will quite literally die. Emily and Ben are both adopted and couldn't be more wonderful companions.

Selecting a cat from a shelter is a special art. First let it be said that, chances are, you will be chosen by the cat and not vice versa. Cats have strong opinions about people. Find one who likes you, that's always a good start.

Decide before you even walk through the door about the type of cat you want—consider temperament and coat maintenance. Try to stay open-minded about color. You will come to love your new cat within days of his arrival home, no matter his color.

If you want a friendly, interactive cat—then go in looking for him. Select a kitten or cat who reaches out a soft paw through the bars, makes eye contact, is close to the front of the cage, and is basically trying in every way possible to interact with you.

If you want a friendly, but not too demanding cat, look for the one sitting observing you from the middle or rear of the cage. When you approach there is no hissing, the cat doesn't crouch lower or flatten her ears. She continues to observe. Perhaps with some small talk and a polite invitation from you she will stir herself and come partway to meet you.

Either one of these cats may break into cascades of purrs when you pet them, or they may not. Although purring certainly is a good sign, I would not turn away a cat who was otherwise friendly but purrless. Some relationships take time to develop.

Sarah Wilson

Who can resist this adorable kitten. He and millions like him are available at shelters nationwide.

A bad breeder:

Tries to sell you a kitten within minutes of getting on the phone. Price comes up early in the conversation.

Downplays your concerns, sidesteps negative issues.

Always has kittens available. Will sell you one just weaned or close to it.

Doesn't require spaying or neutering in her contracts. With the massive pet over-population in this country, no good breeder wants to add to that problem.

Offers no contract, no written promises. Once your check clears they are done with you. A responsible breeder always wants her animals back if at any time for any reason you can't keep one. You won't hear that from a bad breeder.

Avoid the hissing, huddled, or hiding cats. While many of these cats can be rehabilitated and settle into a routine life, these are not as easy to own, taking the special touch of an experienced cat person to bring around. Unless you have the time, patience, and, most importantly, expertise, select from one of the many kind and gentle cats looking for a good home.

VETERINARIANS

Emily, our writing assistant, came from a local vet. She came home with all her shots, spayed and in excellent condition. Many vets that we have known will occasionally have a cat or a few kittens around for adoption.

Your vet *is not* a shelter. Do not drop off stray animals to him. He can only do so much and, as much as it may break his heart, he can't take in all the unwanted, stray animals in your town and stay afloat financially. But try as they might, many vets—due in no small part to their staff ambushing them—end up with an animal or two who needs a home. By all means, take a look.

These cats are no doubt healthy and well cared for medically. Often the animals become the mascots of the staff and are well socialized because of that. All in all, a vet is a wonderful place to find a companion cat.

GOOD BREEDERS

For purebred cats, *the* place to find a good, healthy one is at a good, experienced breeder. As with all things, there are people who do an excellent

job at what they do for all the right reasons and people who do a poor job for all the wrong reasons. How is a novice to sort out who is who?

Start by visiting the cattery if you can. It should look clean and smell clean. It will smell like cats no doubt, but like clean cats. Many of the cats will probably be in cages, but the cages should be roomy, the litter pans clean, the water bowls full. The cats should be well groomed, bright-eyed, and friendly, especially to their person. The person will be friendly, knowledgeable, and eager to help. If she doesn't have a kitten for you, she'll recommend another fine breeder who does.

A good breeder asks questions about your lifestyle and why you want this breed. Price comes up late in the conversation, if, *if*, she decides to sell you one of her kittens. She'll answer your questions honestly, telling you the good and the bad about the breed and about cat ownership in general. She'll have just a few litters a year, spending lots of time socializing and raising each litter.

A written contract that you both sign is an excellent omen. It should guarantee against certain genetic problems, with either compensation or replacement of the animal if such problems arise. It is a good sign when a person stands behind the animals she produces. A section requiring you to spay and neuter your kitten before you get his papers is also a sign of a concerned, reputable breeder.

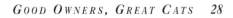

PET STORES

Don't. As cute as that one little kitten is, and they all are, you are encouraging the business of flesh peddling when you buy from a pet store. No good breeder would ever sell a kitten to a pet store to go to some stranger with a credit card. The only animal you can get from a pet store is an overpriced, poorly bred one that has been stressed, frightened, and undersocialized, who has been exposed to numerous diseases and who has an unknown genetic history. If you are a sucker for any kitten, just don't walk in! If you desperately want to save a life from a miserable caged existence, good for you! Go to a shelter and do just that. Don't perpetuate the cycle! Don't give them your business.

NEWSPAPER ADS

Every year millions of kittens are offered free for the taking in local papers around the country. This can be both a fine place to find a companion and a poor place. Deciding which is which is not difficult once you're armed with a bit of information.

Look for home-raised kittens who are in the house when you arrive to see them. Look for older kittens, at least ten weeks old, preferably older. If you have children, finding kittens raised with well-supervised children is a plus. That way the kittens will already know and like kids.

Visit with the mother cat. Her attitude is a pretty good reflection of how the kittens will turn out. The kittens themselves should be confi-dent and playful. When picked up, they should relax quickly. Frightened kittens should be skipped. Keep chanting to yourself: All kittens are cute, all kittens are cute. The next litter will be cute too! Wait for the right kitten to come along.

STRAYS

A stray is someone else's cat who has wandered into your life unannounced. This fine friend shows up on your doorstep or curled in a ball in your garage, takes one look at you, and decides you're worth the trouble.

Often these animals have been neglected, or worse, by their last owners. Or they simply wandered off and got disoriented. There are many possibilities. First thing to do is advertise that you have found a cat. When you run an ad or post a notice, do not describe every feature of the animal. If the cat is black with a white spot on his chest, say "Black cat with white markings." When people call, ask where the markings are. Make them identify the cat carefully before you return the animal to them.

Any stray should be taken to the vet for a full checkup as soon as you can get your hands on him. Also, do not always assume a cat's horrible condition is due to neglect. That can certainly be the case, but if a beloved, pampered house cat got himself lost, he could look a mess in a week or so.

FERAL CATS

There are people with the time, inclination, and just plain God-given

Ben

Most animal shelters across the country are excellent, but the shelter Ben came from was outdated. It was dark, poorly staffed, out-of-the-way, and seldom visited by the public in a struggling town where the animals weren't the only ones suffering.

The semi-toothless staff person waved a hand toward a dim room and said: Help yourself. The cages weren't all full but there were a few cats. Some traumatized adult cats, who looked me over with clear distrust, plus the usual array of kittens, whose charms could not be dimmed even by their housing.

There was an enchanting little calico youngster, an orange tabby kitten, and then, next to them, was a rather plain little tabby kitten with all his whiskers burned off. I spoke to him softly as I opened his cage door. He looked me over, slowly approached, then climbed onto my shoulder to purr in my ear. I felt certain that the flashier kittens would catch the eye of other prospective pet owners but was not sure this plain little abused boy would.

So Ben joined the family. He is our hellion. Whiling away his youth unraveling toilet paper, gutting rolls of paper towels, chasing our other cat down in mock battle, and generally keeping things lively. Ben is a born daredevil. If he were human he'd have been a stuntman or a rock climber, but as a cat, he simply is a force of nature in a house. If I were so foolish as to not put away the paper products before bed, I would open my bedroom door to drifts of white billowing out of the bathroom down the hall or find the kitchen counter cascading with two-ply paper towel, like some kind of waterfall frozen in time.

As behavioral tics go, this was an easy one—prevention and a good vacuum made it manageable. And besides having to learn to use toilet paper in various stages of disarray, it was no real inconvenience. He has since given this up as a hobby—preferring to ambush Emily, catch flies, sleep on my lap, and lounge on the kitchen chairs, one paw over the edge to torture the dogs as they go by. Life for Ben is good.

Sarah Wilson

knack for taming feral—wild—cats. But those folks aren't most folks.

Cats need to be socialized with humans very early in life if they are to accept us. A cat who was not socialized as a kitten feels about as warm and friendly toward you as you would to cuddling up to the average polar bear. Your good intentions aside, feral cats are hard to convince that your hand is for petting, not hurting.

If you are committed to taming such a cat, please read pages 193-194 for more detailed advice on how to do so.

Diane Laratta

Here's a healthy-looking, outgoing little fellow.

How to Select a Kitten or Cat

KITTENS

Ideally, a kitten has stayed with his mother and litter mates for the first three to four months of his life. He has been handled lovingly and consistently by the humans who care for him and he has been exposed to life indoors, including but not limited to the monster in the closet (the vacuum), the storm in a box (dishwasher), and the fully mobile food-dropping furless thing (your toddler).

When you go to see the kittens, look around you. The house should look and smell clean. So should the shelter, if that's where you're going.

If possible, meet the mother, as both her genetics and her personality will greatly influence your new friend.

Now to the fun part—meeting the kittens themselves.

First, simply observe quietly. Take note of the one that comes over to you to investigate and greet. Kittens who are naturally attracted to people make the best pets. Young kittens may not be as fascinated by humans as older ones are. Bring along a cat pull toy and you'll see who is active and eager. If the kittens have been properly socialized, they should be happy to be picked up, relaxing quickly in your hands. If they are stiff or panicked when you handle them, skip the litter. There are plenty of kittens in the world.

As heartstring-tugging as the shy one in the corner is, leave him in his corner. A shy kitten will usually mature into a shy adult. And unless you enjoy feeding and scooping the box for a pet you rarely see, skip him. If the whole litter seems wary, pass them all by.

Remember always that this is a commitment of close to two decades. There is no need to select less than

your dream kitten. There are literally *millions* of kittens looking for homes every year. Your ideal friend is out there. Be patient.

Any kitten that runs away, hisses, or cowers in the corner should be skipped. Any kitten that claws or bites when picked up should be skipped. Instead, choose from the many wonderful kittens that seek out your company, and enjoy being handled. Purring when handled is a wonderful sign.

Select a healthy kitten. These are pretty easy to spot. They are active, with a glossy coat, clear eyes, and no nasal discharge. They are lean, neither scrawny nor potbellied. Timing is everything when looking at kittens, as a sleepy kitten should not be mistaken for a lethargic one. Young kittens play hard and sleep hard, as do most young things.

ADULTS

Adult cats can be selected in much the same way. Before you even go to look at a cat, sit down and envision what your perfect companion would act like. Would she be active, always into mischief? Would he be dignified, gazing at you with all-knowing eyes? Would she love people, or be aloof? Get a clear idea of some of the traits you want, and you'll be better able to select accordingly. If you have a hard time imagining what exactly you want, think about the cats you have enjoyed during your life. What traits did they have?

Now you are ready. With adult cats it is easier, because to a certain extent what you see is what you get, with the exception of an in-heat female. An in-heat or pregnant female can be wildly friendly and affectionate. That doesn't mean she will be when she is spayed (because you are spaying her, right?), but it doesn't mean she won't be either.

Choose a cat who behaves as you envision your cat behaving. This is not always easy to tell, especially in a shelter situation when the cat can be frightened and disoriented, but nonetheless it is a good general rule. If you do find a cat who is friendly, playful, or relaxed in that atmosphere, then you can be sure he truly is that way. He may even be more so once he is home and relaxed.

Common Household Dangers

The old adage Curiosity Killed the Cat still applies to our feline friend today. Cats can get themselves into all kinds of dangerous situations and substances unless we take action to protect them. Luckily, with a little forethought, your home can be made safe for your friend.

CLOTHES DRYERS

Cats adore warm, cozy little spots to curl up in and snooze. Dryers are warm, cozy little spots. Keep clothes dryer doors shut. Give them a quick check before you start them as more than one happily napping cat has met an early demise when the dryer was turned on.

C. J. Puotinen

Pumpkin is adorable, but in danger, when napping in the dishwasher.

TRASH COMPACTOR

The scrapings from last night's dinner can be a powerful temptation to most any cat or kitten. Keep the compactor closed and always give a quick check before using it.

HOUSEHOLD CHEMICALS

Select your cleaning products carefully. Cats are particularly subject to household poisonings because of their careful self-cleaning. They walk across a wet floor, clean their paws, and consume whatever you cleaned the floor with.

ANTIFREEZE

Antifreeze is a terrible poison, made even more horrible by its apparently sweet, appealing taste. Even a small amount can be lethal to your cat. If you even suspect your cat may have drunk some—*run to your vet*. It is your cat's only chance. As safer antifreezes are being developed, seek them out and use them.

UNSTEADY FURNITURE

When cats leap and land on the edge of a shelf or table, they put a surprising amount of weight on it at the moment of impact. If the area is unstable, the cat will find himself in trouble. Test your furniture. Press on the edge of it; if it wobbles, fix it. Other unsteady hazards include books and magazines resting so they hang over the edge of a table. The cat, thinking it is stable, leaps up onto those edges and it all tumbles down. Filing cabinets, with the drawers pulled out, can barely be balanced. A cat landing on the drawer

could well topple the whole thing over with disastrous results.

TOILET BOWL CLEANERS

Toilet bowl cleaners that hang in the tank are extremely dangerous to animals. We would never use one, a permanently sparkling bowl is hardly worth a seriously ill cat. Instead, we clean the bowl the old-fashioned way, with a brush, some cleaner, and a little elbow grease. Afterward, we keep the lid closed for the first two or three flushes, so we can be sure that the chemical is washed away.

WINDOWS AND BALCONIES

People seem to think that because cats land on their feet that they have some wonderful inborn sense of caution about heights. Wrong! Every year thousands of cats plunge to serious injury or death out of open windows and off balconies. Sure, they land on their feet, but from nineteen stories up, it doesn't help much.

Get good, solid screens for your windows. Even a tiny unscreened opening can pose a hazard for a curious and strong-minded cat.

Do not allow your cat on the balcony at any time. Predatory urges will override the dangers of height. A butterfly or bird will entice many cats to leap, with heartbreaking results. Supervision doesn't matter much when a disaster can happen in a second. Avoid any situation where a single moment of misjudgment can end your cat's life. Get him a safe, indoor

Sarah Wilson

Cats and cars don't mix.

window perch and tell him how much better an idea that is.

FIREPLACES

A snug-fitting fireplace screen is something you'll want to get if you have a new cat or kitten for a variety of reasons. First off, a properly motivated cat, normally one in a high state of panic, can and has climbed up into a chimney. Murphy's Law dictates that this will be a white cat and/or that you will have a white couch near the area that the cat will immediately retreat to when it comes down.

Second, ashes make a lovely litter box alternative. This makes for a novel sensory experience next time you start a fire.

Third, warm ashes can seem like an attractive place to curl up, leading to sore feet or worse.

Last, flames are fascinating to more than a few cats. Protection from all open flames is mandatory.

AUTOMOBILE ENGINES

In the rain or on a cold day, the inside of an automobile engine is a cozy hideaway. If it was recently run, it is even a warm hideaway. The obvious problem is: what if someone turns on the car?

I dealt with that horror as a thirteen-year-old. My mom went to the market, not realizing that she left behind on the driveway our black kitten, Snowball. Snowball had apparently been sitting on the fan belt when the car started. Tattered skin hung off her tiny body.

I remember looking out the window and seeing her. I don't remember getting the laundry basket or lifting her into it. I do remember calling people desperately trying to find someone with a car to take us to the vet.

I learned what death smelled like that day. I will never forget it. Today, I am heartless about scaring cats away from cars. If I see them under one, I toss handfuls of gravel or dirt at them, I bang the hood, I make all kinds of noise, I want them to learn to *run* when they see a human near a car. Run! It's not a pleasant thing to do, but a lot better for everyone than risking that kind of death.

MOTHBALLS

Oh, what fun these are. They roll, they make great sounds as they skitter around. They are mouth-sized.

What cat could resist their charms? Not many, and that's the problem. They are poisonous. Keep mothballs well away from your cat.

KNIVES, FOOD PROCESS-ORS, STEEL WOOL, AND OTHER DANGERS

Cats lick and eat things that taste good. Leave a knife you've just carved a roast with on the counter and your cat will likely lick the blade, possibly severely cutting his tongue. Same is true of the blades from the food processor. Leave the steel wool pad you scrubbed the roasting pan with in the sink and don't be surprised it you find it partially eaten. Rinse off knives after their use, store steel wool in a cupboard—take precautions.

BONES

Chicken, fish, pork, turkey bones—any small bone that can be easily crunched—will attract your cat. Small bones like this can splinter, causing internal problems if swallowed. Be sure to throw them away in a garbage can your cat can't get into.

STRING, THREAD, RIBBON, AND YARN

Strings make marvelous playthings when you are doing the pulling but become immediately dangerous when swallowed. This is particularly true if the thread the cat consumes has a sewing needle on the end. But needle or not, a piece of string, yarn, or

OUT PLEASE!

If you have a cat who is fascinated with a particular piece of dangerous machinery—be it an oven, a refrigerator, a trash compactor, or what have you—teach him *right now* what a bad idea that is. If he wants to hop into the oven, open the door *when it's safely turned off and cool,* allowing him in. Then shut the door and for five to ten seconds bang the outside of the door, making a real racket. Then open the door. Your cat will fly out of there like he's being chased. In all likelihood he'll never set foot in your oven again. Good. We hope so.

thread can tangle in your cat's intestines, causing pain, injury, and possibly death. When you are away put these things away. If you find a string sticking out of either end of your cat do NOT pull on it. If it is tangled up inside, pulling can cause internal injury. Instead, bundle your cat off to the vet. This is an EMERGENCY.

THUMBTACKS AND PINS

Cats love anything they can chase. Thumbtacks, particularly the kind with the plastic tops, make wonderful bat-and-pounce toys, at least to your cat. The potential danger is obvious. Keep these put away. Close your sewing box. Put away your crafts.

MEDICATIONS

Never medicate your cat with a human drug unless directed by your vet to do so. Acetaminophen found in Tylenol and several aspirin-free products can be deadly for a cat. Ibuprofen found in Advil, Nuprin, Motrin, and others is just as toxic for felines. Aspirin itself is dangerous for cats. Beware, pills can kill.

Extend this caution to prescription medications as well. Pills and tablets are a lot of fun for cats to chase, but deadly. Keep the lids on tight and store them in a secure area.

DOORS

Slamming a heavy door behind you can kill a little kitten and severely injure an adult cat. Always glance back when you shut the door and shut it with care. A kitten eagerly following his best friend on an adventure should not be injured or worse by mistake. See page 180 for instructions on stopping doorway dashers.

SOFA BED

Open and close with care. A cat curled up under the sheets or who's climbed up underneath can be hurt if the bed is flung open or slammed shut. Check the bed before closing it and give the couch seat a couple of good whomps before opening it if your cat is nowhere to be seen.

STOVE BURNERS

Electric burners can easily burn tender paws. Discouraging your cat from ever being on the stove, not allowing your cat on your counters, and using burner covers all go a long way to preventing a very painful case of hot foot. Keep kettles to the rear of the stove to prevent spilling scalding water.

DANGEROUS PLANTS

There are a surprising number of plants that are toxic to cats in one way or another. Here are a few of the more common ones: amaryllis, azalea, bird-of-paradise, cactus, Christmas rose, crown of thorns, calla lilly, caladium, clematis, common box, daffodil, dieffenbachia, dumbcane, foxglove, holly, hydrangea, iris, lily of the valley, mistletoe, morning glory, nettle, philodendron, privet, umbrella plant, wisteria, yews.

This is only a partial list. If you have reason to suspect your cat is sick from eating a plant, grab the cat and a piece of the plant and rush to the vet. Some plants are extremely toxic, others not so toxic—but let your vet decide which is which.

Holiday Hazards

Holidays, a time of family gatherings, strange human behavior, and odd events, can be a dangerous time for your cat for a wide variety of reasons. So wide, in fact, that we are devoting a separate section to them.

Let's cover one general cats and holidays comment before we go into more specific ones. Overindulgence—avoid it. Most of us can't for ourselves, but we should for our pets. That slice of birthday cake, piece of Halloween candy, leftover whipped cream at Thanksgiving may not sit well with your friend.

If the urge to share in the festivities is overwhelming, offer up a small piece of lean, unseasoned meat or a simple steamed veggie. Anything more and don't blame us for the vomit on your pillow at 2:00 A.M.

For humans, stress is an inevitable part of holidays and your cat feels it too. Even amid the hustle and bustle of holidays, try to take a few minutes here and there to spend time with a probably pretty confused feline friend. It doesn't have to be a lot of time, but a minute or two of quiet stroking and warm words goes a long way to reassuring your companion that all is well.

CHRISTMAS

Anchor that tree! Or put it up in a room that can be easily closed off from the rest of the house. We've

Kodak looks sweet curled up under the Christmas tree, but she shouldn't be left there unsupervised.

POISON HOT LINE

National Animal Poison Control Center: 800-548-2423, has an around-the-clock service. Staffed by veterinary specialists and technicians, this is a great group. A nonprofit enterprise, they do charge a fee for their service—as well they should. It costs money to run a service twenty-four hours a day, every day of the year. We are happy to pay them their small fee.

seen cats take down a fully decorated tree. What a mess! Tinsel or anything thin, long and swallowable is dangerous. Be careful about the ornament hooks, don't leave any lying around. Light cords can be fun to chew, at least apparently if you are a cat. Investing a couple of dollars in some anti-chew sprays available at virtually every pet supply store is well worth it. Spray generously on the cords before you put up the lights. (Slide newspaper under the cord when you spray, as these sprays can have an alcohol base which may damage some surfaces.) Tape the cords to the wall from the socket to the tree to avoid tempting, tangling cords. Unplugging the lights when they are not in use will also help avoid various kinds of mishaps.

Breakable ornaments are, of course, the most dangerous. The best protection is making sure the ornaments are hung securely. If they can't be knocked off easily, they won't break as often. Using small pieces of wire that you can twist onto the branches works well. Green twist ties are easy to use, blend in with the tree well, and most of us have mass quantities of these stuffed in our kitchen drawers.

Several of the traditional Christmas plants like mistletoe and holly are toxic to cats. Keep them well away from your furry friends and check the list of toxic plants for other potential dangers.

CHANUKAH

More than a few cats are fascinated with candle flames. Not only can they burn themselves but knocking over the menorah is a strong possibility. Put the menorah in a catproof room or an unreachable shelf. As an extra measure, anchor it well. Better safe than not.

HALLOWEEN

Keep him inside! Even outdoor cats should be kept in during this holiday, particularly if your companion is black. There are plenty of twisted people who consider harassing cats on this day amusing. Since the front door will be opened and closed often, set him up in a room with all his creature comforts. Then put a sign on the door saying "Don't Open!" With his food, water, litter box, and bed around him, he'll spend a quiet evening napping, instead of getting loose, being frightened by costumes, and running the risk of being a victim of cruelty.

A word of caution here: chocolate is toxic to cats. In fact, just a few ounces can kill a small cat. Keep it away from them.

FOURTH OF JULY

Another keep-him-indoors holiday. Fireworks frighten many animals and, again, people with a mean streak may find it funny to throw firecrackers at your cat. Hard to believe but happens every year. Add a radio or TV on low to his private area so the sounds can help drown out the noise from outside.

THANKSGIVING

One of my favorite cat-versus-the-holiday memories is one Thanksgiving

when my cat Licorice ate the breast out of the family turkey as it sat cooling on the counter. My mother, an unshakable sort, simply flipped the bird over and served it anyway.

Such things can happen, especially with a house full of guests opening and closing doors all the time. Before I start to cook, I set the cats up in their own room with all the necessities, put a sign on the door, and get on with the preparations. This way the cat stays safe, the meal is less hectic—which at Thanksgiving is always a blessing—and I don't have to worry about the cat running outside when Uncle Leon runs out to the car "one last time."

Do *not* give the leftover turkey carcass to your cat. The meat is a fine treat but cooked bones are brittle and can harpoon your cat's insides. When you do throw away the bones, take the trash straight outside into a covered, catproof trash can. Take no chances.

What You'll Need

BOWLS

The best bowls for food and water are stainless steel or ceramic. These are both easy to clean, dishwasher safe, and last a long time. We use stainless steel exclusively as they don't break. In our house that is always a plus.

Plastic is not a good choice. Plastic wears and as the edges get rough bacteria hide in crevices. This bacteria may irritate your cat's skin causing a rash or acne. Skip the difficulties and get another kind of bowl.

For our cats we use small bowls that hold about one cup or slightly more. These are easy to wash and handle as well as allowing me to be pretty precise about feeding amounts. A larger bowl almost always leads me to putting more in the bowl than the cat needs because the portion looks so small in the bigger bowl. The only time we use a larger bowl is for water when we have more than one cat in the house. We like to encourage drinking, so we make sure we have water available to them constantly.

Two bowls is all you need per cat, but we buy more than that so we can have a few in use while the others are being washed.

TOYS

Toys come in all shapes and sizes. Any toys that involve chasing and pouncing are pretty much universal favorites. The instinct to hunt is strong in our felines, giving them an outlet prevents problems from developing.

There are many tried and true cat toys in your house at this very moment. For a listing of these, please turn to pages 66–68.

GROOMING SUPPLIES

Depending on the type of coat your new cat has, the grooming supplies you need will vary. A comb is an excellent tool for combing out a longhaired cat. A fine toothed comb works well for removing dead hair from any length cat coat.

We use flea combs extensively with our cats with good success. A flea comb has teeth so close together that fleas get combed out as you go along. They are then deposited in a dish of soapy water where they drown, an event we do not mourn.

A coat conditioner spray is nice to have around, especially in the winter when static electricity can make grooming a pain for all concerned.

Along with the combs and brushes, speak to your vet about dental care. Many of us aren't used to thinking about dental care for our cats and dogs, yet routine preventive care makes a big difference in your cat's overall health and well-being.

NAIL CLIPPERS

A good pair of feline nail clippers and their regular use can prevent a lot of damage around your home. Large toenail clippers, especially made cat nail clippers, or small guillotine type clippers all work well. Personally, we like the small scissors type of clipper, finding them easy to use.

BITTER APPLE
FOR PLANTS

Bitter Apple is a product made to discourage chewing. Basically, it tastes bad to the cat. Being responsive to the common cat problem (actually owner problem, the behavior doesn't bother the cat at all!) of eating household plants, Bitter Apple has developed a spray that can be applied directly to the leaves. It's a good product.

ODOR NEUTRALIZER
AND STAIN REMOVER

Mistakes sometimes happen. Your cat may vomit. Or miss his box. If this happens, you want to be prepared. Nothing does the job, and we mean nothing, like a specially made pet-stain-removing product. Get some. You'll be glad you did.

VELCRO

Velcro can be bought in rolls, circles, tabs—buy whatever you need. Use it to secure vases, lamps, bookends, and other easily knock-downable items to their tables and shelves. An ounce of prevention is worth fifteen minutes of cleaning up.

FLORIST PUTTY

Used in the same way as Velcro, to attach objects to their attendant surfaces.

WINDOW PERCH

This is a luxury, but one your cat will enjoy. Most cats love to bask in the sun. Setting up a spot by a sunny window for this purpose will please most cats. There are premade perches that rest against the sill and the wall, requiring little mechanical know-how to install. As our bedroom window faces south, we just make sure the curtains are open so the sun hits our bed. Both cats congregate there, following the sun across our king-sized mattress.

CATNIP

About one half to two thirds of cats respond to catnip. The rest show no interest in it whatsoever. But if your cat is one of those who enjoy a good roll in the herb, keep a supply on hand. We have a small pouch of it in the freezer. Every few weeks we take it out and give some to our cats. Ben likes it okay, Emily is wild for it.

Catnip is a nice way for cats to relax and release some steam. We don't recommend giving it to a cat in an aggressive mood, as it can be a disinhibitor for aggression, making incidents more likely, not less. But it can be a help to some cats with aggressive tendencies caused by stress and/or boredom, if given when they are calm.

Carriers

A good cat carrier is one of the best pieces of safety equipment you can get for your cat. A cat in a carrier is a safe cat whether traveling by car, airplane, bus, taxi, or train. That being the case, getting the right carrier is an important investment in your pet's safety. Let's go over them one type at a time.

CARDBOARD

Often given out by vets or animal shelters as the trip-home container. Use them once, if you must, then get a good one. A determined cat can claw his way out of one in no time. Believe us that trying to hold a frightened cat who's half in and half out of a carrier is no fun for anyone.

SOFT-SIDED

Cute, trendy, even fashionable but not effective. Some soft-sided carriers are not self-supporting, and having a carrier collapse on the animal is scary for them. Those soft sides also do not protect you adequately from claws. And lastly, they offer the animal no protection if they tumble off a seat or something slides into or onto it. Cleaning it after a kitty accident is no fun and good luck getting your cat in!

WIRE CRATE

The last thing your frightened cat needs is to feel exposed and helpless. A frightened cat wants to hide, and the wire crates offer them no such option. Wire sides don't offer you much protection from the angry paw either.

PLASTIC-SIDED

Bingo! Here's the one and only winner! One of these will last a kitty lifetime and beyond. Sturdy, secure, protected, cozy, easy to clean—the best and only choice in our opinion. If you would like to know how to teach your cat to get into his carrier willingly, please see pages 104–106. It doesn't have to be a battle.

Scratching Posts

A scratching post is as personal a feline choice as a razor or hairbrush is for you. Cats have a wide variety of preferences, so let's go over some of the most commonly available feline favored versions. New ones are always coming out but the good ones usually have these features.

First off they are sturdy. Cats are not fans of posts that move. So a good scratching object stays put when the cat uses it. For this reason, most hang-from-the-doorknob products are not as universally accepted as sturdy floor or wall models.

Secondly, they need to be tall or long enough. If you want to know what height is best, measure one of your cat's favorite scratching spots. That's his idea of perfect so why fight it? If your pet is new, measure the height of your couch. That's usually a pretty good guess. Oh, and don't throw the post out when it starts to get tattered and shredded. Like an old pair of favorite jeans, scratching posts are just getting good when they start to look bad.

Besides height, it has to be the right material. Here are a few common coverings:

CARDBOARD

Emily loves her cardboard unit. She likes to sit on it and scratch. She's a leather, cork bulletin board, vinyl scratcher, so cardboard works pretty well for her. These little rectangles are inexpensive (especially compared to a leather chair!) and widely available through mail order and pet supply stores.

CARPET

Ben is the carpet king in our house. We have a three-story kitty condo that he loves and that's his choice for scratching. That way when he reaches up, he will often take a moment before or after a good scratch to lean back for a good, slow stretch.

SISAL

An old favorite cat post covering and one cats have been enjoying for years. My only complaint about them is that the roping is usually wrapped around horizontally and the scientific evidence points to cats preferring vertically run materials to scratch. They like to drag their claws downward, shredding the material. The more shred, the happier the cat. However, regardless of how the material runs, millions of cats have used and adored the sisal posts.

BARK/WOOD

Many cats, not surprisingly, love bark and wood. Some cats enjoy using a piece of lumber, others like a log or branch brought in from outside. Finding a log is certainly easy, just be sure that it is not rotten or bug-laden when you bring it in. Whichever you select, anchor it firmly to a wall or stand so that it doesn't wobble or fall.

Litter Boxes and Cat Litter

Here are the most important items for your continued happy relationship with your feline friend. If this equipment is to his liking, all will go smoothly. If it is not, watch for the wet spots!

LITTER BOXES

Boxes range in size and depth. Generally, the larger the box the better, especially if you have a male kitten. You'd be surprised how big he may grow to be, so plan accordingly.

With cat litter boxes there are two basic options: covered or uncovered. Covered boxes can be a godsend to the owners of cats that spray in the box, squat on the edge while urinating or defecating outside the box, kick up a lot of litter, or have a discreet nature when nature calls. They also can help deter the feline-feces-finding Fido.

Covered boxes are bad in only two circumstances. One, if out of sight is out of mind for you. We've seen more covered boxes than we care to remember piled so high with excrement that we could not imagine where the cat stepped when it entered the box. The other is if your cat won't use it. We have seen a couple of very high sided boxes with doors cut in the front. These look great for cats and their owners who would benefit from a covered box but where the feline declines to use it. Such items are advertised in most cat magazines, which are listed in the Bibliography and Resources Section.

If your cat squats to urinate, doesn't kick litter everywhere, and is not shy about using the box, then you probably don't need a covered one. The choice is completely up to you and your cat.

CAT LITTER

It seems that every year new litter box products come on the market. Which one, of the many, is right for your cat? Mostly, that is up to your cat. If he uses it, it's the right one. Here for your information are some of the pluses and minuses of some of the litters available.

CLAY

An age-old favorite, normally easy to find, relatively inexpensive, and widely acceptable to cats, these are fine products. On the downside, it is heavy and some brands also have a tendency to be dusty, which is not good for your cat.

Without getting into too much detail, let it be said that clays do differ from area to area and brand to brand so if you and your cat really like one, stick to it. Don't assume all clay litters are the same.

CLUMPING LITTERS

These are touted as making litter box maintenance a breeze. We are told the cat's urine will form a scoopable ball that's easy to lift right out of the box and dispose of. No urine, no odor, no need to change the litter weekly.

We used this litter—briefly. Our neutered male, Ben, had not read the

CHANGING BRANDS OF LITTER

There are two basic ways to approach this. One way is to mix a bit of the new in with the old. By changing the litters over slowly, the cat has time to adjust to the change. Praise her enthusiastically for every successful trip! Your support will help her adjust more quickly.

The other way is to set up two litter boxes side by side and see which litter your cat prefers. If there are no pressing reasons to change litters, let the cat decide.

It may not be a bad idea to confine your cat in her room for a few days if you see any resistance to using the new product. That way mistakes will be limited.

Happy scooping!

directions on the package. When he urinated, he flooded a corner of the box, making not one lovely little ball but a urine mass that broke up when we tried to scoop it out. If our timing was off, the lumps were also broken up when Emily used the box. Because these litters are extremely fine, the pieces that broke off fell through the scoop. The odor problem was lessened slightly, but we still needed to change the box regularly. And that posed our next problem. This stuff is like cement. Washing the box is a pain because you can't get it out, and then all the particles solidify in the sink. Which is difficult to handle and, we worry, none too good for our pipes. We were not impressed so we never bought it again.

In its defense, I know many cats and owners that swear by the stuff. Your choice, but either way, it isn't the discovery of the century it is touted to be.

RECYCLED PAPER, PELLETIZED CORNCOBS, WHEAT HULLS, AND WOOD SHAVINGS

All of these are biodegradable, most are flushable in reasonable amounts, lightweight, and absorbent—not bad.

Many of these have a pleasant odor to them. Some are more easily tossed around by a digging cat. All have their pluses and minuses.

OTHER CAT BOX ACCESSORIES

LINERS

Great idea! Certainly a go for owners of declawed cats, but our cats tore holes in them as they dug to cover their leavings. Maybe yours won't. Certainly worth a try.

CAT BOX DEODORANTS

In short, if your cat's box stinks— clean it. Deodorants give folks the impression that if they just sprinkle some of this in there everything is okay. Not true. Skip this product, just do the work.

LITTER SCOOPS

Love them. Wouldn't have a cat without one or more. We get the biggest one we can find and keep it right next to the box. Makes our life simple and keeps the cat box clean.

When I was working in the pet supply store once, a nice, older Spanish-speaking woman came in. She went around the store obviously looking for something, spied the scoop and started asking me all kinds of questions in Spanish. Unfortunately, I don't understand Spanish. So after a few minutes of mutual frustration, I called a friend who was fluent and handed the customer the phone. She spoke for a few moments, made a few surprised sounds, nodded, handed back the phone and left. When I picked up the phone, my friend was still laughing. Turns out the woman was looking for a pasta spoon and had mistaken the litter box scoops for them.

Only in New York.

Frequently Asked Questions

Do cats always land on their feet?

Not always, but a lot more than you or I would. Cats have a wonderful sense of balance. A survival feature no doubt that nature selected for in this naturally climbing species. But how do they do it?

Cats land on their feet due to a tiny chamber inside their ear that communicates the animal's head position to the brain very precisely. This allows the cat to always know where its head is in relationship to the ground. Once his head is right side up, his body naturally follows.

I've heard that cats had something to do with the Black Plague. Is this true?

Absolutely. During that period, cats were persecuted as being the animal sign of the devil. Believing that, people hunted down and killed cats in great numbers—mostly drowning them or burning them alive. As the feline population diminished, rodents enjoyed a boom in numbers seldom seen before or since. With those furry hordes came uncountable fleas that carried the plague with them. When those fleas infested homes throughout Europe, much of the European population died a slow, grisly death.

Feline retribution, perhaps?

My friend says there is a breed of cat with short legs like a Dachshund. Is that true?

It's true. They are called the Munchkin cat. A genetic mutation started this breed, as it has many others. It is a controversial cat, as some people argue that encouraging what they consider to be deformity will lead to health problems down the road. Others argue that uniqueness is not necessarily a bad thing. Our thought on the matter is that the further away an animal is from what nature intended it to be, the more health problems you are likely to run into.

My Persian seems to breathe funny, almost like snoring. Is that normal?

Normal for a cat, or normal for a Persian? Because of their shortened nose, some Persians do have breathing problems. If you have concerns, ask your vet about it.

My last cat never scratched anything, but my new kitten is climbing all over. Is he just a bad kitten?

Your kitten is a normal, healthy, red-blooded kitten. Sometimes as an older cat matures, it is hard to remember the antics they went through as a kitten. In rare instances, kittens aren't particularly active but that would cause me to run to the vet. A well-behaved kitten is not the norm and if you actually had one, don't ever expect to have one again. Your new kitten isn't bad. He's just normal: needing supervision, directed play, and confinement. Age will mellow him. It mellows all of us.

My cat lies down on every book I read, how can I stop this? It's cute but makes it hard to get through a chapter.

Cat joke. Be consistent and firm about removing your cat and he'll get the idea. If he's persistent about it,

Next time your spouse complains about all the animals you have, show him this!

use a quick blast from a can of pressurized air. That will work without disturbing the quiet of the moment.

My kitten likes to chase flies, is this okay?

In general, fly chasing is a natural and harmless occupation even if your kitten is successful in his efforts. The only time we would curtail this is if we had just sprayed with some sort of heavy-duty pesticide that we didn't want our kitten consuming in even small amounts. However, we don't use such toxic chemicals around our house and can't imagine using a household chemical so toxic that a fly's amount could hurt the kitten. That would be some pretty scary stuff. In that case, surely the cure is worse than the disease! Nonetheless, we state it here for the record: read all warnings on pesticides and herbicide products before you use them.

Why does my cat seem to gravitate to my friends who least like cats?

A classic question, a classic cat behavior. Even aloof cats seem to relish the entrapment of felinephobes. If the poor person is allergic, the cat is likely to be particularly persistent. Why? We believe it is because cats have a twisted sense of humor.

Why is my cat's tongue rough?

Your cat's rough-surfaced tongue has many useful purposes. Since cats are self-cleaning creatures, a rough tongue gives them a built-in miniature scrub brush for working on stubborn dirt. It also is an excellent loose hair remover—a mixed blessing for your cat. It helps get the dead hair out of the coat, but then the cat may swallow a large amount of it and develop a hairball.

Drinking is facilitated by that tongue as well, as those bumps are like hundreds of tiny little cups that help bring water into the cat.

And lastly, but certainly not of least importance for wild felines, that rough surface helps them lick the last morsel of flesh off large bones. *Don't* give your cat bones please, but for the wild cat it serves that function. Pretty amazing bit of physiology, huh?

2 🐾
Kittenhood

Kittens are a riot. Charming, mischievous, active, adorable, occasionally painful, purring imps who rule your household with an iron paw. They arrive knowing only kitten things. Important things like food—on a plate or in their dish—is for eating. Vertical things, including pant legs, are for climbing. Most everything is for chasing. Your ankles are for ambushing. And you—you are their best friend, most comfortable sleeping spot, ever-vigilant protector, regular supplier of meals, best playmate, and favorite scent post.

The antics that irritated you ten minutes ago really don't matter when you have a tiny ball of warmth curled against your neck, purring a huge purr. Or when the kneading on your leg with tiny pinpoint claws becomes delightfully painful. Or when you

hear the tiny mews of a temporarily lost friend who is looking for her one and only person. Things such as these make all the chasing after, shooing off of, reaching under, and cleaning up behind worthwhile.

Enjoying this period fully while avoiding as much chaos as possible is largely a matter of planning ahead and accepting the inevitable. Kittens explore—going into, behind, on top of under, and over anything and everything they can. They chew on plants, wiring, strings, and tassels. They are nocturnal, being prone to midnight madnesses and early-morning songfests. They want to climb everything from your shower curtain to your most expensive drapes. So, get ready! A little understanding and planning can make this possibly trying time a wonderful, fun, and safe one.

Getting Ready!

Your kitten will, we promise you, get himself into places you didn't think he possibly could. Classic kitten predicaments include: stuck behind virtually immovable bookshelves, lodged up into old-fashioned box springs, wedged atop warm car engines, and immobile behind the refrigerator. And these are only a few of the seemingly endless possibilities.

Prepare for your new arrival. Walk through the house with a kitten in mind. Block all likely spaces you can; small cardboard boxes or cardboard cut to fit the opening will do the trick. Work hard to block behind the heaviest pieces of furniture, as these are the hardest to move and the first place kittens seem to seek out. When you can't block it, put double-sided tape down or a piece of contact paper, sticky side up, to deter exploration.

Now, check all the horizontal surfaces. Remove and store any small, easy-to-play-with objects as well as the easily breakable. Lamps and other necessities can be anchored with Velcro stickers, double-sided tape, or florist's clay. Check your bookends; make sure they cannot be easily moved, and if they are, fix them so they can't be. A cascade of books could cause injury to your new little dynamo.

Toss drapes up over the rods for the first few months to take them out of range of eager climbers. A good floor-to-ceiling climbing post with shelves for sitting can easily be made the focus of your cat's climbing needs. Kittens will climb, so you might as well get them something you don't mind them romping on. Are those expensive? Some are, but not compared to new drapes.

Also, get the name of food and litter the kitten is used to from wherever he is from. Pick up a supply of both. Changing homes is stressful enough without adding the unnecessary stress of changing food or litter.

Buy some extra film for your camera. You will thank us later when your cat matures into his dignified adult self making it hard to remember him as a silly little ball of fluff. Of greater import though, a photographic record is a good idea in case the little one gets lost. In such cases, a picture really is worth more a thousand words.

Set up his room, as described on pages 52–53. Not only will having his own room make him feel safe and secure, but it will prevent bad habits from developing, which is half the battle. Ask any smoker: never starting a habit is thousands of times easier than stopping one later.

Purchase an anti-chew product from the pet supply store. These have names like Bitter Apple, Sour Grapes, Bitter Lime. Spray telephone cords and electrical cords with this stuff before the kitten even enters your home. Repeat the spraying every week or more often, as needed. Kittens adore pouncing on cords of all kinds and the sooner they learn that such things taste terrible, the safer they will be. Chewing electrical cords is a potentially deadly game for a kitten and having your phone re-

Sarah Wilson

You may sometimes feel like climbing the wall, but kittens really do!

Installing childproof latches or magnetic mechanisms to cupboards is an excellent idea, especially if you have dangerous substances stored there. Anything that you would keep away from a child should be kept away from your kitten, including cleaning products, paints, weed killers, insecticides, medications, household chemicals. Kittens and cats are more prone to being poisoned since they lick their paws and coats often. Anything they touch, they end up consuming.

Antifreeze is one of the most lethal substances around. Less toxic ones are now available; select from these. Insist your mechanic use them. Do not put your loved ones at risk.

If you are a craftsperson or do needlework—put your projects away. Don't count on a closed door to protect your kitten; doors can be left ajar. A swallowed needle is no fun for anyone. Even if your kitten comes out of your craft basket in one piece, your crafts may not. If something is important to you, protect it. Don't think about what you think a kitten *might* get into, think about what he *can* get into.

Keep dresser drawers closed. If you find one open, close it carefully. A tiny kitten who has climbed into the back of the dresser can be hurt if the drawer is slammed shut. When I was a child, my family and I rescued more than one kitten from the recesses of a bureau, where it was captive. We could hear a muffled mewing, but it took several minutes to locate the prisoner.

Install screens or storm windows in all your windows. Kittens can, will, and do tumble out of open windows

DOING THE KITTEN WALK

Don't lift up your
 toes
Keep your feet real
 low
Kinda slide them to
 and fro
Make your steps
 a little slow
And that is how it
 goes
when you're doing
the kitten
WALK!

A little silly perhaps but serious. Do the above whenever you have a tiny, fuzzy, feline underfoot being in your home.

peatedly disconnected by your feline friend is beyond annoying. Another good safety measure is nailing wires to the walls, running them through a plastic conduit, or wrapping up the excess—anything that removes the extra enticing dangling sections.

The most dangerous of all cords are the ones attached to small household appliances such as lamps, hair dryers, or the worst of all—irons. These are deadly in more ways than one, but anything heavy that is often rested on a counter or table is dangerous. If it can tumble when the cord is yanked on—be careful!

every year. Serious injury and death are common results. Prevent that now.

Ode to Confinement

If you want to keep your kitten safe when you can't supervise him, limit the potential damage to your home, and develop good habits, you will confine your kitten.

Confinement can be either in a large crate that has ample room for a bed, bowl, and a litter pan or in a bathroom. For continuous, day-to-day use I prefer a bathroom that has been kittenproofed. A bathroom is ideal, as it is normally tiled, making it both easy to clean up if the need arises and unattractive to most kittens as a toilet.

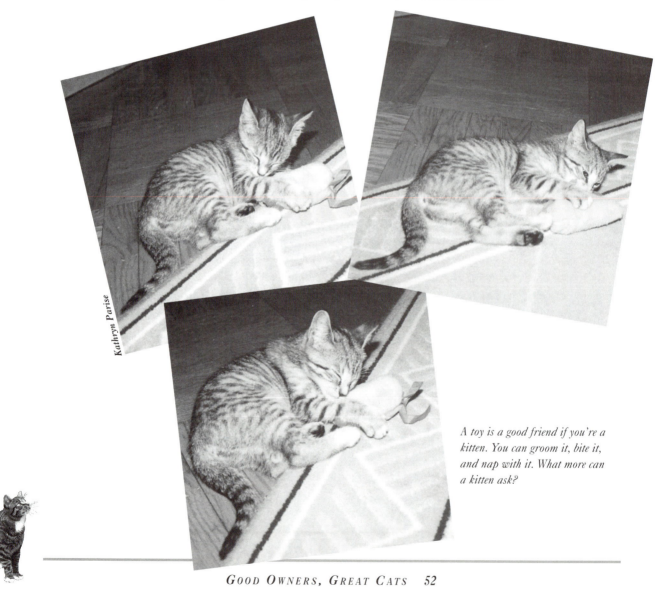

Kathryn Parise

A toy is a good friend if you're a kitten. You can groom it, bite it, and nap with it. What more can a kitten ask?

To kittenproof a bathroom you need to remove everything from every surface. Kittens will reach all those areas you think, Nah, he'll NEVER get up there. Put away soap, shampoo, razors, toothbrushes, knickknacks, plants, deodorant, cups, etc.... Roll up and store any bath mats or rugs.

Make sure that cabinet doors close tightly. If they can't be closed tightly, either install a childproof latch on the inside, tie them shut, use a hook and eye that has a tab so it can't just be pushed open—do what you must to secure those doors!

Toss the shower curtain over the rod so the kitten can't climb it. Slide shut the shower door. Close the toilet so it doesn't inadvertently become a swimming hole.

Store the toilet paper, as the kitten *will* rip that to shreds—guaranteed. We've used an inverted coffee can to cover ours, but that's hardly high fashion. There are prettier toilet paper covers available at most bed and bath departments.

Now that you have kittenproofed, it's time to make it kitten-friendly. Put the litter box in a corner, as out of the way as you can. Bowls of food and water should be put away from the box. No one likes to dine next to a toilet. The kitten's scratching post belongs next to his bed. Cats often scratch when they first wake up, so close proximity to the bed will help.

Safe toys can be left as well. Any strings, wires, ribbons should be put away, as they can be chewed into pieces and eaten, possibly harming your kitten. Toys with buttons or plastic noses or eyes—anything that can be swallowed—should not be left with your kitten. Kittens, especially solo kittens, enjoy the sheepskin toys that are made for dogs. These are big enough to wrestle with as well as curl up next to. Easy to maintain too, just toss in the wash when grubby.

A radio left on a mellow station can help keep the kitten company. Set it on the floor or secure it to the surface, for it will surely be knocked about. Be sure to spray the wires with an anti-chew pet product or use a portable. Chewing wires is a dangerous, but unfortunately favorite, kitten pastime.

The First Day

It is best to pick up your new addition in the morning, preferably at the beginning of the weekend or a vacation so you two have time to bond before you go off to work.

Keep the kitten in the carrier all the way home. You'd be amazed how quickly a frightened kitten can get out of your grasp and into trouble. Line the bottom of the carrier with a few layers of newspaper covered by an old towel. This will keep him dry if he has an accident.

If the kitten dirties a corner of the crate but can stay away from the mess, you may want to leave it. This all depends on the length of the trip, the attitude of the kitten, your experience with cats, and how much the car smells. If the kitten is obviously terrified, yowling, cowering, pupils dilated, skip cleaning up, as it will just add more stress. If the kitten seems okay, then go ahead with a quick cleanup.

WHAT YOU NEED FOR THE TRIP HOME

PLASTIC CRATE
Your kitten can interfere with your driving, climb up inside the seats, get hurt if you suddenly stop, or squirm out of a barely opened window. Keep him crated until you are safely home.

PAPER TOWELS
We always have a roll or two in the car.

ODOR NEUTRALIZER
You'll be surprised what a big stink a little kitten can make. Bring along a spray bottle of a some good, store-bought odor neutralizer.

EXTRA TOWELS AND PLASTIC BAGS
Both necessary if you have to toss out a stinky towel.

BOWL AND WATER
A cool drink on a long drive home is often welcome.

See this? Don't count on this the first few nights!

There is really little you can do to convince a frightened kitten that all is well. He has just been taken from the world he knew into a noisy, moving metal thing to a place he cannot imagine with a person he has never met. Who can blame him for being spooked? Once he knows how wonderful his new home is, he'll settle in with a purr, but don't expect that the first car ride.

For the cleanup, stop the car. None of these one-hand-on-the-wheel, one-hand-opening-the-crate routines please. We all share the roads with you. Then, keeping all the doors and windows closed—clean up. If you are alone, try to avoid removing the kitten when you clean the carrier. Kittens can get themselves into some tiny spots in your car that you never even knew you had! Whenever possible just

reach in, roll up the towel. Take it out, put in a new one, and close the door. Put the soiled towel in one of the plastic bags you brought with you. Speak quietly and be matter-of-fact, this will have a calming effect on the kitten.

Now continue on your way. When you arrive home, take him to his quiet, kittenproofed room. Set down the crate. Open the door. Get comfortable, read a magazine. Don't try to force him to come out. He'll come out soon enough. Let him set his own pace. When he does venture out, simply observe him for a few minutes as he explores. Once he gets comfortable, gently lift him up and set him in his litter box.

This is not the time for a neighborhood "Meet the New Kitty" party. Be respectful of his situation. Let him gain confidence about his new home first. In a few days, invite over a friend or two at a time. Do not allow overeager people, of any age, to pursue the kitten "just to make friends." If the kitten retreats, respect that. It is his way of saying, "Help! I'm overwhelmed." The sooner he learns that you will keep his world safe for him when it gets to be too much, the sooner he will trust you.

The First Night

Ah, the first night. It is a wonderful thing to get sleep the first night the kitten is home, but we doubt you will. Your kitten's a stranger in a strange land and is likely to play mini-insomniac or, at the very least, sing you ballads of sadness from behind a closed door.

Depending on your temperament, you can do one of two things. You can set him up in his own room, leave a radio on low in there, and tuck him in for the night. Putting a worn sweatshirt or old sweater in a small box or basket will give him a great sleeping spot. Warmth helps to induce sleep, so wrapping a towel around a hot water bottle can help the little one settle in.

The first few nights he may cry and scratch at the door. Ignore this. I know it's difficult, but if you let him out because of these shenanigans, you'll just be rewarding him for fussing. Next time he'll cry longer and harder, hoping for his freedom. The best course of action is to give him plenty of attention, playtime, and cuddling in the evening and then just calmly put him to bed. That's it.

He has everything he needs in there, he's safe, he's fine, go to bed. The sooner he understands that nighttime is sleep time, the better off you'll all be.

Or you can have him curl up with you. Nothing like curling up next to someone to make you feel like buddies. The downside to this is that your night is likely to be sleepus interruptus at best. Cats are nocturnal creatures and the mood is likely to sweep over your kitten at 3:00 A.M. to pounce on your toes, clean the inside of your ear, or play hockey with your hairbrush.

Your choice. Either way is fine.

Nine-to-Five Kittens

Kittens and cats have the reputation for being able to spend long hours alone without a problem. While it is true that they tolerate long periods of solitude, that doesn't mean it is easy or ideal for them. This is especially true for people-oriented active cats like Siamese and Abyssinians.

The reality is that kittens want and need companionship. The other reality is that you have to work to bring home the canned food. How can this be resolved?

The best solution for all concerned is for you to consider adopting or purchasing two kittens at once. They will entertain each other while you are gone, making everyone's life more stress-free. Getting two kittens from the same litter ensures that they will be especially companionable.

SOCIALIZATION

The more exposure your kitten gets to different people, the more people-oriented she will become. Invite cat-loving friends over, supply them with treats and favorite toys. Soon your kitten will thrill at the sound of a doorbell, eagerly trotting over to see who has come to visit her!

Of course, all this should always be done at your cat's speed, with the greatest respect shown to any doubts or fears. Engage her, tempt her, play with her, but do not force her, hurt her, or frighten her.

If you cannot get two kittens at this time, do not be disheartened. There are many things you can do to make your singleton companion happy.

FOOD

Kittens who spend many hours alone need regular access to food and water. We recommend leaving a dry kitten food out all day for snacking or using an automatic timed feeder available at many pet supply stores.

ENTERTAINMENT

Everyone gets bored, your cat is no exception. Set up a window perch by a busy window. Leave the TV or the radio set at low volume to a talk or classical station. Rotate his toys so he gets different ones every few days.

EXERCISE

Exercise is one of the greatest stress reducers known. Nine-to-five kittens are usually under some amount of stress. Making sure that they get at least one good play session a day can help the kitten relax and handle his time alone better. Two ten-to-fifteen-minute sessions a day, one in the morning and one in the evening, are ideal. The more aerobic the game the better. Ball chasing, toy bouncing, drag toy pouncing are all wonderful and almost as fun to watch as they seem to be to play.

QUALITY TIME

If you have a solo pet, particularly a young one, try to avoid coming home on a weekday and going right back out. This is very hard on an animal who has been basically waiting all day for you. Without taking it to an extreme, attempt to set up your social life on your day off or have friends over to your place.

A nice way to spend some time is to groom the kitten. He'll come to look forward to those few minutes spent together and so will you.

Now that's *entertainment!*

Nancy Gugh

Introduction to Other Pets

CATS

Before you introduce any new kitten to your older cats make sure all your animal's vaccinations are up to date. There are several serious, contagious diseases in the general cat population that you want to make sure your cats are protected from prior to welcoming a new feline into the family.

Before bringing your kitten home, take him directly to your vet. Have any necessary tests run and vaccines given so you can be assured the kitten is healthy. Follow the vet's recommendations, which may involve leaving the kitten overnight until the test results are back or isolating the kitten in a separate room at home for a few days. Either way, do it. It simply isn't worth the risk.

The second advantage to putting the kitten in his own room for a while is that once the health clearance is in, the cats can sniff at each other through the door. Every day, the older cats can be put in the room and the kitten can be brought out for some socialization and bonding time with you.

You can also help the process along by making them both smell similar. This can be accomplished by rubbing one with a towel, then the other, then the first again. Or rub them each down with a towel spritzed lightly with cologne/perfume or a feline flea spray. Go easy with the stuff—cats' noses are sensitive! A light spray on the towel is plenty. Any of these techniques may help the acceptance process.

You can try letting them see each other after the veterinarian gives the go-ahead. Expect some growling and hissing, that is normal. Cats have a strong sense of territory and it is the rare feline that greets a newcomer in his or her world with glee. Aloofness, puffing up, casual curiosity, hissing, growling, retreating to a higher surface, exiting the room at high speed are all normal responses. Just let them be, they'll figure it out on their own—most of the time.

Attacking, stalking, and ambushing are not to be tolerated. Do not scold your cat for this; rather, watch for signs and stop it before it starts. A book dropped, a wall slapped—any sudden noise is likely to startle your cats out of any plan of action, allowing you to separate them. Scolding the established cat for defending his turf will make him more tense, not less.

A sturdy box or wastepaper basket kept handy to carefully drop over an intently aggressive cat can save everyone involved wear and tear. Once you have the aggressor penned in, remove the intruder. To attempt to remove the agitated cat is to risk further upset and possible injury.

Whenever possible, let them work it out at their own speed. When Emily arrived she spent over a week in the linen closet. She came out for necessities but nothing else. Ben would try to say hello but she would have none of it. We just let her be. Eventually she came out and stayed out. She never hid in the linen closet again.

Another technique that fosters acceptance is to feed them in the same

Being new, Emily was not sure of Ben's intentions at first.

Sarah Wilson

room. We go strictly to wet food when we do this. We feed twice a day in a quiet room. At first, set the bowls across the room from each other. Every few days, we move the bowls a foot or two closer until, eventually, they are dining right next to each other.

As they are happily eating, warmly praise both of them. Let them know how pleased you are that they are getting along. Lavish praise and support at this juncture is always helpful.

A little feline vocal blustering during meals is okay, as long as the eating continues. That's a victory. If at any point one of the cats refuses to eat, preferring to glare at the other, calmly remove the glaring cat. Say nothing. No more food until the next feeding. At the next feeding, move the bowls back a foot or two and begin again. It is important that you don't scold the cat. Remain neutral.

You have no opinion about this, all you know is that uncooperative cats go hungry. It's quite amazing how a growling stomach can influence one's perception of dining partners.

Most cats grumble a bit, make a few faces, throw out a couple of cuss words, and then settle into a companionable peace with each other. Just let it proceed at its own rate. Love them both, but don't try to rush their friendship. It'll arrive in its own perfectly appointed time.

DOGS

Kittens and dogs frequently become the best of friends, but, as with many relationships, it may not have started out that way. All things are made easier if either the cat or the dog have lived with the other species before, but if this is the first time for both of them, fear not. It can work.

The first order of business is to protect the kitten from an overly enthusiastic or misdirected dog. All dogs should be kept on lead around kittens until you are 100 percent sure they will not cause injury. A well-trained dog is a joy to live with in general, and a much safer companion for your kitten.

Teaching your dog the "Leave it" command and a good solid "Down/Stay" (both of which are taught in detail in our dog training book, *Good Owners, Great Dogs*, Warner, 1992) are the *minimal* control commands you will need to make this work. Start training long *before* the kitten arrives. If you can't control your dog when all is quiet, you won't have a chance when a kitten enters the home.

If you don't have control over your dog, go to a local training class and get some. Even a dog with the best of intentions can harm a kitten. Dogs with a history of cat aggression or who have killed small animals need the direction of a professional trainer or behaviorist immediately! Be particularly careful if your dog is possessive of his food bowl. A small curious kitten exploring his bowl can trigger aggression. Don't wait for a disaster—take action now, get help!

To make introductions easier, make sure the kitten has clear escape routes available. Being cornered by something frightening brings out the worst in everyone. Do not attempt to hold the kitten. Let him handle the situation as he wishes.

Be sure that you praise your dog warmly for all gentleness and calm he shows—even if it is fleeting. The vast majority of dogs desperately

Brian Kilcommons

Caras and Spot were fast friends. Here they both take a nap with Sarah.

want to please you, they are just at a loss as to how to do that. By praising them, whenever you catch them doing something right you give them a clear picture of what you want. When you cannot carefully supervise the dog and kitten together, confine one or the other. In a week or so they'll have it worked out, but till then, you need to oversee the process.

BIRDS

Let's state the obvious; cats are predators. That said, some cats are more predatory than others. Until you know what your cat's abilities and interests are regarding hunting, best to keep any smaller, caged animals well out of reach.

Bird cages need to be hung well away from any shelves or tables the cat can leap from. Hang them securely so they can't be knocked down easily. A simple way to do all this is to put a large screw eye in the ceiling and then hang the cage from a cord that runs through that eye and to a hook on a wall. This makes it easy to raise and lower the cage, allowing you to hang it away from any stand or table.

To ensure your smaller pet's safety, make sure the bars of the cage are close enough together to keep your cat from sticking his paw inside. The door should latch securely so if a mishap does occur the door won't fly open.

Cats should be corrected for stalking or looking at the bird with a squirt of water from a plant mister, or a shake of the shake can. (See "Your Behavior Changing Arsenal" on pages 144–145.) Do not verbally scold or chase the cat because then the cat will link you to the correction and resist stalking the bird only in your presence. You want the cat to think looking at the bird is wrong, period, not that you disapprove. If you hide the shake can or plant sprayer behind you, and look away after you correct the kitten, he won't realize you had anything to do with this unpleasant situation.

SMALL ANIMALS

Sarah lost more than a few gerbils as well as a hamster in her youth to the intrepid Captain, a mighty hunter and the decimator of small pets. A tight-fitting, secure lid to their cage, weighted down well, is the best protection for a small vulnerable pet. Well, not *the* best, *the* best is closing the door to the room where the small pets are kept. But we humans are imperfect and, when the door inevitably gets left open, a good lid can save the day.

Booby-trapping the area around the cage with double-sided tape or some strips of inverted contact paper may well convince your cat that the whole area is off limits. Skip the inverted mousetraps, as we don't want to give your gerbils nightmares. For extra safety, make sure the cage can't be pushed off the table or bookshelf it rests on by nailing a narrow piece of wood into the shelf along the front of the cage, making a sturdy sill.

Litter Box Training

Kittens want to be clean. Given an opportunity, most kittens will happily use a litter box all the time. Your job is to give them that opportunity.

Before we discuss other details, let's cover praise. Kittens respond to positive words and touches, just as the rest of us do. Rewarding a kitten for a successful trip to the box encourages him, reinforcing the habit. Do not praise him until he is finished or he is likely to be distracted from the business at hand. Praise him in a way he enjoys. He'll let you know. If you are too loud and enthusiastic, he'll scoot away. If you are too mild, he won't seem interested. The correct type of praise for your kitten will attract him to you with a head rub and a purr.

Set the box up in an easy-to-reach but quiet spot. Too much traffic may distract or frighten a kitten, too far a hike may just not seem worth it to tiny paws. If you live in a multilevel dwelling, consider putting a box on every level for the first few months. This way your little one won't be caught short in the basement with the box on the second floor.

When setting up a box for your new kitten, make sure the sides are not so high that it is difficult for him to get into it. Kittens grow quickly and will soon be ready for an adult-size box, but if your kitten is small, start off with a cut-down cardboard box. Along with making it easy to get in the box, make sure that it is easy to get *to* the box. Keep the door to the room where the box is open at all times when the kitten is out and about.

Go easy with the litter. Tiny kittens don't need to wade around in pounds of the stuff, sinking like a little kid in soft sand. An inch or less of litter is more than adequate. The kitten will be happier; a happier kitten is a cleaner kitten.

Keep the box(es) *clean!* Nothing is more disgusting than walking into a public restroom and finding a burgeoning unflushed toilet. Your kitten feels the same way. Make it a habit to scoop the box whenever you walk past it. That will keep odors down and usage up. Consider keeping a small, lidded wastebasket lined with a plastic bag next to the box if that makes it easier. Personally, we keep the box in the bathroom and use a flushable litter. Easy for everyone.

Along with making the box accessible and clean, making other areas you don't want used as a toilet uninviting is critical.

Either clean the ashes from your fireplace or put up a good, solid screen that your kitten can't get around.

Hang any house plants you can out of reach. Large potted plants can be made unattractive as a toilet by any one of these methods: placing wire mesh over the soil area, putting in a thick layer of gravel, running double-sided tape crisscrossed on the top of the pot, or using an indoor repellent. One of these should do the trick.

Use luggage or boxes to block the space behind the couch or bookshelves or any other tight little spot a kitten might love to crawl into, look

around, and say, "Hey, no one else is using this area for anything, guess I'll poop here!"

Confining a kitten when you cannot supervise him has been discussed and is the best way we know of to prevent bad habits and encourage good ones. Cats with good habits get more freedom in the long run than cats with unwanted behaviors.

Occasionally, even with the best-made plans, a mistake will happen. As annoying as this may be to you, a kitten is a baby, so treat him accordingly: no spanking, no nose rubbing, no scolding. Such punishments only make him fear you, teaching him that you don't like it when you catch him eliminating. Often this makes a kitten shy about using the box in front of you. The logical extension of this message is, "Don't let my owner see me urinate or defecate," which forces him to start going out of sight, like, say, in your closet.

If you catch him in the act, don't say anything. Instead slap a wall or clap your hands. A loud noise will startle him, stopping him midact. Then *calmly* scoop him up, take him to the nearest box, and *gently* deposit him within. If he finishes his business in there, praise him well. If not, oh well, next time.

If frequent mistakes are occurring, shame on you! Supervise him more closely when you are home and confine him to his room when you can't keep an eye on him. Always remember—he's a baby. A litter box error is just that, an error, not a felony and not a capital crime. He'll get the hang of it soon enough. Patience and prevention are the keys.

If the problems continue, a trip to the vet many be in order. A low-grade urinary tract infection or tummy upset might be causing these mistakes. Make sure that a stool sample is checked for worms. It is nearly impossible to train any animal if they have worms.

For proper cleanup of mistakes you *must* use an odor neutralizer. These can be purchased from a pet supply store or veterinarian. Cats have a wonderfully acute sense of smell. If the area is not properly cleaned and deodorized, the kitten will be drawn back to it. Never use ammonia to clean up a pet mistake. Ammonia is in urine, which will simply draw him back to the area!

Always wipe down any area where there has been a mistake, even if you can't see or smell any residue. Our noses are quite primitive compared to a cat's, so you can't take your nose's word for it. Carpeting may well have to be soaked through and then the floor cleaned underneath. Wall-to-wall carpeting is a pain, as urine can soak through into the padding and there's no way to get to it. A professional cleaning may be called for if your kitten has had frequent mistakes in one area. Tell the cleaners ahead of time that you are dealing with cat urine. Make sure they are using an odor neutralizer in the cleaning solution.

Preventing Bad Habits

Do not encourage your kitten to do anything you don't want your adult cat to do. This makes sense, but it is all too easy to get into bad habits because of a kitten's overwhelming charm.

Here's a classic example: Lying in bed you shift your feet. Your kitten spots this movement, gets into her "I'm a leopard" pounce position, then takes a flying leap. She partially misses her mark. You laugh, shifting your feet again. She repositions herself and tries again. Pretty soon you're laughing and she's pouncing—both of you are having a great time.

What's the problem? The problem is that you just taught her to attack movement under the covers. So don't blame her when you awaken

As cute as this is, playing under-the-cover pounce games as a kitten leads to problem pounce games as an adult.

with a squeal sometime in the hazy dawn with an adult cat with adult claws and adult teeth latching on to your toe.

FEEDING

Feline blackmail is rampant worldwide. Early-morning yowling, the cat version of a gun to your head, has trained millions of owners through the ages to get up to feed that kitty! We have even spoken to some helpless humans who keep cat food in their bedside table so they can pour it out without opening their eyes.

All this can be avoided. It's simple. It's magic. It works. Don't feed your cat first thing in the morning. Instead, make it a ritual to feed him just before you leave for work. Let him associate your getting your keys with being fed. Not only will this prevent early-morning blackmail but it will give your cat a pleasant association with your leaving, which will lower any stress he may feel about being alone. Alternatively, feed mostly dry food and only give the wet food at night. Either way, you'll actually be able to get some sleep.

For those of you who are already being held hostage by your cat's internal alarm, please see pages 182–184 for instructions about how to fix this mighty annoying cat habit.

GROOMING

Teaching your cat to accept all kinds of handling is best started when he is relaxing on your lap. Stroke him gently all over. Always stroke, slowly and calmly, in the direction the hair goes.

Rapid, short, abrupt stroking aggravates most cats.

Gently handle his paws, run your hand down his tail, look in his ears, lift up his lip. The secret to this is being calm, moving slowly, speaking kindly, and stopping anytime your cat's tail starts twitching or he otherwise looks annoyed. Mix this type of handling in with his regular stroking. The point is to slowly, over a period of days or weeks, get him used to being touched everywhere. Do *not* try to get everything accomplished in one forced session. Force a cat too far, too fast and you'll have a bigger problem than when you started.

Why do this? Because you will have to clip his nails, medicate his wounds, comb his fur, and clean his ears throughout his life. If this type of handling is introduced early, in a pleasant way, he will accept it. A cat that is easy to handle is a pleasure for you and your vet and suffers less stress than one who fights the simplest procedure.

The basics of grooming need to be introduced as soon as possible. You can incorporate these exercises with your regular handling exercises.

Daily, as a part of normal petting, gently apply pressure to the toe so the claw unsheathes. Immediately let go and praise and stroke your friend. If your kitten is sensitive about his feet, then slowly start getting him used to it. Start off just stroking his legs and paws as a part of petting. When he is relaxed about this, then add in some toe touching a little at a time, mixing plenty of warm words and regular stroking into the mix. Doing this regularly will not only help your cat adjust to this handling but will train you to handle your cat all over. Once you incorporate that into your normal petting sessions, handling in general will become easy.

Along with the specific paw handling that prepares your cat for having his nails clipped, you also need to introduce brushes and combs. This is especially critical for the longhaired kitten. Your kitten may not yet have enough coat to get tangled but she will, and when she does, grooming—often daily—will be mandatory.

As you are petting your kitten, telling him how wonderful he is, pick up the brush and gently stroke him once or twice with the back of it. Then put it down, and continue hand stroking. If he does not mind the back of the brush, then use the front. Again, just one or two light strokes, then lots of praise. Your goal at this point is to get him to think of brushing as pleasant, it's not to get the whole job done at once. As soon as he accepts this without complaint, you can increase the number of strokes. But watch his tail! If he starts lashing it about, stop! He's getting annoyed. Your kitten's ears and tail will tell you all you need to know, if you pay attention.

Kittenhood is also the best time to introduce the blow-dryer to your kitten. Accepting a blow-dryer is a great convenience when the animal matures—making post-bath dry-offs and kitchen sink mishaps much more easily dealt with.

The best way to desensitize your kitten to the sound and feel of a blow-dryer is to keep the kitten in with you when you blow your own hair dry. Do not point the dryer at his face, he

It's never too early to develop good scratching habits.

won't like it. He will love it though if you give him treats throughout the episode.

Another neat trick is to bring the blow-dryer into the kitchen with you and run it when he is eating his meals. Start with the dryer across the room from him so it is not scary. As he gets used to the sounds, bring it slowly closer over a period of days or weeks. As with everything potentially frightening, go slowly. If you rush and frighten the kitten you will be worse off than when you started. Do not test the kitten to see how much you can do until he gets scared. Your goal is to always stop *before* he ever gets scared.

Basically, if you do it right, you'll feel like you are doing very little.

Once he is relaxed about being near the hair dryer, you can scoop him onto your lap and blow him gently and briefly—dryer set on low or cool only please! Just a second or two followed by calm stroking and warm words will go a long way toward relaxing him. Slowly increase the time he tolerates until he accepts the whole process without too much complaint. Now you've just made both your lives a little easier.

PLAY

Games that give your kitten an appropriate outlet for his predatory urges are the best. Ping-Pong ball chasing, rag pouncing, and such like are all excellent. The more games you teach your kitten while he's young, the fewer games he will need to make up out of boredom. Made-up games are not nearly as pleasant for you as ones you select. Made-up games usually include things like curtain climbing, ankle ambushing, and knickknack hockey.

Avoid any game that makes human flesh the target prey. Hand pouncing, finger fighting, foot wrestling are all bad. If the game could draw blood played with an adult cat, don't teach it to your kitten.

USING A
SCRATCHING POST

Have a scratching post at home before your kitten arrives. Use confinement during the early months to prevent unwanted scratching habits

from developing and to encourage the habits you want. More than one post strategically placed near likely scratching spots—like corners of couches—and any appropriate spot near your kitten's favorite sleeping area will help focus your new friend in the right direction. Most cats like vertical, sturdy scratching posts, but for every rule, there is an Emily. Our Emily likes horizontal surfaces. And, unlike Ben, who is a fabric fan, Emily likes leather, cork, cardboard, and the like. She adores her catnip-enhanced cardboard scratching box, where Ben doesn't give it a second sniff. Whatever the price of the posts, they are cheaper than reupholstering the couch!

Tried-and-True Toys

The best news about great cat toys is that so many of them cost so little! Fortunately, cats are pragmatic beasts with no desire to social-climb (why should they, they're already at the top!), so the cost of trinkets does not impress them. Not that there aren't fabulous toys available at virtually any pet supply store across the country, there are. Our only point is that cats have been having fun long before there was flashy packaging. Here are some of the old-fashioned favorites that have amused kittens and their owners down through the years.

PING-PONG BALLS

The lowly Ping-Pong ball is one of the great cat toys—lightweight, makes a great noise, moves easily. They are

hours of fun in a single package. Go to your favorite sports equipment store and buy a few boxes. You won't regret it.

PAPER BAGS

The paper, not plastic, grocery bag is another fine way to pass time. Place it open on its side and rattle the back of the bag from the outside. Rolling a ball into the bag is a great way to start the fun. When you are done, put it away so if your cat decides to take a snooze inside his new play house he won't be inadvertently stepped on.

BOXES

Cat forts, cat beds, cat perches—boxes are many things to many cats. Try turning one over and cutting a doorway in it for the cat to retreat to. Or cut two doorways and drag a thing-on-a-string toy through. This should pique your cat's interest. Or cut many doors and roll Ping-Pong balls back and forth.

LIGHT

A handheld mirror reflecting a dancing spot of light or a flashlight in a dark room can provide much amusement for both you and your cat. Cats and kittens never seem to figure out that they can't catch the light. In fact, that makes the light even more challenging for them. Give it a try!

BALLS OF ALUMINUM FOIL OR PAPER

Lightweight, interesting movement, easy to scoop up with an outstretched paw, a ball of aluminum foil has given many a cat many a happy hour. Don't play with foil that has been used in cooking or wrapping food. The idea here is for the cat to play with it, not eat it.

EMPTY SPOOLS FROM THREAD

For as long as thread has come on spools, cats have gleefully batted the empty spools around the house. Since thread can tangle in the cat's tummy, only give him a totally empty one. Other than that, enjoy. They are a great size, weight, and shape for endless hours of feline fun.

WINE CORK

Eminently chaseable, soft enough to be able to sink claws or teeth into, light enough to toss around—corks are great. If your cat is one of the few that really likes to chew things apart, supervise his use of the cork. It's unlikely he would chew off a big hunk and swallow it, but why risk it? For most cats, though, this is plain old fun.

ROLLED-UP SOCK

Roll a sock up into a ball, maybe put a little catnip inside if your cat enjoys it, and then roll it across the floor. Cats who like to pounce, bite, and carry will especially enjoy this toy. Or, for cats that need an outlet for aggres-

sion, stuff an athletic sock with a few rags, tie a rope to it, and use it as a drag toy. It's large enough for a cat to grab and kick his back claws against. Good for a rough-and-tumble cat.

STRING

Millions of cats for hundreds of years have been amused by a piece of string dragged seductively across the floor. If supervised, string chasing is a great aerobic workout and, frankly, it's just plain fun. But...

CAUTION: Never leave string or yarn around your cat unsupervised. If a hunk is chewed and swallowed, the string can tangle in your cat's intestines, killing him. So, when you are through, roll it up and put it in a

Kodak demonstrates the correct way to play with a spool and some yarn. Such games are great cat fun, but only under supervision!

DANGER! PLASTIC BAGS!

Plastic bags, especially the grocery store bags, make wonderful noises when pounced on and can billow around seductively but... *never allow your cat to play with one.* Cats can and do suffocate every year in all kinds of plastic bags. Store them safely in catproof drawers.

Wells Wilson

SPAYING AND NEUTERING

Every year millions—yes, MILLIONS—of healthy, wonderful, friendly cats and kittens are killed because there are no homes for them. Please, if you love cats, spay or neuter your kitten—as early as your vet will allow.

Neutering is now being done on kittens as young as eight weeks of age, with no ill effects, although six months is still the norm. But each veterinarian has his or her own age preferences, so do as they recommend. But do it.

Neutered cats live longer, have fewer health problems, and are just as well adjusted as intact animals.

All of our cats are neutered. Please join us in our fight against unnecessary killings. This is one problem we can all do something about.

drawer. If your kitten starts to seriously chew on it, game's over for the day. Like so many toys and tools, it's wonderful when used with a little commonsense precaution.

First Trip to the Vet

During your kitten's first trip to the vet, he'll get a thorough looking over. His ears and mouth will be looked into, his heart and lungs listened to, his coat checked, his abdomen palpated, his temperature taken.

If you can, bring a stool sample to be checked for worms. It should be fresh. If you find a new pile in the morning, wrap a small piece in a plastic bag and put it in the refrigerator. If you haven't brought the kitten home yet, just bring a sample by in the next couple of days. Starting out worm-free makes everything easier.

Blood will probably be drawn so it can be tested for feline leukemia virus (FeLV) and feline immunodeficiency virus (FIV).

Both FeLV and FIV are serious, complicated diseases. In both cases, a cat who tests positive can live for many years with the problem, or can become rapidly and suddenly ill. Chances are the tests will be negative. But if they aren't, you and your vet will want to discuss the best course of action.

There are many vaccinations that help to prevent disease in cats. Which vaccinations your kitten will get this visit depends on his age, vaccination history, your veterinarian, and your

area. Here are a few of the more common vaccinations. (See pages 96–98 for a more complete discussion of these diseases and why vaccinating your cat against them is essential.)

ESSENTIAL VACCINATIONS

RABIES
Every cat, indoor or outdoor, should be vaccinated against rabies. No exceptions! Even an indoor cat can be infected by a mouse or bat wandering into your home.

FELINE LEUKEMIA VIRUS (FeLV)
These shots are given after nine weeks of age, three weeks later, and then boosted yearly. Get this vaccine.

FELINE IMMUNODEFICIENCY VIRUS (FIV)
There is no vaccine on the market at the time of writing, but they're working hard on it.

FELINE PANLEUKOPENIA VIRUS (FPV)—ALSO KNOWN AS FELINE DISTEMPER
These boosters are given every three weeks or so from six to eight weeks of age until the kitten is over fourteen weeks old. If you want to know why so many shots are needed, see the Frequently Asked Questions section, page 76.

FELINE INFECTIOUS PERITONITIS (FIP)
This is a nasty virus-caused disease that not too much is known about yet. Protect your cat from this, it's a deadly one.

Selecting a Veterinarian

It's a good idea to select your vet before you get your new companion. This way you can ask their advice about bringing the kitten home, and what to look for when selecting the kitten. One of the best ways to select a vet is to ask for recommendations from other cat-owning friends and neighbors. Often a certain name or two will keep cropping up and that is who I would call.

DOES THE VETERINARIAN OWN CATS?

Cats are unique, and owning one is a sign of a real cat lover. Of course there are many non-cat-owning vets who are excellent, but it is a mark in their favor if they have a cat or two.

IS THE CLINIC CLEAN?

It should be clean and smell clean. If it's not too busy, chat with the front desk personnel. They often have much to do, but a few minutes of conversation will give you a good idea of the atmosphere of the clinic.

MAN OR WOMAN?

Your personal preference. The sex of your vet makes no difference in competence.

YOUNGER OR OLDER?

Both have advantages. As a sweeping generality, younger vets have been exposed to newer methods and cutting-edge techniques, while older vets have the benefit of years of experience and hands-on work.

DO THEY HAVE TWENTY-FOUR-HOUR COVERAGE?

This is a BIG plus, as animals inevitably fall ill in the middle of the night or over a long holiday weekend. Sometimes the vets with twenty-four-hour call are too far away to be convenient. But keep their number handy anyway. I hope you'll never need it but if you do, you don't want to have to hunt for it.

Fantasy land is a vet who'll make house calls. A joy for cat owners, especially those of us who have more than one cat. Such marvelous doctors do occasionally crop up. Take good care of them, they are wonderful to have around.

Feeding Your Kitten

Let's start at the beginning: feed kittens food made for kittens. Almost every cat we've met prefers canned food to all others. Around our house, we feed canned food exclusively. However, canned foods spoil if left out, and are more expensive and messy than dry. Dry food keeps well in the bag and the bowl. It is less expensive than canned, is simple to use and store. Semimoist foods are as convenient as dry and as accepted by most cats as canned, but are usually full of colorings, additives, and flavorings to make them that way.

Fresh water is an often overlooked kitten necessity. Even if a kitten drinks out of a dripping faucet, fresh water should be available all the time in a bowl. Change the water and rinse the bowl daily. This is especially true if you feed a dry food. Drinking adequate amounts of water helps prevent urinary tract problems. Fresh water is important for all cats, but it is critical for males, who are more prone to such problems.

Milk, a mythical kitten food, can cause diarrhea. Give your kitten clean, fresh water rather than milk.

Kittens teethe between three and a half months and six months. During that time, chewing may be intermittently painful. If you are feeding dry food and your kitten seems to want to eat, but then only takes a few bites before walking away, try soaking his food in warm water for a few minutes. This will soften it, making it easier for him to eat. This is of course much less of a problem with canned food, which is already soft.

Like any teething baby, his mouth may hurt. He may chew on things to try to relieve the pain. He may cry or be fussy. He may have a little loose stool, or be more lethargic than usual. And during this period, his breath may be less than sweet. All this will pass. If you are at all concerned, give your veterinarian a call. He'll be able to sort out whether your kitten's symptoms are normal or cause for alarm.

A young kitten, under three months, should have food available continuously throughout the day. His energy and growth demands are so high that he is unlikely to overeat; rather he'll be tearing around the house burning off calories, as any healthy kitten should. If, however, you need to feed him separate meals for some reason, feed him at least three times a day.

After about six months of age, you can switch a kitten over to twice-a-day feedings, the same as we recommend for adult cats. At six months his rapid growth period is over. He is still developing, but more slowly. Feeding meals allows you to control the amount your kitten consumes. This may not seem important now, but obesity is a common problem plaguing adult indoor cats. An ounce of prevention now is worth a few less pounds of cat later.

Set the meals to suit your schedule but, as we've already said, *never* feed a kitten right when you get up. If you do, your kitten will quickly realize that he eats when you wake up, so WAKE UP! 5:00 A.M. is not too early for a bit of breakfast, is it?

If your kitten does wake you in the middle of the night do not feed it to quiet it. This will start a habit that is hard to break. Cats have long memories when it comes to food. Instead, feed him just before you leave. Don't let him link your waking with his eating and all will be well.

In the evening, the same rule applies to your return home. If you feed him right when you walk in the door, he'll start becoming anxious if you are late. Anxious kittens are kittens who misbehave. Rather, feed him when you eat or feed him after the latest time you return home during the week. For example, if you are normally home at 6:00 but twice a week you stop by the gym for a workout and roll in around 7:30, then feed the cat at 8:00 every day. That way the routine stays a routine.

Where you feed is important. If you don't want him on countertop cooking areas, then don't feed him on any part of the counter. Same rule applies for kitchen table and such. Your cat will and should feel comfortable going to his food dish, and if that dish is near to something you don't want him on, you'll create problems for both of you.

If you have a cat-food-addicted dog, put him someplace else when you feed your cat. That way you can keep the food on the floor. That's another advantage to meals, the dog can't steal the food if it isn't left out. Millions of cats have convinced their people that they must have access to their dish twenty-four hours a day. It simply isn't true.

Another word to the wise, don't start feeding your kitten from the table. Just keep repeating to yourself, twenty years, twenty years, when you see those big green eyes looking up at you. Unless you want a couple of decades of hassling from your feline food addict, skip treats from your plate.

Grooming Your Kitten

Now that you know from pages 63–65 how to get your kitten used to grooming, let us now explore the basics of what type of grooming is needed.

SHORTHAIR

Even though a shorthaired kitten's coat isn't going to mat or tangle, brush him at least once a week, more often during shedding season. This will stimulate the skin, distribute coat oils, remove dead hair, teach him to accept handling, and give you a chance to give your kitten a thorough once-over.

The tool I like is called a grooming glove. This is usually a square canvas mitt with sisal bristles on it. This is gentle and effective and most cats don't mind it too much. The sisal, unlike plastic or rubber, does not develop a lot of static electricity. To clean the hair out of these, scrape it down the edge of a hard object.

LONGHAIR

Some longhaired cats do not have a very thick or soft coat so they rarely get tangles. Others, like Persians, seem to mat simply by walking across the room. These need daily attention to look and feel their best. Only get a Persian if you have the time and desire to groom daily; it is not fair to the animal if you don't. Groom them daily or don't get them.

NAIL CLIPPING

Clipping an indoor cat's nails on a weekly basis will limit the amount of damage your cat can do to your belongings or to tender human skin. With a cooperative cat, it takes about a minute to do, so why not? If your kitten resists this process, see the section on teaching him to enjoy it in the Preventing Bad Habits section on pages 63–65. For your basically cooperative kitten, use clippers made for the job. When you clip, cut off just the thin, clear end of the nail. Stay away from the pink inner part, as that is flesh and nipping into it is about as pleasant as someone pulling your nail off below the quick.

It's a good idea to have some styptic powder handy, as a nicked quick (the inner part of the nail) bleeds impressively. Be sure to keep up your happy banter as you clip. The sound of your calm voice is comforting to your kitten.

EARS

Check the ears weekly for any dirt or discharge. Ear mites are not uncommon in kittens. Heavy black waxy discharge is a clear signal to get to the vet. A weekly wipe with a moistened cotton ball around the visible area of the ear is a good idea. Never go deep into the ear or further than you can see. The ear is delicate, and injury is possible unless you know what you are doing.

Kathryn Parise

EYES

Cats' eyes usually require little maintenance. Some of the shorter nosed breeds, in particular Persians, may need the folds under their eyes wiped out on a daily basis with a cotton swab. Have your veterinarian, breeder, or groomer show you what's needed.

BATHING

Unless absolutely necessary, don't bathe a kitten. If you must, be quick, keep him out of drafts, and get him dry! If you've done the hair dryer training and your kitten accepts it well, dry him off that way with the dryer set on low.

If he isn't used to a handheld hair dryer, set him up in a towel-lined carrier in a warm, draft-free area under a lamp to dry. Keep a close eye on him—you want him to be cozy, not roasting. If he's curled up asleep near the light all is well. If he is panting, trying to get away from the heat source, he is too warm. Move the carrier back away from the lamp a few inches. If he is shivering and crying, he is too cold. Move the lamp closer to the crate or take him to bed with you and cuddle him under the blankets until he stops shivering. But best of all, skip the whole routine until he is six months or older.

Sienna demonstrates careful grooming.

Frequently Asked Questions

Is wearing gloves a good solution to a kitten playing a little too rough?

Yes and no. Yes, it works as a short-term solution, because the kitten can't hurt you, but and this is a big *but*, it does not allow you to teach your kitten how to play appropriately. Unless you teach a kitten to play gently with human flesh, you are just postponing the inevitable lesson and allowing your tiny one to grow into a large scratching and biting cat.

Even though my kitten eats a lot, he still seems skinny and his coat is dry and dull. What is wrong?

Sounds like it's time for a trip to the veterinarian. One of the common causes of this is worms or other internal parasites. Bring a small stool

The urge to hunt is part of every kitten.

Sarah Wilson

Even though kittens are fastidious, it's important to start grooming them early.

sample with you for the veterinarian to test. Most kittens will have worms at one time or another. It's nothing to worry about, it's just something to deal with. Do *not* use over-the-counter medications. Leave the diagnosing and prescribing to the veterinarian, he's had the training.

My kitten seems to be trying to nurse on my dog, is this normal?

Common enough, although maybe not normal. Kittens need to stay with their mother and litter mates much longer than puppies do. People tend to separate them too early, like at five to seven weeks. This early separation can lead to nursing behavior throughout the cat's life. Whenever possible, get a kitten who has been left with his mother for at least ten weeks. Twelve to sixteen weeks is even better! But, bottom line is, as long as your dog doesn't object, why should you? It's really between them, don't you think?

Why does my kitten need so many shots for feline distemper?

Good question. What happens is that when your kitten nurses from his mother, he gets a certain amount of maternal antibodies that protect him from diseases, including feline distemper. The trick is that no one knows how long those antibodies will last. Sometimes six weeks. Sometimes twelve. And until those maternal antibodies fade away, the kitten's own system won't recognize the vaccine and build his own defenses. So the vaccine is given repeatedly, because eventually the maternal antibodies will be gone, and the kitten will react correctly to the vaccine and create his own antibodies.

My kitten won't let me brush my teeth without batting at the water with his paw. I thought cats hated water!

Many cats do hate to be put into water, but that doesn't mean they aren't fascinated by moving streams of it. A great number of cats adore playing in a trickle of water and even more like to drink from such a stream. Luckily, cats are under no obligation to make sense.

I think kittens are so cute, don't you think a cat should have babies just once?

NO! All kittens *are* adorable, but there are already millions too many in the world. If you love kittens, volun-teer at your local shelter to play with the ones there. They need the attention, handling, and love. Please don't bring more lives into the world for your own amusement when so many kittens die every year for want of a loving home.

Instead, neuter your kitten at six months. Neutering is a much more loving thing to do. Neutered cats are less prone to certain cancers and other health problems. If you love cats, and kittens in particular, you'll neuter yours promptly.

Won't neutering my kitten make her fat and lazy?

No. Too much food and not enough exercise will make her fat and lazy. That is just one of the many myths about neutering that keeps people from doing the right thing— spaying and altering their cats. There is no reason not to, and about five million (that's about how many cats we kill a year because there aren't enough homes) reasons a year to do it. So don't delay!

My kitten doesn't bury her waste. Is this normal? Can I teach her to cover it up?

Normal, yes. Teach her to cover it? Nope. As with everything feline, cats are rugged individualists. Some cats dig for minutes, scooping, tossing, sometimes even just pawing at the air in an instinctual urge to bury their waste. Others just drop it and go. Be grateful. It's easier to scoop, less use of litter, less flinging of litter, and generally just easier to deal with. If you don't like the look of it—wonderful! That will motivate you to scoop.

Or, and there's always an "or" isn't

there?, it could mean she doesn't like the litter. If she appears to dislike walking in it, shakes her paws vigorously after she steps out, tries to squat in the edge of the box, or doesn't cover her waste, you may want to try a different litter. Set up two boxes, one with the litter you use and one with a different one. If she covers it in the other box, you have the answer. Litter avoidance. If she just lets it sit there in either box, might be it's just the way she is.

Several times a day, my kitten runs around the house like a wild man. Is this normal?

Oh yes! Welcome to F.R.A.P. attacks—Frenetic Random Activity Periods. With kittens, and some adult cats, these happen several times a day, most frequently in the early-evening or morning hours. These times correlate to the times in the wild when the cats would hunt.

Your kittens, and thousands of others worldwide, all of a sudden get the uncontrollable urge to run amok for a few minutes. Up and over the couch, across the floor, spinning in place, and off again in the opposite direction. If you're in the way, you become a piece of exercise equipment. Over your lap, up your leg, across your shoulders— whatever is easiest to reach.

These don't normally last more than a few minutes, ten at most. Best to just enjoy the youthful fun of it all and try to stay out of the line of fire. Attempting to pick them up while they are in this state will probably lead to some form of feline protest, so let them burn it off. If you like, you can direct this mini-mania by rolling a ball or dragging a thing-on-a-string in front of him. Chances are he'll focus on it and pounce. Lots of fun for all. However you elect to cope, enjoy them—they end all too soon anyway.

3 🐾
Adulthood

Cats are an ever-present cord in my life. My childhood memories are landscaped with cats: playing with kittens for hours, trying to do homework with a cat batting at my pencil, kissing a high school sweetheart with a cat purringly interfering. I slept every night with a warm cat curled into the crook of my knees or pressed lovingly against my neck. I have more memories of my cats than I do of some family members. But then, my cats were always there, always a comfort, ever an amusement, and incorruptible friends. They remain so to this day as Emily lies happily across my lap, head resting on my forearm, making it awkward to type, but who's complaining? She is comfortable; I am happy in a way that people cannot make me happy, so I don't move her. Blissfully, trustingly asleep, she makes me feel graced, in a life that sometimes lacks that. For me, it is very true, a house is not a home without a cat.

Life in the City

Cats have lived with people in every possible habitat. They are survivors and adapters, so life in the city is no real problem for them *if* you keep them inside. Life on the streets is hardly a place for a human, never mind a feline. All city cats should be strictly house cats—pure and simple.

Small apartment or large brownstone, it doesn't really matter. Cats adjust. As long as you care for their basic needs and anticipate some of their instinctive desires, you can have a happy and healthy cat in any urban home.

Space may be the final frontier but it is in short supply in most apartments. Getting all of your own stuff in is hard enough, so where is the cat to go? A good plan for all concerned is to invest in one of those floor-to-ceiling cat roosts. Not only will this offer climbing exercise for your cat but it enriches his environment, giving him an excellent retreat when it is needed.

Once installed, you can encourage your cat to use it by hiding special treats on the perches, dragging string up the post for him to chase, or rubbing catnip into it. Any of these will reward him for investigating the perch and give him a good feeling about it.

Your most important city cat safety items are good, solid screens that won't pop out of place if a cat sleeps against it or throws himself into it while attempting to chase a pigeon. Cats can and do fall from extraordinary heights with predictably unpleasant results. Protect him well, install sturdy screens. NEVER leave your screenless window open even a crack! Cats can slink out of surprisingly small openings, or can push the window up and make their escape.

Because of the smaller area of most city housing, be sure to set up a private place for your cat that she can retreat to when strangers arrive. Many cats have no love of strangers and will feel stressed if they can't hide. If setting up your bedroom as an escape hatch isn't an option, consider a corner of a closet. Leave the door ajar, and rig it so it can't accidentally be closed. Put a bed with a worn T-shirt of yours in and a bowl of water within easy reach. That should be fine for short periods of a few hours.

If your cat retreats, house rules should be that no one approaches her there. This should be a guaranteed safe zone for her. People mean well, but approaching a cat who is trying to hide is a terrific way to create aggression and other stress-related problems. Wait for her to come out on her own and then invite her over for a pat and maybe a treat or two. Remember, it is perfectly normal and acceptable for a cat to be wary around strangers. It is neither a problem nor a defect. Just let your cat be. She's fine just as she is.

Like us humans, city cats can be victims of stress. The stress caused by long periods of isolation, close quarters, sudden loud noises, constant sounds out in the hallway or on the street, and air pollution can all add up to a cat more prone to developing behavioral problems than one not struggling under these conditions.

Fortunately, these stresses can be made more manageable through proper diet, exercise, play, environment, and routine. Diet is important to all of us, and your cat is no exception. When your cat is stressed is no time to skimp on her nutrition. Get the best diet you can, which in our opinion is a natural one as free of artificial coloring and flavoring as possible. Many companies are creating excellent versions of such foods and we highly recommend them. Be sure your cat has cat greens to munch on as well. Fresh, clean water is as important as any of the above.

Exercise and play are closely linked in cats. Things-on-a-string are loads of fun both for the chaser and the human end of the game. Any sort of chase game is good, especially if the cat can run over and under things, making it even more interesting and tiring. We don't actually expect you to exhaust your cat doing this. Few cats will play that long. But a good artificial hunt once or twice a day fulfills an instinctual drive

in your cat that nothing else can.

Environment, as discussed above, either makes your cat's life easier or more difficult. Supplying your cat with ways to hide and to climb creates a natural environment for your cat in an unnatural one.

And lastly, routine is calming for any stressed animal, except perhaps the stress of boredom. If your cat is frightened or anxious, creating a predictable routine will give her daily events to count on. Try to prepare your schedule—her schedule—in such a way that you will be able to maintain it most of the time. Meaning, for example, don't feed her at 7:00 A.M. during the week if you intend to sleep in on the weekends. Either feed her as late as you can on weekdays or get an automatic feeder, which can be set to a reasonable time. Work on making her world as predictable as you can because predictability translates into a sense of safety and security to your cat.

Life in the Suburbs

Of all the places cats live, I think suburbia poses the most dangers. Why? Because people think of themselves as being out of the city, the yard looks quiet, the neighborhood nice—surely letting the cat outside will be just the thing. Wrong!

Suburbia has a high density of cats, meaning that territory is well staked out and the boundaries are taken seriously. Your cat will either step out the door into another ani-

mal's area or have to fight for his piece of land. Either way, fights are inevitable, especially with males.

There are many roads and lots of traffic in suburbia. Traffic is never good for cats, most of whom do not understand the danger that oncoming vehicles pose.

There are poisons in these areas from lawn pesticides your cat strolls through, then later licks off her feet, to chicken bones in the garbage that your cat can eat and impale her innards with: your cat is walking through a mine field when she's out in suburbia.

Then there are cat-hating neighbors. Our friends have neighbors who enjoy taking potshots with a BB gun at any cat that crosses their tiny piece of grass. Stupid? Yes. Dangerous? Absolutely. But these people aren't exactly focused on social welfare and it's your cat who'll come home injured— or not come home at all.

Add to this the wandering dogs in many neighborhoods, and you have a beautiful area that is quite deadly for our feline companions.

Do your cat a favor and keep him inside or build him a nice covered outdoor area where he can enjoy the breeze and chase the occasional fly without getting himself into any real trouble.

Also, things are changing in the world. Communities are passing laws banning the free wandering of cats. This is no real surprise. Have you ever tried to sleep through the love

Not all cats love the great outdoors; Emily hates it, staying hidden at all costs.

Sarah Wilson

songs of a female in heat or the battle cries of the males who want her? Maybe you find a ripped-open trash bag with the contents strewn across your driveway an acceptable part of cat ownership but I doubt your non-cat-owning neighbors will be so tolerant. What if your toddler scooped up a pile of cat feces out of his own sandbox? These are real-world concerns, and unless all of us start being more thoughtful of our neighbors, the tide of pet intolerance will keep growing.

Living with cats is an acceptance of responsibility, not just for their health and well-being, but also for their actions.

Life in the Country

The country, that is, homes on several acres or more surrounded by homes also on several acres or more, on a quiet lane, well away from busy streets, are somewhat safer for cats.

Such areas, though, are still a risk for cats if less so than the suburbs. There are fewer cars, more space, and usually a lower cat-per-acre population, which means boundaries won't be so easily crossed or hotly contested. There are still many dangers, however, that should be considered when you think about whether or not you want to allow your cat out-of-doors.

But being away from human-made dangers does not mean your cat is safe. Now you also have to worry about nature's dangers, which primarily take the form of wild animals, although sometimes the dangers are closer to home.

Kodak, the beautiful black and white cat seen in the front picture in the Required Reading section and in other pictures throughout this book, lives in a rural area of Vermont, on the top of a small mountain, off a tiny dirt road. She has enjoyed a life of freedom for many years. Yet a few months back she had an accident. She got butted by one of the rams on the property. For those of you who haven't seen a ram lately or been butted, it is not a fun experience. These are large animals, well over a hundred pounds, with large horns and the natural ability to use them. When they run at you, you can be seriously injured. When they run at a cat... well, Kodak is lucky to be alive. She did, however, lose an eye.

Why did this happen after years of living peaceably together? Who knows. Kodak had been seen in the company of a skunk earlier, and the theory is that she smelled foreign when she entered the barn. The rams defended themselves from what they thought was an intruder.

The skunk itself is another issue. Skunks and raccoons are notorious carriers of rabies, a disease that is alive and well in many parts of North America.

And then there are traps. Some states still allow the use of leg-hold traps. These traps lay hidden until the animal steps in them, then it snaps shut on a paw. Of course, there is no way of determining who the paw belongs to. All kinds of creatures get caught in them, suffering slow, miserable deaths—dying of thirst,

Cats love milk, but milk does not always love cats, as it causes diarrhea in many.

trauma, shock, or hunger. There are more humane options available if trapping must continue, and all of us should demand those options be used. There is no excuse.

Basic Needs

Just as a parent is responsible for the health and well-being of their infant, you, as a cat owner, are responsible for those things in your cat. As a parent, you watch over the infant, keeping him safe, since you know he can't protect himself. You carefully feed him what he requires. Tending to his bodily needs, watching carefully for signs of illness, amusing him, educating him, taking him to the pediatrician—without thinking about it. After all, you are the parent, those are your responsibilities.

And so it goes for you, the cat owner. It is a good rule that you

should do for your cat, in general, what you would do for an infant. If you won't let your baby sit in a dirty diaper, don't allow your cat to have a filthy box. If you bathe your baby, brush his hair, lotion his skin, clip his nails, then do the appropriate grooming for your cat: brushing him, clipping his nails, giving him a bath as needed and as recommended by your veterinarian.

There are limits to this analogy. We certainly discourage you from allowing your infant to climb up on the backs of couches, chase after balls of aluminum foil, or hang off the draperies, but you get the general idea. A cat is totally in your care. His health, well-being, and very life depend on you. While a pleasant responsibility, it is also a serious one. Don't let your cat down.

A cat in your care has a few basic needs he must have to be a happy, contented companion. These needs

include good food, fresh water, snug shelter, adequate exercise, regular grooming, professional veterinary care, as well, of course, as your love and attention. Without any one of these basics, you can expect your cat to become stressed physically and/or mentally, inevitably leading to illness or behavioral problems.

Food and Water

Water is one of the most important keys to good health and one of the most overlooked necessities for the average cat. Since most of us don't drink nearly enough plain, clear water ourselves, it slips our mind that our cats need it as well.

A healthy water intake can help to prevent bladder problems, flush toxins from the system, control the appetite, and generally clean the body system.

Water should be supplied in a ceramic or stainless steel bowl. Change the water and rinse the bowl daily. Many cats are real sticklers about the water being fresh, turning up their noses at a stale bowlful.

If your cat is not a bowl drinker but loves water fresh from the faucet, set it on a trickle for a few minutes several times a day for him. The more he drinks the better.

Our cats get their food twice a day for half an hour and then we take it away. Emily tends toward the matronly end of the scale, as she was a stray, and has the classic stray viewpoint of "eat now, who knows when the next meal will be." When she arrived, she would, not infrequently, eat until she vomited. Ever-present bowls of food will as inevitably cause obesity in some cats as an open tub of ice cream will for some of us humans. If it's there, it will be eaten. This is especially true with cats as they age.

We feed our cats meals instead of leaving food available round-the-clock because of our dogs. Virtually all dogs adore cat food and will go to great lengths to attain it. We have my office set up as a dog-free zone but no system is perfect. A mistake on my part means I suffer the canine gas that cat food often brings on. Now that's a good correction!

On a side note, did you know that dog food isn't good for cats? Adult cats need about five times as much protein as adult dogs. Cats also need an amino acid called taurine in their diet, dogs don't. Cats need more of other things

Don't use food to love your cat to death. Instead, love him to life by keeping him slim.

Shirley Minatelli

like B vitamins as well. All in all, don't feed your cat dog food. A few bites every so often isn't going to hurt but it is not a complete diet for cats.

If your cat does not overindulge and you don't have a cat-food-scarfing dog, then by all means free-feed. It's certainly easy and convenient. The best people to ask about proper diet are your breeder, if you have a purebred cat, or your veterinarian. Follow their advice.

Table scraps can be given if done so intelligently. More than one cat owner has created a mono-diet monster by offering yummy bits of leftovers from their own plate. Cats, not being stupid animals, soon figure out

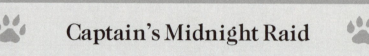

Captain's Midnight Raid

When I awoke, the woods around our suburban home were filled with spotlights. Dark figures moved behind those lights. I could hear hurried whispers downstairs and a distant thumping. Random but loud, like a fist being pounded against a wall.

As I crept downstairs to see what was happening, I found the disconcerting sight of my father, not quite fully dressed, in conference with a police officer. The thumping continued; it was coming from the basement.

A plan of action was agreed upon. The officer, with his partner close behind, slowly opened the basement door. The thumping stopped. The policemen exchanged serious glances with each other and proceeded down the stairs.

The tension in the house was palpable. We peered down the stairs, listening for what exactly we did not know, but for something—something dangerous. We were baffled when we heard laughter. It was the two policemen. They called us down to see our intruder.

There, in the laundry room, was Captain, our ever-hungry cat, with his head wedged firmly in a box of dry food. As we watched for a second, he struggled yet again to get free, whomping the box against the side of the washing machine with a mighty whack. When we freed him, he took one look at the uniformed strangers in the basement and disappeared as only a frightened cat can.

We offered the police officers a cup of coffee and promised to keep the cat food in a closed cupboard from then on.

that waiting for the end of your meal is much more interesting than eating their own. Owner mistake. Cats who begin to show cat-food-boycotting tendencies should be cut off immediately from all treats. The more your cat complains about this change in menu, the sooner you should have changed it. Once your cat is eating his own food without complaint, you can start offering him the occasional extra.

Grooming

Although cats do an excellent job of self-grooming, you still need to assist them in their quest for perfect hygiene. While all cats need some attention in this area, longhaired cats predictably need the most. Here are a few tips for basic grooming. Seek out more detailed advice from a local groomer, veterinarian, or breeder.

SHORTHAIRED CATS

The majority of cats in the world fall into this category. Easy to own and care for, these animals benefit nonetheless from some weekly grooming—especially during shedding season, which comes in spring and fall. A natural-bristle brush or what is called a hound glove are both effective tools while being gentle on the cat. Also, a fine-toothed comb is a good, cat-acceptable tool for removing dead hair.

LONGHAIRED CATS

Longhaired cats vary in their grooming needs immensely. Some have a thinner, harsher coat that rarely tangles and others have this soft, luxurious Persian-type coat that mats easily. Prime mat areas are underneath the neck, belly, and chest, behind the ears and the hind legs. Maybe it's just easier to say that the top of the head, the front of the legs, the tail, and the back are not as likely to mat—but you still have to watch those spots, especially during shedding season.

Getting a longhaired cat used to being groomed is an absolute necessity. Too many times I have seen a longhaired cat shaved due to his owner's failure to groom, and a shaved longhaired cat is not, I repeat, NOT, a thing of beauty. If it has to be done, do it. It's for your cat's health and comfort but shame on you. If you choose a longhaired kitten, then you also choose the daily grooming that comes along with him. If you are not the kind of person who enjoys daily tasks like that, by all means get pictures of longhaired cats, but don't get a live one.

Before you invite a Persian into your life, spend some time with a breeder to see exactly what grooming is required on a daily and weekly basis. One little trick of the trade is using a soft-bristle toothbrush to groom the face. It's gentle and works well.

On massively coated animals, trimming the rear of the cat to create a poop chute may be necessary. A monthly trim is so much more pleasant than picking out a bit of clinging feces after a trip to the litter box. When trimming around your cat's anus, work with the scissors pointed downward, away from the cat's body; that way a squirm is less likely to result in an injury. If you have any reser-

REMOVING MATS

Here's a little tip for trimming out mats from your cat's coat. The safest way to do this is to grasp the mat at the base near the skin. Then, leaving your fingers there, trim just above them. This guarantees that no skin will be lost when you cut away the tangle.

Another effective and safe method is, using a sharp pair of scissors, slide one of the blades under the mat, sharp side of the blade facing out, and then lift away from the skin. This splits the mat safely. Done repeatedly, the mat can be broken down into brushable or combable sections.

vations, take your cat to your vet or local groomer. This is not an area where you want to make a mistake. Your cat thanks you in advance for being so careful.

NO-HAIR CATS

There are a few cat breeds that have little or no fur. Often an acquired taste, these elegant animals obviously have little problem with shedding, hairballs, or fleas. On the flip side, they have little tolerance for temperature changes, need to be protected from sunburn, and may need lotion applied to keep them from drying out.

Cutting Nails

If you've been handling your cats' feet from kittenhood on, then this will not be too much of a battle. If not, then you may want to look at pages 63–65, Preventing Bad Habits. It's never too late to teach your cat something new, so don't despair, just get started!

It is best to begin this process with a tired, relaxed cat. No reason starting off at a detriment by trying to handle an excited feline. When your cat is calm, start to gently stroke her, keeping your voice and hands calm.

Gently press on one paw to extend her nails. Taking a clipper, clip off the end of one. Put the clipper down and continue to stroke her. Do this a couple of more times, then quit for the day. It isn't written anywhere that you have to do all the claws at once. We strongly encourage owners to quit when they are ahead. The nails will

be there tomorrow. Taking it slow is a terrific way to train a cat to accept this process, so that a month or so from now you'll have a cat who lounges happily while every nail is clipped.

Bathing

I don't know who hates baths more—the cat being bathed or the owner doing the bathing. Most cats, the majority of cats, detest being placed in water, and although some cats learn to accept bathing when done regularly and from a young age, few ever learn to enjoy it.

The good news is that most cats, naturally tidy animals, rarely need bathing. That said, if your cat gets grimy, has an oily coat, is inundated with fleas, or is full of dandruff, a bath will be in order.

Young kittens and older cats should not be bathed at all unless absolutely necessary. If you do have to bathe them, be extra careful about drying them well and keeping them in a warm, draft-free area for the first few hours after the bath. For older or young animals we recommend you consult your vet before proceeding.

Here's what you need before you start your bath:

A CLOSED ROOM

If you leave the door open and the cat gets loose, good luck! You'll be trying to talk a soapy, irate feline out from behind the couch.

A WELL-GROOMED CAT

Washing a matted, tangled cat will only make matters worse. If you can't

Even though Maverick loves to drink from the sink and play with water from the faucet, that doesn't mean he'll enjoy a bath. Cats are funny that way.

get the mats out, take her to a groomer and have them removed professionally. Then, next time, keep up with your grooming responsibilities. Brushing out the loose hair, checking for small wounds, cleaning the ears, and clipping the nails are all normal prebath exercises.

A Shower Attachment, Hand Sprayer, or Hose

This should be a gentle spray, not a shower massage! But this tool is a gem, especially if you are bathing the cat by yourself. It allows you to rinse the cat well without ever loosening your grasp. When you use the sprayer, turn it on against the bottom of the tub, and then bring it up close to your cat's body. If you hold it back away from your cat, expect your cat to panic.

For cats who detest the sprayer, use a simple hose attached to the faucet for wetting and rinsing. This will give you a good supply of water with no noise or pressure attached.

A Big Sponge or Small Bowl

If your cat refuses to accept a handheld sprayer or hose, wetting and rinsing may be done with a sponge or bowl. Both work well, it just takes a little more time to rinse underneath the cat. That problem can be solved by allowing a few inches of water to accumulate. Not too deep please, that will scare your friend.

Cat Shampoo

Use a product developed for cats and that says so on the label. This is particularly true of any flea or tick products, since products made strictly for dogs can be toxic to your cat.

A Thick Towel or Window Screen

Cats aren't fans of slippery footing. A towel folded on the bottom of the tub

Deskunking

If you are reading this section with anything more than idle curiosity, we extend our heartfelt condolences. Luckily, cats rarely get themselves into this state, but if they do, you deserve some help. A skunked cat is a misery for all concerned. And frankly, no matter what you do, that smell will haunt you on humid days for months!

First, put him in a crate *outside*. Make sure he's sheltered and shaded but don't bring him in any part of your house. If he's in already, take him out. That smell clings to everything it touches.

Put on old clothes you've been meaning to throw out. Gather up some old towels you can live without. Slap a finger full of Vicks VapoRub under your nose on your upper lip and enter the fray.

A bath is obligatory here. Use rubber gloves if you have them, they'll make you more bearable after this ordeal. Many people have opinions about what removes the smell of skunk. Here are some of the favorites: One pint vinegar to one gallon of water; undiluted tomato juice; undiluted orange juice. Some vinegar-based douches are said to be excellent, but you may have to explain to your pharmacist why you need four or five packages of the stuff!

In any case, soak the cat down all over, carefully avoiding the eyes. Let it sit on the cat for a few minutes. Rinse. Repeat. Finish up with a good bath with a cat shampoo. This won't completely kill the smell but it will make it tolerable.

As heat helps to destroy this particular smell, blowing your cat dry with a hair dryer set on low will help your cause. Don't go overboard and dry him on high, you could add to his misery by burning him.

If you want to save your clothing and towels, then give them a good vinegar-and-water soak and hang them in the sun to dry. You may have to repeat this, but it will help. I'd keep them out of your washer-dryer until they are bearable again, no need to stink up your machines. Then soak yourself in a hot bath, you deserve it!

or sink will give him some feeling of security. Many people swear by a window screen leaned in the sink or tub. The cat grabs on to that and pretty much stays put. Anything that keeps the claws occupied is a great idea!

A Hair Dryer

Plug it in nearby, but not too close to the water, please.

Fresh Towels Within Easy Reach

One for the cat, and one or more for you—you'll probably be wet too by the time this is all over.

A Good Hold on Your Cat

The best way to hold a cat during a bath is by the nape of the neck. Hold the skin there gently but firmly and do NOT let go. If you do let go, don't try to grab him. Any attempt at recapture while the animal is in a panic will just frighten him more, never mind the high likelihood of damage to your person.

GIVING THE BATH

Now you're ready to begin. Get your cat. Be relaxed and friendly. Take a few moments to stroke him and tell him how marvelous he is. Go into the bathing room and CLOSE the door. Continue to speak to him calmly throughout the whole ordeal. Your gentle voice will help him stay calm.

Get ahold of the nape of the neck and set the cat down into the tub facing away from you. That way, if the cat becomes frightened and gets away, with any luck he'll flee away from you.

Run the water lukewarm, nothing hotter than that. Cats have sensitive skin and water that is comfortably warm to us may seem scalding to them. Now, using the sprayer close to the cat, wet him down. This is the time you'll get the worst fighting. Once the cat is wet, most cats resign themselves to the inevitable. Avoid wetting the head; this will keep the cat calmer. Most animals hate water in their ears and eyes.

If your cat is infested with fleas, however, the head will have to be washed. In that case, use a sponge to wet the head. Carefully soap it up first, making sure no soap gets into the cat's eyes, nose, mouth, or ears; then do the neck. Fleas, being as much interested in survival as the rest of us, seek high ground when confronted with water. High ground, in this case, is the head, so blockade that area with a good lather first and you'll cut off the little devils at the pass.

Use as little shampoo as you can in order to get a good lather. The more shampoo you use, the longer and more difficult the rinsing process is—so go easy. A good way to use the shampoo is diluted in warm water. This makes it spread through the hair more easily and encourages a good lather. Massage in the soap all over. With longhaired cats, squeeze the soap through the coat. Scrubbing is likely to tangle long hair, making your work harder later.

Rinse well, then rinse again. Leaving any soapy residue can lead to itching and skin irritation. Don't rush this part—give your cat a good rinsing. Always spray the water away from the head, with the lay of the fur. Be sure to carefully rinse the belly, and under

DEALING WITH FLEAS

One of the great, unsung tools of flea control is the flea comb. Use this daily on your cat, dropping any you catch into a dish of soapy water; this will help keep the flea population down to a dull roar. Along with combing, daily vacuuming of your cat's favorite sleeping areas will help. Fleas tend to hop off and lay their eggs wherever your cat likes to nap.

Once you have been invaded, more drastic measures are called for. Ask your vet what chemicals he recommends for your cat and your house, since both will have to be treated— repeatedly. Successful flea control means commitment on your part.

Fleas are another good reason not to let your cat outside. If the fleas never come into your house, you'll never have a problem.

VOMITING

You will be amused to know that when I entered my office to start work on this book today, there was a stream of cat vomit that started from the top of my monitor, down the screen, ending in a decent-sized pile on the layout for this book.

Emily's work no doubt. Periodically, she gorges herself and then rethinks the process. Cats can vomit when they want to, so it is not nearly the big deal to them that it is to us. The occasional vomiting of a healthy cat is normally nothing to worry about. If it becomes frequent, if the cat vomits several times in a row, seems lethargic, depressed, isn't eating, isn't drinking, or there is blood in the vomit— call your vet. But the once-in-a-while, down-your-computer-screen kind of vomit is usually pretty normal.

the tail and armpit areas where soap can lurk.

Once rinsed, lift the cat up and onto a clean towel. Wrap the towel around the cat snugly, and then and only then release your hold on him. Now, lovingly pat him dry. Again, don't scrub long fur, you'll mat it. Remember to continually speak softly and calmly to your cat. Tell him all kinds of wonderful true things like how good he has been about this and how gorgeous he will look clean and fluffed.

If you can, blow him dry with a hair dryer set on low. Or towel him dry as best you can and then put him in a warm, draft-free area for several hours. Putting him into his carrier, with a soft blanket or towel, and then setting the whole thing under a small lamp can be cozy. Check on him regularly to make sure he isn't getting too hot.

And you are done! Congratulations! Go put your feet up for a few minutes, you deserve it.

Health Care

Cats rely on you to notice when they are not well. They cannot ask for help in words but many a cat asks pleadingly in other ways. Here are a few things to observe daily in your cat:

Healthy	*Not Well*
Well-groomed. Cleans self thoroughly.	Unkempt. Dirty. Not clean behind.
Eats normally for him.	Becomes voracious. Or won't eat at all.
Drinks what he normally drinks.	Drinks excessively. Won't drink.
Is normally vocal.	Is excessively vocal or uncharacteristically quiet.
Uses the box normally with normal results.	Goes to box frequently with little or no results. Strains in box. Has diarrhea. Stops using the box.
Vomits occasionally, seems normal afterward.	Vomits repeatedly. Has blood in vomit. Seems lethargic.
Maintains weight.	Gains or loses more than 10 percent of normal weight in a month or less.

Be alert to your cat's normal habits. If your gut tells you something is amiss—trust it. Call your vet and discuss the changes. He'll be able to determine whether you should bring him in for a checkup.

There are certain problems that occur fairly frequently in the general cat population, and as an owner it is a good idea for you to know their symptoms.

HAIRBALLS

Some cats end up swallowing a large amount of hair when they groom themselves. This hair can wad up inside the cat, forming a large hairball. This large ball can block, or partially block, the cat's intestines, making him feel generally lousy. Symptoms include lethargy, vomiting, lack of appetite. Thorough daily brushing, especially during shedding season and for longhaired cats all the time, can help control this problem.

If you suspect your cat has a problem, go to the vet. He'll be able to confirm the problem and recommend the correct treatment.

EAR MITES

These nasty little beasties live in your cat's ears. They bite through the skin in the ear canal, which causes the area to become inflamed and painful. Cats react to this discomfort by shaking their head, scratching vigorously at their ears, and rubbing their head against the floor or furniture. Ear mite infestation is accompanied by a dark waxy discharge from the ear.

You will need medication from your vet to clear up this problem.

Have her show you how to properly administer the ear drops or ointment as well as how to clean the ear safely.

DIARRHEA

You know what the symptom is for this, right? Hard to miss, harder to clean up. Diarrhea can be caused by any number of things, from eating bad food to an internal parasite. Take a stool sample to your vet and follow his instructions about how to handle this problem.

VOMITING

Vomiting can mean you have trouble on your hands, or it could mean nothing more serious than your cat ate too much, too fast. A good general rule is if your cat vomits occasionally, and otherwise seems fine, don't worry too much about it. If it becomes frequent, happening repeatedly in a few hours' time, if there is blood in it, or your cat seems uncomfortable or sick in other ways—call the vet. If you have any concerns—call the vet.

FELINE UROLOGIC SYNDROME (FUS)

If your cat strains to urinate, cries more frequently, is urinating in inappropriate places, has blood in his urine, or can't urinate at all—go directly to the vet. These are symptoms of serious, potentially life-threatening problems. Go!

TAKING YOUR CAT'S TEMPERATURE

Before you start this adventure into cat care, make sure you have the correct equipment: a *rectal* thermometer,

SCOOTING

You'll know what I'm talking about if you've seen it. The cat sits, rear pressed against the floor, and drags himself around. This rather disgusting behavior, inevitably performed on your most expensive carpeting, may be a sign that your cat's anal glands are irritating him.

Every cat has a set of glands inside his anus. These glands serve as scent markers as well as panic buttons. When a cat is terrified, he may well express his anal glands. These glands can become impacted, leading to swelling and pain. Cats then scoot and lick at themselves. Take the poor thing to the vet. The contents of an impacted, infected set of anal glands is nothing you want in your home.

Scooting and licking may also be a sign of worms. Either way, go to your vet and have it dealt with.

lubricant (like petroleum or K-Y Jelly), paper towels, alcohol, a clock or watch, and a large towel for wrapping up your cat.

First shake down the thermometer. Then lubricate the end. Now, get your cat. Do not expect him to think that this is a good idea! Using the large towel to bundle your cat, wrap him securely around the neck and body. Now lift the tail, and insert the lubricated bulb of the thermometer into the rectum. Insert it gently but firmly, right into the center. Your cat will resist for a few seconds, that's normal don't you think? Then the thermometer will slide in. Do not push it in far, not more than an inch, as just the bulb needs to be inserted. Hold on, if you let go the thermometer could be pushed out or disappear in! If the latter happens, which it *very* rarely does, do NOT try to get it out yourself. Take him right to the vet. If that glass breaks inside of him, you'll have a real mess. This *will not* happen if you keep ahold of the end sticking out of your cat.

Leave it in for two minutes. Remove slowly, wipe down with the paper towel, and read it. Normal is somewhere between 101 and 102 degrees. There is some natural variation given excitement level, temperature, exercise, and such. But, if it's over 103 or below 100, call your vet! Anything over 105 is an emergency!

Then, after jotting down the results on the paper (because who wants to forget and have to repeat this procedure?), wipe the thermometer clean with the alcohol and put it away.

As always, stroke and speak kindly to your cat for a few moments before freeing him. This will have a calming effect.

MEDICATING YOUR CAT

Medicating your cat is not the most fun either of you will ever have. But there are tricks to this process that make it easier for all concerned.

How to Pill Your Cat

Pilling an unwilling cat is—well—unpleasant. To make it easier, practice the age-old art of deceit. While a spoonful of sugar may make the medicine go down for us humans, a tiny ball of cream cheese works best for cats. Burying the pill in the soft cheese or a small amount of canned food is often a perfect solution. You get to feed your cat a medically loaded treat and your cat gets to think that something wonderful just happened.

Of course, many cats know a Trojan Horse when they smell it and look at your offering with utter disgust. In this case, a more direct approach is needed.

For this, you will need a large bath towel, the thicker the better. Technique varies, but I wrap it under their chin like a bib and then back over the shoulders until the cat is completely bundled in the towel with just his head peering out. Now hold on.

Having a partner in this process makes things easier, but it can be done alone. I put the cat bundle in my lap, head facing away from me. Then, reaching over, I use one hand to open the mouth. The easiest way to do this is to reach over the nose, pressing the lips in, just behind the

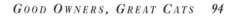

long fangs in front. Pressure at that point will cause a cat to open his mouth. Then with the other hand put the pill down one side of the tongue. Keeping the pill on one side makes it go down better, although it is by no means a perfect system. Once the pill is in, close the mouth and, pointing the nose skyward, stroke the cat's throat until he swallows. If he licks his lips or nose, he's swallowed. Now, keeping him bundled, watch for a second. He may well spit it back out.

There is a little tool called a pill gun, which is a handy-dandy plastic doodad that holds the pill firmly so you can insert it down the throat more easily, while keeping your fingers safe from those sharp feline molars. These are inexpensive and well worth the trouble of getting. Although it allows you to put the pill further down the throat, never put it further than you can see.

Once the pill is swallowed, take a minute to stroke your cat calmly and tell him what a magnificent, wonderful animal he is and how much you appreciate his cooperation, as unwilling as it was. If he will take a small, special treat, so much the better. Then slowly unwrap him and release him. If you have trouble with this, and you might, ask your vet to show you how to do this.

The other option is to crush the pill and mix it in with his regular food. This often works just fine if the medication isn't bitter. Or you can try mixing it with a special treat like baby food. We have a pill crusher, another inexpensive and useful thing to have around. Setting the pill be-

tween two spoons and pressing down will crush most pills. For more stubborn cases, you can crush it by folding it into a piece of paper and then tapping it with a hammer. There is no need in most cases to really bash the thing; most pills come apart with a fairly gentle tap.

GIVING LIQUID MEDICATIONS

If you thought pilling your cat was a challenge, just wait till you two go for a liquid medication. It can be done, though, with a bit of patience and persistence.

First, wrap your cat up in a towel as described in the section on pilling. This is not optional, as most any cat is going to protest this procedure. Do *not* attempt to use a spoon for medicating a cat. It doesn't work well and makes a mess. Instead, ask your vet for a syringe without a needle. This will allow you to precisely measure out the medication as well as administer it to your cat a bit at a time. Make sure your vet shows you exactly how to do this when he gives you the medication.

Now, while speaking softly to your cat, reach over his head and place the thumb and index finger behind each of his big canine teeth. By applying pressure there, the cat will readily open his mouth. He won't like it though, so be ready to insert the tip of the syringe into the corner of his mouth and depress the plunger a bit. Put down the syringe, let him close his mouth, and, pointing his nose to the ceiling, stroke his throat. This will cause him to swallow.

IMPORTANT: Do not squirt too much down your cat's throat at once,

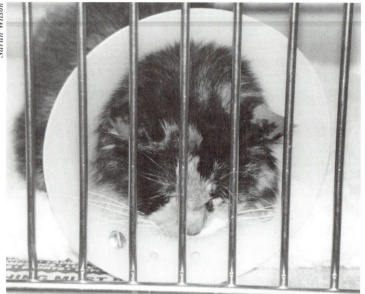

Cats hate these, but sometimes they are unavoidable.

then dab a bit of margarine or Vaseline on each front paw. Most cats will attend to those first. Having cleaned the paws, the cat may relax, feeling like a job was well done, or move on to a complete toilette. Hope for the first, expect the second.

You can also purchase an Elizabethan collar for your cat. Cats hate them with a passion, but it will keep the medication where you put it. Ask your vet how long the collar has to be on for the medication to be effective. If the answer is all the time, so be it. Your cat will heal up. The horror of the collar will pass. Just tell her it's a fashion statement.

DISEASES AND VACCINATIONS

All cats, indoor or outdoor, need several vaccinations to have a long healthy life and to assure that the cats he comes into contact with also have a long healthy life. These vaccinations include those for rabies, feline infectious peritonitis, feline leukemia, feline distemper, as well as feline upper respiratory diseases.

RABIES

Most everyone has heard of rabies, the deadly disease that makes animals crazy before they die. That "crazy" stage, commonly called the furious stage, lasts for a few days before death. Rage, weakness, irritability, twitching are all part of this horrible illness.

Rabies is spread through saliva, primarily through bites. Like most viruses, it has an incubation period, sometimes up to twelve months.

as this may cause him to inhale some of the medicine, potentially giving him serious lung problems. Do a little at a time. Do not lift the cat's head up as you give the medication, as this can cause the medicine to go down the windpipe. If at any time he seems to be really panicking or trying to cough, stop *everything*. Let him cough all he wants. We don't care how much medication he spews out. Then, once all is well again, try once more.

A cheater's way of giving small amounts of thick medicine is to put it on your cat's front feet. He licks it off, you win.

APPLYING TOPICAL MEDICATION
The problem with putting ointments on cats is that more goes *in* the cat than *on* the cat. This is normal, but not always acceptable. Here are a few tricks to cats and creams.

First is to put the medicine on and

Since most people are careful about vaccinating their dogs for this deadly disease, cats now lead the chart in the companion animal most commonly infected with rabies. There is no excuse for this. Rabies kills and it's one of the few diseases that can kill you and your children too. Hardly worth risking just because it's a pain to get the cat to the vet, is it?

FELINE INFECTIOUS PERITONITIS (FIP)

Feline infectious peritonitis is the second main cause of infectious disease death in cats. Until 1991, there was no vaccine. But now there is, so use it. Transferred animal to animal by the usual routes of saliva, urine, or feces, this stalwart little killer can survive for many weeks in the environment, which is one of the reasons all cats should be vaccinated. It's a nasty illness that shows itself as fever, depression, anorexia, and generally feeling miserable. Most cats die once infected.

FELINE LEUKEMIA VIRUS (FeLV)

Feline leukemia virus is passed most easily by blood or saliva, but can also be found in urine and feces. Consequently, the virus is passed between cats by eating or drinking from the same bowl, using the same litter box, grooming, or fighting with an infected cat.

Infected cats can act and look healthy for years, but during that time they can infect other cats. This is why every indoor-outdoor cat should be vaccinated and any cat coming into your household should be tested and vaccinated. But why

take the chance? A vaccination exists, use it.

FELINE PANLEUKOPENIA VIRUS (FPV)

Also called feline distemper, this highly contagious disease causes fever, diarrhea, anorexia, nausea, vomiting, and the dehydration that comes with those symptoms. This is a hardy virus that can wait in the environment for many months for a cat to come along to infect.

FELINE VIRAL RHINOTRACHEITIS (FVR)

Even after a cat recovers from this virus, he is a carrier for life. This disease causes the feline version of an extremely nasty cold with coughing, sneezing, running eyes and nose, difficult breathing, to name a few of the symptoms. Protection from this disease is normally included in the feline distemper vaccination.

FELINE IMMUNODEFICIENCY VIRUS (FIV)

Here's one you can't protect your cat from through vaccination; feline immunodeficiency virus. This virus, similar to the AIDS virus in people, is deadly among cats. It has, at the time of this writing, no known cure. It cannot, however, be passed between species so you and your dog have no worry if your cat is ill. As there is no vaccine yet, your best defense on your cat's behalf is to keep him indoors and to test any cat before adding him to your family.

In a recent U.S. study, more than one out of every five cats was found to carry either the feline leukemia virus or the feline immunodeficiency virus. Regardless of where you live, all your cats should be thoroughly tested and vaccinated. It's for your cat's well-being; it's for all cats' well-being.

Daily Interaction

Cats, like humans, differ greatly in their need for daily interaction with others. If the cat has been raised with loving, cat-oriented people, his social needs will be entirely different from that of a barn cat. However, for the purposes of this book, we are assuming that the cat is attached to you and vice versa.

For such animals, daily interaction is necessary to their mental and physical health. Daily and consistent interaction, that is. Consistency is important, as cats are creatures of habit, getting used to and enjoying routine. If you give your cats tons of attention on the weekend and then dash off to work on Monday, don't be surprised if you get a stress behavior from your cat on Monday or Tuesday. Something chewed, knocked over, or wet are not uncommon early-in-the-week events.

This is not to say that you should ignore your cat on vacations or weekends, just be aware of how confusing this schedule business is to companion animals. Most of the week you wake up friendly when she purrs in your ear at 7:30 A.M. and then on the weekend you scowl and remove her from the bed. What's a cat to think?

So attempt to be consistent. All week long, give most of your attention and playtime in the evening when you will usually be home or in the morning after breakfast. If you give it before your breakfast, you'll start having early A.M. cat revelry as she tries to get you romping.

This is all made more important if your cat lives alone with you indoors. In this case, you are about the only really interesting thing in her day. She offers you companionship, amusement, and a glimpse into the natural world right in your own living room. In return, she needs your attention. An excellent trade, as millions of us cat lovers can attest, but a trade that it is easy for us humans to renege on. Other things in life are more overtly demanding. Jobs, friends, outside commitments all pull on us, while our cat sits quietly cleaning herself on the top of the TV. It is easy sometimes for them to slip your mind. Don't let it happen. It only takes a few minutes of play a day to keep most adult cats happy. A small price to pay for friendship, available twenty-four hours a day, 365 days a year.

Exercise and Play

All cats, but especially indoor cats, need outlets for their energy. Like children, you can either direct them to games you like or live with the games they invent themselves. Cats invent games like Wild Cat: Master of Your Ankles; Spider Cat: Climber of Expensive Drapes; or any number of self-amusing but owner-unacceptable games.

Finding painless, nondestructive entertainment for cats is not too

Nermal—Who Wasn't

Nermal entered the Johnsons' life by veterinary technician plotting, which is how more than one animal has found a loving home. Mrs. J. took her dog in for boarding and, while waiting by the front desk, noticed a litter of charming kittens playing in a box. As she watched this group, enchanted, a homely calico kitten in the gangly stages of growth came up and introduced herself. When the technician came out, the little calico was happily curled up in the crook of Mrs. J's arm. "She likes you?" gasped the tech. "She doesn't like anyone. She's yours!" "Oh, no!" said Mrs. J. "I already have a cat." But then she looked down at the kitten. "But… if by the time we get back from vacation she still hasn't found a home, I'll think about it."

When she went to pick up her dog after her vacation, there was the kitten with a big ribbon on her neck with a small tag that read, "I belong to Mrs. Johnson." That, as they say, was that.

It took several months for Nermal to really settle in. She was distrustful of people, of men in particular. Although she came to trust her family, she remained terrified of strangers, loud sounds, and sudden movements. Despite her rough start, she was an extremely bright cat who demanded extra attention. Here are just a few of her self-taught tricks:

Ringing the doorbell to come in and out. While cute, this rapidly became annoying. Mr. Johnson finally had to disconnect the bell for the sake of the peace.

When banished from the laundry room/bathroom so a person could have a bit of privacy, she would run upstairs and slide down the laundry chute to say hello.

If feeling impish, or if you needed her for some reason, she hid underneath the Oriental rug in the dining room, forcing all to look for lumps in the carpeting when walking through. She did the same thing under bedspreads.

Nermal demanded and needed daily interaction with her family to be happy. The Johnsons gladly gave it to her and she gave them her utter devotion in return.

difficult. Cats favor hunting-type amusement. Games that involve stalking, pouncing, chasing, batting at, or biting into objects are held in universally high feline esteem.

Few cats can resist the simple fun of a piece of string dragged across the floor or a ball of paper rolled across linoleum.

FELINE WORKOUT

STRETCHING

A cat who is running, leaping, pouncing, and chasing is stretching. If you can catch him lying on the floor, then you can encourage good stretches by drawing toys a bit out of reach. With any luck he'll stretch to reach them.

Other stretching can be accomplished by slowly lowering him toward the floor. Most cats will reach toward the floor as they get close. Alternatively, you can hold him near and slightly below the edge of a bed. Most cats will reach up and pull themselves up. Anytime your cat does what you want, praise him warmly. Your encouragement will help him understand what you want from him.

CLIMBING

By using a drag toy, you can direct your cat to climb up just about anything. First get your cat to pursue something intently. Dangling it just above his head, or slowly dragging it in front of him will get even the most uninterested cat involved. Now, drag it up his scratching post, bounce it off the top, be annoyingly tantalizing.

The more your cat reaches for it, the better a workout he is getting.

AEROBICS

Keeping your cat active for ten to fifteen minutes gives them a good aerobic workout, and chances are you'll be getting one too! Chase toys are the best for this. The more interesting the chase, the more involved your cat will be. Or take a good-sized cardboard box and cut several cat-sized doors in it. Now roll a Ping-Pong ball into it, drag a toy through it, dangle a toy into one of the doorways—have fun, your cat will! And if, in the midst of it all, the box is pretty well destroyed, who cares? There are more where that comes from.

Cat Training—Strengthening the Bond

Cat training? Can that be done? Sure, why not? Absolutely! Don't expect Lassie or anything but you both can have a great deal of fun teaching your cat what a few words mean.

To start with it is important to understand that commanding a cat to do anything is not going to get you too far. It is much more effective to suggest. Suggest to a cat, teach him why it is a fine thing to do, and you'll be on your way. Tell him, and you'll be sitting alone.

Why teach a cat behaviors? Isn't that undignified? Let us answer that one at a time. Why? Because it is fun—for both you and the cat. It develops communication between the two of you, makes you a team, and increases trust, when done properly. It exercises your cat's intelligence, of which he has a great deal but which largely goes untapped in the cat-human relationship. And, lastly and most importantly to us, it strengthens the attachment between human and cat.

This brings us to the next point, isn't it undignified? I don't think so. The cats we've worked with haven't thought so. And as long as your friends don't laugh at the cat, he probably won't ever think so. But I guess that kind of depends on how you approach it. With Ben, I thought him so smart for learning so quickly, I felt nothing but pride in him and his accomplishments. If you think teaching the cat is stupid—skip it. You won't be able to hide it from your cat anyway, and when he gets a whiff of that, forget it!

But if you think developing some shared understanding, a communication bridge between two species is a worthwhile endeavor—go ahead. I bet you'll be surprised at how much untouched talent lies in your feline friend.

USE YOUR VOICE PROPERLY

Your voice is your most effective training tool. It is versatile, readily available, and easy to use. There are just a few things you need to know to use it properly in this scenario.

CAREFUL WITH VOLUME
Normal cats have excellent hearing, much better than ours. Yet, we often treat them as if they were deaf. We may speak too loudly—like someone might speak too loudly to a visitor from another country in the hopes that will help them understand. It doesn't. And with cats a raised volume usually means impending trouble. This makes them tense. A tense cat is not one who'll learn much. Speak in a normal tone, that's all that's required.

BE AWARE OF YOUR LANGUAGE
Language is quite confusing for a cat. It is not their natural mode of communication. The fact that they can learn it at all is a tribute to their intelligence. Smart or not, your cat can use all the help he can get. Make it easy for him by speaking clearly, using simple words. Be 100 percent consistent about your words and your cat will become close to 100 percent consistent about his response. If the word you are teaching with is "Sit" don't say "Sit" one time and "Sit down" the next. That is confusing.

SAY THINGS ONCE
Cats, not knowing language, learn exactly what you teach them. So if you say "Sitsitsit" and then guide him to do so, he'll think the command is "Sitsitsit." He won't respond to a simple "Sit" because he won't recognize it as the right word—any more than Bee means the same thing a B-B.

WATCH YOUR TONE
While cats may not naturally understand language, they do understand tone quite well. Use your tone to your best advantage. Words you are teaching the cat should be said in a neutral tone—not a request and not a

THE MYTH OF SPITE

Spite is the age-old explanation of animal misbehavior. The cat urinated on the new quilt out of spite. Or the dog chewed up the remote control while you were gone out of spite. Although an easy answer, it is not a correct one.

Humans are spiteful. Animals are not. They do react to stress, new situations, and fear in certain predictable ways, none of which is spiteful. Your cat urinated on the new quilt because he was marking his territory, in this case a large new object in his private domain. He ate your pot roast because you left it out and it tasted good, not because he was trying to get you back for having people over.

Whenever you start to think, "He did it from spite...," think again. Spite just isn't in a cat's vocabulary.

command. A statement is best. We, as polite human beings, have a tendency to ask our cats questions. "Sit?" we say. Far better and more effective is "Sit." Try to use the same tone each time, that will make it much easier for your cat to learn what is wanted. Praise in a warm, higher tone, similar to the "Here Kitty, Kitty!" that has worked on thousands of cats through the years.

MOTIVATING YOUR CAT

What motivates the cat to work with you? That depends on the cat. But in most cases the immediate motivation is a reward of some sort, food being the easiest and most reliable.

Some people have a negative reaction to food-based training, saying that they don't want to "bribe" the animal. Well, I have shocking news—all training and teaching whether for people or animals is based on a bribery system, or what we prefer to call positive reinforcement. I've never understood why some folks resist training their pet with food, yet consider a weekly paycheck okay. Getting paid is positive reinforcement. How many of us would continue to go to our job without a paycheck?

In school, grades are the "bribe." You work hard, you get a good grade. Somehow that is fulfilling to most of us. Alternatively, affection may be the positive reinforcement used. Warm praise for some cats and most dogs may be plenty of motivation to repeat the behavior. But whatever the teaching situation, positive reinforcement is almost always in place.

Food is the positive motivation we will work with, however. By all means praise your cat as well. In fact, if you praise your cat as you are giving the food reward, he will soon consider the praise almost as wonderful as the

This is a dangerous place for your cat to be.

Sarah Wilson

food itself. An obvious point, but an important one, is that since you are using food, it is best to work with your cat when he is hungry. Five minutes of teaching before a meal is plenty. Sessions don't have to be long to be surprisingly effective. A week or so of five to ten minutes a day and you'll have a cat who joyfully plays the I-say-it, you-do-it game.

Correction or Punishment?

Many of us have had the misfortune of being trained, at one time or another, through largely punitive methods. Because of this, we are indoctrinated to believe that punishment is key to learning. Not true and *really* not true with felines.

Punishment normally means some emotionally charged physical and psychological attack intended to make the attackee feel unhappy, embarrassed, threatened, or just plain stupid. You try this with a cat and she will leave. If she can't leave physically, she will leave mentally. And if she can't do that either, she is extremely likely to respond aggressively. Ten points for the cat.

Something to keep in mind with cats is that when they put their mind to it, they are infinitely better equipped to attack us than vice versa. Anyone who has been seriously assaulted by a cat can attest to that. Such assaults are rare, but remember, we domesticated predators to share our homes. Respect is due them.

A correction is an unemotional

negative reinforcement that educates rather than frightens. The ideal correction is perfectly timed, is appropriate to the deed, and communication to the cat what you intend to communicate. Figure out these three aspects of a perfect correction and you will be halfway home to changing behavior.

In all teaching, timing truly is everything. The best time to stop a behavior is just as the cat starts to do it. The second best is just as the cat does it. The most common, and least effective, is after the cat has done it.

Here are examples of each of these types of corrections for the on-the-counter cat:

THE BEST:
You see your cat walk into your kitchen toward your counter. You grab the water bottle and, staying out of sight behind the doorway, get ready. He positions himself to jump and just as he is beginning to take off you squirt him a couple of times and duck behind the door. He scoots under the table, wondering what just happened. That's perfect. He associates something unpleasant with the act of jumping. If you can teach him not to jump at the counter, you will never have a countertop cat.

THE SECOND BEST:
You see your cat walk into your kitchen toward your counter. You grab the water bottle and, staying out of sight behind the doorway, get ready. Your cat gets ready, jumps, and lands on the counter. You squirt him a couple of times and duck behind the door. He scoots off the counter, under the table, wondering what just

happened. Not bad, but that teaches him to get off as soon as he gets on. With a bit better timing, as described in the first example, you can teach him not to get on in the first place.

THE WORST:

You see your cat walk into your kitchen toward your counter. You grab the water bottle and, staying out of sight behind the doorway, get ready. He hops up, stays there for a few seconds, you leap up yelling "NO!," squirt him a few times, he jumps off, and you pursue him, squirting him a few more times. What has he just learned? Mostly, that you're crazy. That you leap out of nowhere and attack him for no reason that he can figure. The minute you frighten him he is linking the fear with *you* and not with getting on the countertop. By pursuing him, he gets no reward by jumping off the counter. If the correction does not stop the instant your cat complies, how is he supposed to know when he did what you want?

A good correction stops the cat from proceeding, but doesn't cause other problems in the process. If you overcorrect—screaming, charging, or otherwise terrorizing your cat—he will become frightened. He may quite logically link that fear to you and not to the deed. Another common example are cats who won't use the litter box in front of their owners. What often happens is the owner catches the kitten making a mistake and overreacts, scolding, slapping, or rubbing the kitten's face in his own mess. What does the kitten learn? That you get mighty upset when you

see him eliminating, so he now goes to great lengths to make sure you don't. You may still get mistakes, only now they'll be out of sight. People then call this hiding the mistake spiteful, cunning, and proof that the kitten knows he's doing wrong. Not at all. He's just responding to your teaching and hoping that out of sight is out of mind.

Equally bad is the ineffectual correction, which makes no impact on the cat whatsoever, teaching him simply to ignore you and go about his business. Continuing with the counter example, you see the cat on the counter. You walk over saying, "No, baby, no, no," in a sweet, slightly chiding voice. You lift the cat from the counter, set him on the floor, and stroking him say, "Counter's not a good spot, honey. The floor is good." What did the cat learn? That he gets a wonderful amount of attention and love when you find him on the counter.

Carrier Training

Getting a cat into her carrier is one of the jobs that most owners dread. You pull out the carrier. The cat heads for the hills. You extricate the struggling cat from behind the sofa, trying to tell her it's okay—a sure sign to your cat that it isn't—and you approach the crate. Your normally sane cat becomes an acrobat. Paws fly out in every direction, claws grab on to your clothing. You attempt to put the cat into the carrier. You get one paw tucked in, another flies free and blocks the entrance. It's a nightmare

We taught Ben to like his carrier — he goes in and out just for fun.

for you both and by the time you are successful, if you are successful, everyone is traumatized.

Good news though! It doesn't have to be like that. You can have a cat who wraps himself around you excitedly as you bring out his crate, eagerly hops in when you open the door. Impossible? Hardly. Just takes a few days, a few treats, and a little practice.

INTRODUCE THE CRATE

For cats with no crating experience, this is easy. For cats who look upon a crate as a close second to the gates of hell, getting them used to it may take a little longer. But not to worry, either way, it's ridiculously easy.

Take the crate, removing the door if you can or propping the door open. Set it on the floor. If you only have cats in your house, great. Put treats all around and in the crate. Put treats in a three-foot circle around the crate. When the treats are all gone, put them out again, only this time in a two-foot circle. Repeat until there is no circle, and all the treats are in or on the crate. When your cat happily climbs on and into the crate to get the treats, wonderful. Now, for just another day or two, store the treats inside the crate, near the rear. He does that fine! Perfect! Move on to the next step.

TEACH THE WORD "CRATE"

It doesn't matter what word you use, all that matters is that you use the same word consistently. Say "Crate," "Bed," "Home," whatever you like, just always say it and never change it. Now, get your cat's attention with

CRATING AN UNWILLING CAT

Getting an unwilling cat into a carrier is something like trying to stuff a woodchuck into a sock. Teaching your cat to happily enter a crate is so much less trouble than attempting to wrestle him in. But if you haven't had the time to teach him yet, here's a trick.

Using a plastic crate with a front gate, set it up on its end. Then, lifting the cat up by the scruff of his neck and supporting his rear with your other hand, lower him down into the crate. Since he doesn't see it coming he may not realize what's happening until it is too late. Holding him by the scruff has a calming effect. The trick is to release the cat and get the gate shut. Little stress or strain on either of you and success. Who can argue with that?

some really wonderful treat. Whatever makes his heart sing. Depending on the cat, that might be a small cube of chicken, beef, or a raisin. Don't argue the matter, just use whatever he likes. Show it to him and in your happiest voice say the command, we call it "Crate." Keeping the treat at his nose level, guide him over to the crate. When he gets within a foot, give the treat. Praise him and tell him how brilliant he is. Pick him up and move him a few feet away from the crate. Repeat.

Once he becomes confident coming that close, put the treat on the ledge of the doorway. Let him take it from there. Heap on the praise and petting. You're really getting somewhere now. Now, toss the treat inside and let him go in to get it. Marvelous. No more worries. Go on to the next stage.

CLOSE THE DOOR

Reinstall the door if you took it off. Repeat the previous exercise just to make sure the door doesn't spook him. If it does, go back a few steps and reteach the approach to the crate on command. He'll move through the stages very quickly this time, as it is old turf. He may not notice the door at all, but if he does, don't worry. It'll only take a day or two to get back up to speed.

Now, once he's going all the way in to get the treat, practice softly shutting the door behind him. Keep up the happy banter. Try tossing in several small treats to keep him busy. Do not keep the door shut for long, no more than a few seconds. Then open it and allow him to come out if he wishes.

You're done. Now you have a cat who'll happily hop in his crate anytime. Only took a week or so and there was no bloodshed. We call that time well spent!

If you want to keep up his positive attitude toward the crate, feed him in there with the door open. Put a blanket in there and set it in the sun. Put catnip in there every so often. Always have a couple of yummy treats tucked inside. Tell him to hop in, close the door, carry him down the hall, and let him out. Reward him well, praise him and fuss over him. Basically, continue to make it a positive place for your cat and he'll continue to think of it in a positive way.

Teaching "Sit"

Teaching a cat to sit is amazingly simple. The premise is basic anatomy. Picture your cat's spine like a seesaw with his head at one end and his rear at the other. Now, as the head lifts up, what happens to the rear? It goes down, always and inevitably.

In order to teach your cat to sit at your suggestion, all you have to do is teach him to lift his head up and back, then let nature take its course. Food is the easiest way to accomplish this task. Using a treat he finds especially compelling, hold it between your fingers and to his nose. Say "Sit" once, clearly and calmly. Now, lift the treat slowly up and back, keeping it close to his nose. When he sits, praise him warmly and give him the treat immediately. The closer you can get to having that treat in his

Hold the food at nose level ...

Photos by Brian Kilcommons

Say "Sit" and bring the food up and over his head ...

When he sits, give him the treat, stroke him, and tell him how incredible you think he is.

mouth the moment his bottom hits the ground, the quicker he will link the two events. Bottom on ground—treat in mouth. Once he gets that formula, you're home free.

COMMON "SIT" PROBLEMS

BACKS UP INSTEAD OF SITTING

If your cat backs up when he looks up, either practice this against a wall where he can't back up or gently run your other hand over his rump scooping him into position. Once he is seated, immediately give him the treat and praise! A couple of times helping him out and he'll soon understand what is wanted.

Sarah holds the treat a bit high, forcing Ben to sit up. By lowering the treat, she'll help him into a sit. Ben won't get the treat until he's sitting.

SITS UP

If your cat sits up for the treat, don't despair. That's a pretty cute trick in and of itself. He's just telling you that you are holding the treat too high. Bring it lower, right up over his

nose, and he should respond as you wish.

BITES FINGERS

Hold the treat further back in your fingers so he can smell it but not see it. Then use your hand as the lure to guide his head up and back. He'll follow the smell, but be less likely to bite. If he continues to nip, he may be too hungry. Stop, wait a few minutes, give him a small meal, then try again. A little food should take the edge off his appetite without making him completely uninterested in food.

Also, try using a firm, negative tone of voice along with withdrawal of the food. There is no need to be loud here, just firm and direct. Always stay calm with a cat; if they sense you are upset, things will get worse.

GRABS WITH FRONT PAWS

Use a firm, negative, but not loud tone and, bringing your hand down and away, disengage the paws. Be sure to reward him the instant he sits but doesn't put his paws up. The good trainer always waits for any instant of good and rewards it instead of waiting for the bad and correcting.

For insistent grabbers, use a ruler or pencil to block his front paws. Block, do not whack them, please. Usually once the cat has been rewarded a couple of times for the behavior you desire he'll be more than happy to comply with your wishes.

Teaching "Down"

"Down," meaning lie down, is a convenient behavior to teach your cat to do on cue for grooming, trips to the vet's office, as well as to amaze your friends and impress your relatives.

The easiest way to start teaching this is to have your cat sit, then for you to take a treat between your thumb and forefinger. Showing it to your cat, slowly lower it straight downward. Ideally your cat's head will follow the treat. Once your hand reaches the table, slowly pull it out away from the cat. The path of your hand should write out a capital L shape. If all goes well, your cat will follow the treat right into a down position. The moment your cat is down, praise her warmly and give her the treat. A few times of this and she'll get the hang of it.

An alternative method is lifting the front paws and easing the cat down into position. When you grasp both front paws at once, be sure to keep one finger between them. That will serve to buffer any pressure between the two. Once the cat is down, praise and give the treat as usual. Your cat will soon understand what it is you want.

COMMON "DOWN" PROBLEMS

STANDS UP INSTEAD OF LYING DOWN

Your cat is so limber she can simply stand up without moving from that spot; this allows her head to lower

Start with the cat sitting, putting the treat right up to his nose...

Photos by Brian Kilcommons

Say "Down" and slowly lower the treat straight down ...

Once down, stroke him, give the treat and praise him warmly for being so wonderful.

further downward in pursuit of the treat without actually lying down.

If this happens, slow down. Rest your free hand on her rump while you guide her slowly with the treat. Do not hold her by or apply pressure on her rear, this will only cause her to struggle. The hand just rests there as a reminder.

Alternatively, use the lift the paws method. Use whichever method gives you success. Be sure to stroke, praise, and reward your cat for any compliance. She'll soon catch on to what you want.

LOWERS HEAD BUT DOESN'T LIE DOWN

Very common to start with. If your cat lowers her head but won't actually lie down, don't worry. Here's what you do. When she lowers her head, give her the treat. Next time, make her lower her head a bit more before she gets the treat. Do this and in a session or two she'll be lying down like a champ. Always keep in mind: this is not a race. It doesn't matter if it takes three sessions or five or ten. Who cares? Praise, patience, and fun are the keys to success!

REFUSES TO LIE DOWN

This will happen if you try to force your cat to comply. Don't attempt to press down on his shoulders, that won't work. Don't get into a battle of wills with your cat. If he becomes annoyed, end the session. The last thing you want is for him to think that this is no fun. Keep the lessons short and upbeat. Take your time. Reward every small improvement. Soon he will relax and lie down. And

if he doesn't? Does it really matter? Take a break and come back to this behavior in a few days or a week.

Teaching "Come"

Chances are your cat is trained perfectly to come. Just use the can opener if you feed wet food or jiggle the box of dry food and your cat materializes from many rooms away, ready and willing.

This is interesting. Why does your cat come so consistently to those sound cues? There is a clear motivation. Coming to those sounds is always followed by a meal. There is no downside for the cat. He is never scolded or disappointed. If you smacked your cat every time he came when he heard the can opener, and you didn't feed him, he would soon—very soon—stop coming when he heard that noise. Now, of course you wouldn't smack your cat, but what if you called him and immediately put her in a bath or in the car to

go to the vet, or sprayed him with flea spray. Get the idea? If you call a cat to you and then do something unpleasant, what is his motivation to come to you again?

The can opener is 100 percent consistent. It always sounds the same. Consistency when teaching is terribly important. The cue is unemotional. The sound of the dry food in the box or the can opener never changes. But your voice can. If you holler at a cat to come to you, he won't. Cats are no fools, and they will not come to an angry, frustrated, or cranky human being. When training an animal, keep your voice as consistent as possible. A pleasant tone of voice makes teaching easier for you and your cat.

The good news is that if your cat has learned to come to the sound of the can opener, he can learn to come to the sound of your voice. You just have to learn to be half as good a teacher as the can opener is.

Start by getting a suitable reward. Let your cat's preferences direct you.

If he's a fool for fruit, use that. If he's a glutton for mutton, why fight it? This is not the time to get persnickety, use what works.

As with any complex behavior, start at the end and work backward. Sound funny? It's true. For "Come," that means starting with your cat very close to you and working backward till he'll respond from a distance.

If your cat won't come one foot to you to get the treat, why try ten feet? Also, if your cat won't come one foot to you for the treat, either he isn't hungry enough or he doesn't like the treat. Either way, make some changes. Feed him after the training session. Feed him less on the days you train. Use another type of treat. Make it work.

Once he is eager, begin. Starting with him right next to you, use his

For "Come," put the treat right up to your cat's nose. Say "Come" and back away...

Praise him as you continue to back away. Keep the treat at his nose level ...

After he has come a few feet, stop, and, raising the treat above his head, say "Sit."

Once he sits, stroke and praise him some more. That was great!

name and say "Come!" in a cheerful tone but normal volume. Then immediately give him the treat. Repeat this a few times, until he is eagerly taking the treat when he hears the word "Come." All you're doing now is linking the word "Come" with a verbal praise and a food reward.

Once this is working well (for some cats it will be minutes, others a few sessions) step a few feet away from your cat. Say "Come," show him the treat, and guide him to you. I like to have the cat sit when he arrives, so I add "Sit" right away.

When your cat does this perfectly, take a few more steps backward as he approaches, so that he is now coming five to six feet and sitting on command. Now, begin using "Come" when your cat is across the room. If he comes right away, give the treat and praise! If he doesn't, go over to him, put the treat up to his nose, and back away to where you first called him. Praise and encourage him to fol-

low you. If he does, reward him. If he doesn't, stop the session, put away the treats, and try again later.

Now you can start having some fun. When he is in the mood and eager to please, play some come-to-me games throughout your house or apartment. Start off easy, but make it harder as he gets better. As he is watching you, step out of sight around a corner or behind a door and call him. Praise him as he is looking for you, even if you can't see him. Praise is important here, especially when you are out of sight. When he finds you—praise him and give the reward. Build on this, until he'll come and find you wherever you are.

It is important to continue praising him while he is looking to give him an idea of where you are and keep his motivation up. Sitting there silent is no help and you may find yourself sitting there alone for a long time. This is not a test, it is a game. If your cat is having a hard time find-

This is the first time Ben's ever been on lead, and he's having a pretty typical reaction ...

With a little sweet-talking and a large chunk of cheese, he begins to relax ...

ing you, make it easier for him to succeed. Nothing succeeds like success. Think play, not complexity.

One funny side effect of you being the only person in the house training the cat is that your feline friend may well believe that "Come" means, literally, run to you—regardless of who says the word. Don't be surprised if he makes a beeline to you the first few time a new person says "Come." This is easy to change. Just have the person start off at the beginning with a few very short "come"s with lots of treats. The cat will understand quickly what the new game is.

Teaching "Let's Go"

Some cats enjoy a nice walk on a lead outside. Having a cat who accepts a lead and harness is a convenience, especially when traveling. We suggest using a harness with a cat, as a collar can cause a cat to panic when pressure is applied.

We also recommend the H type harness with separate straps that buckle around the neck and chest. The figure-8 type harness with just one buckle is easier to put on but it can tighten around the neck or chest uncomfortably when pressure is applied. The best lead is a thin nylon one with a small clip. You're not towing a truck here, you're walking your cat. You don't need a thick lead with a huge buckle.

The harness has a magical effect on many cats, causing them to stay motionless for a long period of time. To skip this stage, and to help the cat have a good feeling about being harnessed, we recommend harnessing him every day for meals. If necessary, add some extra scrumptious food to his regular fare for the training period.

Leave the harness on for half an hour or so after the meal. This helps your cat adjust to the feel of it on

Now he's relaxing and Sarah can begin guiding him with the food and praise ...

And away we go — a steady stream of conversation and the cheese held in plain sight makes our first on-lead outing a success!

him. Once he is at ease with the harness, start adding the lead. Now, harness him before meals, attaching the lead, then setting him down two or three feet from his bowl. Let him walk over dragging the lead. Pet him well for this accomplishment. Once he is walking to his bowl comfortably, start saying the words "Let's go" and holding the lead as he walks.

Next, put down his dinner, pick up your cat and harness him just out of sight of his dining spot. Put your cat down, say "Let's go," and encourage him to walk to the dish. If he refuses, have a helper rattle the dish while you verbally encourage the cat to go to it. If all else fails, pick him up, show him his dinner, then set him down a few feet away.

The goal is to teach him that when you say "Let's go" that there will be something good at the end of the road if he walks there. As he is heading for the dish, praise and encourage him. As he gets better at this game, start setting his bowl down in different parts of the house. Now you're ready to go places.

At first, make these walks short and easy. Throughout the walk, give him treats, praise him warmly, and play with his favorite toy. Try to praise and play with him when he is moving. Your cat may stop to eat his treats, but give them to him when he moves forward; don't wait for him to stop and then feed him, as that will only encourage him to stop. As he improves, make him walk further and further for fewer and fewer treats.

COMMON "LET'S GO" PROBLEMS

CAT FREEZES IN PLACE

Expect your cat to freeze at least a few times during this training. That is a normal reaction to feeling something around her body. Be patient, she'll get the hang of it. If she freezes in place, leave the lead on her and allow her to drag it around for half an hour or so. *Be sure to supervise her* during this time, as the lead could get caught up on something.

CAT PANICS

If she starts flipping around, panicking, wait for her to stop, then praise her. Leave the harness on, allow her to get used to it. Again, always closely supervise a cat dragging a lead. Wearing a harness is unlike anything she's ever felt, so give her a chance to adapt. She will if you are patient and encouraging.

CAT PULLS AWAY FROM YOU

This is to be expected. Any animal's first response to being restrained is to attempt to get away. Be patient, use treats she really enjoys, make sure she's hungry and take things slow. Reward her anytime she takes even a single step forward. As she conquers that, reward her anytime she takes two steps forward. Keep building her compliance step by step. Soon she'll be walking on lead with ease.

Teaching "Off"

Here's another spot to put a training table to good use. (Training tables are described in the section on teaching "Down.") "Off" for our purposes means four feet on the floor pronto! Using the training table makes this both fun and easy to teach.

Start with one hungry cat. Put him on the training table. Show him a treat, tell him "Off," and then guide your hand toward the floor. Chances are he'll jump off the table. Praise him, give him the treat. Extol his brilliance! He's one in a million. Repeat once or twice. Cats have little tolerance for endless repetition. The moment your cat appears bored or begins to lose interest—stop! You can do more another day.

Once he gets good at this, leaping off readily for his reward, tell him "Off" but don't lower your hand to the floor. Instead, do a fake—move your hand toward the floor but only partway. He'll probably jump anyway. Praise him and give the treat. Over a few sessions, shorten your hand movement until he is jumping when he first hears "Off." Now you have it. That wasn't too hard, was it?

COMMON "OFF" PROBLEMS

CAT WON'T JUMP OFF

If your cat stares at the treat but can't be bothered to actually jump off, do one of two things. You can try a lower table if your cat's not a big jumper. Or you can gently ease him off the

Teaching "Off" is not hard. Put your cat on something, hold a treat below him, and say "Off."

He'll hop off to get to the treat ...

When he does, praise him and give him the treat. Won't take long for him to learn this!

Photos by Brian Kilcommons

table, then praise him and give the treat as if he did it himself. We use a flat hand behind his butt and gently push him off. This is to help him along if he just can't seem to get the idea; this is *not* a punishment in any way. There is no swatting, shoving, or scolding involved. Help him, then praise him. He'll figure it out quickly.

Ben and Training

Ben was a great deal of fun to train. He adored the food treats, which made it simple to direct and reward him. He already had complete trust in me, so fear didn't get in our way.

Typically, he learned quickly. Cats are extremely bright, and as long as you ask them to work *with* you and not *for* you, things can move along quite well. The only behavior he had any real problem with was "Down." He wasn't interested in that position, but we worked it out with some time, patience, love, and rewards. But actually, doesn't that work most things out?

The side benefits of working with him were tremendous. He became more people-oriented in general and more me-oriented in particular. Previously a bit aloof, he now seeks me out for extended feline lovefests, insists on curling up on my belly during TV times, and otherwise gets himself involved.

The only minor problem we had was that Ben took his training quite seriously. He saw it not as degrading but more like higher education. It became immediately clear that laughter was *not* allowed in the training area. Anyone who ignored this rule was met with a cold stare. Then Ben lay down, closed his eyes in a slow blink, and refused to participate any longer. It was hard for me not to laugh the first time this happened! Now I give strict instructions to all our audience that this is to be viewed with respect and not amusement.

Multi-Cat Households

Running a smooth multi-cat household is not usually a difficult task. Most cats adapt to each other—eventually. There are a few tricks though to making it run smoothly and these we will share with you here.

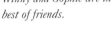

Winny and Sophie are the best of friends.

LITTER BOXES

With two or more using the toilet, you have to be even more diligent about keeping it clean. Ideally, a box for every cat is nice but at a certain point that becomes a bit unwieldy. But if you do have many cats you will need many boxes. In a multi-cat household, a good rule to go by is scoop as many times a day as you have cats. Two cats, scoop twice a day. Three cats, three times a day. All this scooping becomes mandatory as your numbers increase. It's a dirty job, but you're the one who has to do it. It's a heck of a lot better than cleaning urine out of the rug.

If you are getting mistakes, and you're not sure who is making them, try feeding each cat separately and adding some natural food coloring to each cat's food. That way you'll know who is responsible for what.

Alternatively, you can confine one cat at a time, each for a few days. When the mistakes stop, you know you either have the culprit under lock and key or the instigator. The instigator may not be the cat making the mistakes but may be the cat who torments his housemate to such a point that she makes errors. Either way, once you know who is going where, please read pages 147–153 for complete guidelines for how to handle the problem.

ADDING A NEW CAT

Consider having a friend bring in the new family member. Or, if that is not possible, bring the cat in her carrier into "her" room, open the carrier door, and leave her. In an hour or so you can open the door and see what your first cat thinks about this all. If you are concerned, put the newcomer back into the crate for the introduction. That way they can sniff each other but can't cause any real harm.

As with all things to do with cats, you must take an "everything in its own good time" view of the situation. Some cats accept a new member quickly, others take several weeks or months to work it out. As long as no blood is being shed, don't worry about how they feel about each other too much. Actually, it's between them, isn't it?

For more detailed information about introducing a new cat to older, established household felines see pages 57–58. In the case of adding a new cat it is a good idea to follow the old advice "Hope for the best and prepare for the worst."

TERRITORIES

Cats like to have their own spots. Providing high-up hideaways will be a great comfort to your new cat. When cats are stressed they like to go up, if possible. When Emily is stressed she climbs to the top shelf of my bookshelves. When I go over with one of my dogs to my friend Audrey's house, her cats all hide up behind the facade on the top of a large cabinet she has. Ben doesn't ever climb—I don't think insecurity is part of his nature.

If your furniture does not provide such a retreat, consider building or buying a floor-to-ceiling cat climber with a high perch. Not only does this allow your new cat to tuck himself away, but it keeps him out of the established cat's territory.

Remember, your older feline friend is going to have to at best share some space and at worst lose some territory in this deal. Neither option sounds too good to him. Give him time to adjust.

Because scratching furniture is largely a territorial-marking exercise, you can expect some increase in this activity when a new cat enters the house. Placing a few posts at critical points in each cat's area helps direct the cats to the proper surface. Probable places for scratching to occur are near the door to the new cat's area of confinement (on both sides of the door), the most commonly used entrance into the established cat's favorite area, and beside his favorite sleeping spot. Prevention, redirection, and praise for the behavior you want is the best way to handle it.

Punishing a cat at any time rarely works and punishing a cat who is under stress already almost guarantees you more trouble!

FEEDING

Once you get a couple of cats, you will no doubt have a range of appetites at your table. Almost every multi-cat group has a glutton. At our house it is Emily, since, as stray, she never seems to get used to the idea that the food *will* most definitely be back again in a few hours, that she doesn't have to gorge herself.

Feeding meals, instead of leaving food out all the time, is an easy way to cope with these different eating styles and needs. A separate bowl for each animal works best. Put down the food for the slow eaters first, and the fastest eaters last. Of course, your glutton is going to want to dive into the slow poke's bowl. This can easily be handled by taking him away from the bowl and showing him his own bowl. Normally that will focus him on the bowl you have and he will forget his previous desire. That way with a bit of timing you can get your cats finishing up at close to the same time.

As you put down each bowl, say the cat's name. A week or so of doing this, and the cats will pick up the routine and eat in an orderly fashion.

Another simple solution is just feed your gluttons in a separate room.

Dogs and Cats

Most dogs and cats learn to live peaceably with each other—given time and some clearly understood ground rules. Every cat adjusts to the presence of a dog at her own rate. You cannot force her to like the dog, and any efforts to do so will inevitably lead to increased tension between them.

When introducing a cat and a dog make sure of two things. First, that the cat has a safe harbor to retreat to, and second, that the dog is restrained.

A safe harbor for your cat can be a tall shelf or table, or a separate room set up with a baby gate across the doorway so the cat can jump in and out but the dog cannot. If your dog can leap the gate, then use a large hook and eye to clip the door open enough to allow the cat to enter but not the dog.

A guaranteed safe place allows the cat to relax and gather her wits about her without the stress of the dog being able to approach. Make sure that the cat isn't cornered when she meets the dog. Being cornered brings out the worst in any frightened animal. Having an escape route will make her feel bolder and more secure.

Restraining a dog is critical. This always means a leash and collar. Holding the dog or relying on verbal control is *not adequate*, as a dog in the mood to chase a cat is hard to manage. Most dogs are going to be curious about a new cat, that is natural.

But in some dogs, curiosity can quickly change into aggression. Almost any dog is going to get excited if the cat runs away from it. This is particularly true in dog breeds created for their aggression level, such as some of the working/guard breeds and terriers. That doesn't mean that they won't become fast friends, only that when the dog is in a high level of excitement he may not always make the right choice.

In an ideal world, you've been training your dog all along. But the world isn't ideal, so chances are you haven't done much training or have let it slip. Get to it! Now is the time you need good verbal control over your dog and the canine respect that comes with it.

Our first book, *Good Owners, Great Dogs*, gives you all the information you need to train your dog to be reliable around cats. Almost every dog can be trained to obey "Wait," "Leave it," "Out," and "Down" on command. Not only is such training a good idea for all dogs but for cat chasers they are a must!

ADDING A CAT TO A HOUSEHOLD WITH A DOG

Confining the cat in "her" room allows the cat and dog to sniff each other through the door. Put down two blankets or towels for them to sleep on and switch them every few days so the animals get familiar with each other's scent. If they refuse these beds, then simply rub the animals down with the towels and switch them anyway. The effect will be the same. Allow the cat to settle into her new home and to get comfortable

SCRATCHED EYES

Dogs can get their eyes seriously scratched by a cat, although, knock on wood, we've never had that happen. Most cats will only seriously scratch a dog in self-defense. If you make sure the cats feel safe and can always retreat, fewer accidents will occur.

This type of problem is a particular danger for short-nosed dogs like Boxers, Pugs, Cavaliers, Lhasa Apsos, Bulldogs, and the like. Be extra careful with them as well as with all puppies, whose combination of rambunctiousness and immature facial structure puts them at higher risk as well.

Keeping the cat's nails trimmed is particularly important if you are introducing new animals or have reason for concern. Controlling and training the dog goes without saying!

with you *before* you attempt to introduce the dog. One stress at a time, please!

If your dog is crate-trained, great. Crate him for an hour or so in the evening. This gives your cat a chance to explore without worrying about pursuit. If your dog isn't crate-trained, confine him to a room. Give him a special toy to play with. If he barks and scratches at the door, you definitely want to train him. He's confused about a few things. Last choice is to put him on a lead and keep him next to you. This isn't the best because the cat won't be able to come over and visit with you and may beat a hasty retreat when she spots the dog. But if that's the best that you can manage, it's better than nothing.

Another nice gift to your cat is having the dog sleep in your room with you, leaving the house free for your feline to explore. These explorations will give your cat more confidence, allow him to scope out the good hiding places, and get him accustomed to the dog's smell.

Any canine cat chasing should be handled immediately in a no-nonsense way. Such behavior is not allowed. As much as we would love to give you complete directions for this process, they are lengthy and it is not within the scope of this book to cover them. Suffice it to say: "Get help."

A SPECIAL WORD ABOUT KITTENS

Kittens are fragile little fireballs. Even a sweet dog can inadvertently harm a kitten with an overenthusiastic paw. Supervision—strict supervision—until the kitten gets bigger,

sturdier, and more able to defend herself is an absolute necessity.

ADDING A PUPPY TO A HOUSEHOLD OF CATS

Limiting the pup's access to the rest of the house makes sense both from a housebreaking and a cat-chasing perspective. Crate him when you cannot directly supervise him. Close doors and put up baby gates when the pup is with you so he cannot wander. Keep him on lead with you when you take him into the rest of the house. This way you can correct any cat-chasing as it starts. Let him know right off the bat that harassing the other family members is not allowed. If you are not sure how to do this, or are having a hard time, seek out a good local trainer for assistance. Ask veterinarians and local humane societies for a recommendation. They usually know the better professionals in the area.

COMMON DOG-CAT PROBLEMS

DOG STEALING CAT'S FOOD

This is an easy one to stop. Either feed your cat two meals a day in a room away from the dog or put the dog in confinement when you feed the cat. If your dog is walked morning and evening, put down the cat's food just before you go out for the walk. Pick up the bowl the minute you return. Painless and simple. One trick: Keep your dog on lead when you return and correct him for rushing at the cat's bowl. Instead, have him sit and give him a treat for sitting patiently.

Dogs learn this deal quickly and soon sit nobly waiting for their treat.

LITTER BOX RAIDING

Here's a truly unappealing, but almost universal, dog-versus-indoor-cat problem. The best solution is to keep the box out of your dog's reach. For small dogs, keeping the box in the bathtub can be effective. As long as you remember to remove it before running your shower, it's a great answer to a disgusting problem.

As we have larger dogs, we put the cat box in the bathroom closet. A heavy string looped over the doorknob and then around a nail in the door frame works well. The best method is a long hook and eye. This is ideal because it can't be accidentally shut nor be easily opened by a dog. Installing a cat door is a bit more of a project but is another excellent solution to the problem. There is no reason a cat door can't be used inside the house.

DOG PLAYS TOO ROUGH

Many youthful, wonderful dogs just play a bit rough with the cat. This is really between the two of them as long as no harm is being done. Most cats will set the limits clearly. But if your cat is declawed, extremely tolerant, or just being lovingly mauled by an enthusiastic but mildly dim dog, then you will have to intervene on your cat's behalf.

One thing to do that works well is to down your dog. A dog playing from a down position is usually gentler on the cat than a pouncing, bouncing, standing-up dog. If you insist on the "Down" command when the play starts and then praise the

dog for downing, the dog will soon start downing himself when he feels playful.

The other option is to stop the games altogether with a "Leave it" followed by "Come" and "Down." This is best if your dog is truly out of hand when he plays. If enforcing this is hard for you, seek out a good local training class. I know it can seem impossible to get that kind of control on your dog, but we promise you it isn't.

CAT STALKS DOG

Some cats amuse themselves by stalking and tormenting the family dog. Some dogs are quite flustered by this and it is best to intervene on their behalf. A spray of water is the right correction for the stalking cat as it corrects the cat without frightening the dog the way a shake can or air horn might. Don't say anything when you spray the cat. This will help him associate the correction with the act of stalking the dog.

DOG PUSHES BETWEEN YOU AND YOUR CAT

One hard and fast rule around our house is that one animal can't butt in on private time between us and another animal. Once this is clearly established, much pushy behavior stops. Any animal who attempts to stick his head between one of us and another cat or dog is told to "go away" in no uncertain terms. The buttinsky is *never* petted, spoken to, or cooed over. It doesn't take long for them to all realize that everyone will get their fair share, but not all at once. Therefore we have no such problems between any of our four dogs or two cats.

IT'S ALWAYS SOMETHING

One night, after a long day, Sarah treated herself to an early-evening zone-out in front of the TV. She got the thick down comforter, made herself a cup of tea, unplugged the phones, and settled in for a relaxing few minutes. Corrie, just a pup at the time, came wagging over and asked, pretty politely for a pup, if she could come up. "How sweet," thought Sarah, "this will just make the moment." So Sarah arranged a spot and invited Corrie up. Corrie gleefully sprung onto Sarah's lap, cuddled up close to her chin, and proceeded to regurgitate half the contents of the litter box onto her chest. What a mess!

All About Emily

Omnipresent Emily helps with the writing of this book.

Sarah Wilson

As I write this, our cat Emily is lounging on the computer mouse pad, purring to herself and rubbing against my hand when I offer it. She is our newest household addition, a stray, found in a dumpster, kept by some bighearted folks at the Orange Community Pet Hospital for five months, until we came along.

She didn't have a classically cute face or a very pretty color but she was extremely sweet, which is our main criterion. That is how we got to Emily as a name. There is a line in the play *Our Town* that goes something like this: "Mama, am I pretty?" asks Emily. "Pretty enough for all normal purposes," replies Mama. That line came back to me with clarity looking at our Emily. She is pretty enough for us and has grown in beauty in our eyes as we have gotten to know her.

Upon arriving in our home, she took up immediate residence in our linen closet. Who could blame her with our crew? Although frightened and disoriented, she never offered a claw or a tooth in our direction—then or ever. She is a lady to her marrow and if she were human I am quite sure she would wear white gloves and use lace doilies on her tables. As is true of many such ladies, she is not a gifted athlete.

Emily jumps on a hunch, and often finds, in midair, that she has greatly misjudged the height or stability of her target. She has since become more careful in her efforts, but initially this led to all manner of mishap as she explored the house.

It took her two weeks in our home to purr. She was polite—always—and sweet and I didn't even really miss the purring until it started one day. A delicate little purr that you feel more than hear. A purr she does to herself, a feline mantra of happiness and the first sign to us that she knew she was home.

As I finish this, she is draped across my printer, resting her tiny head on an outstretched paw. Opening one eye in my direction—"Yes?" she seems to say, "are you writing about me?" Then she pulls in the paw, curls into a ball, and falls fast asleep.

Traveling with Your Cat

It is the rare cat who likes to travel. But if you happen to own such an animal, or if you are going for a long stay someplace and want your cat to come with you, then there are certain things you can do to make the trip easier and safer for all of you.

One of the keys to safe travel with your pet is to keep it cool. We would not even attempt a summer car trip without air conditioning. Even a few minutes in a hot car can overwhelm a cat, leading to heat stroke or death. If your cat is particularly susceptible to getting overheated (Persians are, for instance, with their long hair and short noses) freeze some cool packs and put one in the bottom of her crate wrapped in a thin cloth. Put a few others in a small ice chest. This way she'll be cooler and more comfortable during the ride. Even with this, never leave a cat in a car in the sun or on a hot day in the shade for even a few minutes. You would be horribly surprised how quickly an animal can get overheated and in serious medical trouble.

TRAVEL CHECKLIST

CURRENT PHOTO OF YOUR CAT

If, God forbid, your cat gets lost, a good, clear, reproducible photo of your cat will make putting together a lost sign much easier. If you can, bring along the negative too so you can have someplace run you off a bunch of copies.

LIST OF IDENTIFYING MARKS AND PATTERNS

Sit down for five minutes and study your cat. Make note of any unusual or unique marks.

HEALTH CERTIFICATE AND RECORDS

Some states and all other countries require your cat to have a current health certificate. These are simple to get, requiring just a quick trip to the vet, an exam, and check on all the vaccinations. Bring along copies of relevant records if your cat has any chronic medical problem along with your regular vet's phone number. The stress of travel can cause flare-ups of problems and you'll want all the information you need at your fingertips if that happens.

REGULAR FOOD

Some cat foods are harder to get in different parts of the country. Since many cats are finicky about their diets and since a sudden diet change can trigger a nasty diarrhea attack, something you *definitely* don't want in a car, it pays to plan ahead. Pack enough food for a few extra meals, that way if any spills or if you extend your trip you won't be caught short.

DISPOSABLE LITTER PANS

A disposable box is a real convenience. If you can't find these boxes, use litter box liners. If your cat doesn't shred them, it is a simple matter to pick up the contents of the box and throw it out. Also, don't feel like you have to use a ton of litter in the pan—half an inch or less is fine.

CAR SICKNESS

If you have a cat prone to car sickness, we suggest the following:

CRATE HIM
Not being able to see the world going by has a stomach-calming effect on some cats. Get a crate that is the right size for car riding—small. As long as the cat can turn around in it, it's big enough.

SKIP A MEAL
If you're worried about a gun going off, don't load it. If you're worried about a cat vomiting, don't feed him for at least four hours before the trip.

GET HIM USED TO CAR RIDES
Take frequent trips. Feed him after each trip. A few rides like that and he may begin to think differently about the whole affair.

MEDICATE HIM
Ask your vet about medication, which may help your cat cope better.

Start making these changes slowly during the few weeks before your trip. This way your friend will be used to the new kind of box or liner and the smaller amount of litter before you pack up the car and go.

WELL-FITTING HARNESS
Buy a properly fitting H type harness. These are the most secure and most comfortable for your cat.

SOLID CAT CARRIER
The solid plastic cat carriers are by far the best. These will not collapse if a sudden stop throws a heavy suitcase against it, and they have outer rims that allow for air flow even if bags are packed in around it (not a good idea by the way). They take a lot of wear and tear, are easy to clean, keep the mess confined if the cat spills his water or vomits, and generally are simply the best tool for the job.

CAT-SIZED RETRACTABLE LEAD
Retractable leads are great inventions. They come in several sizes, you'll probably need the smallest one. These allow your cat more freedom than a regular lead and rarely tangle, another big plus. Take a human friend for a brief walk around your home or yard before attaching your cat. It takes a few minutes to get the hang of using the brake and the locking mechanism.

WATER BOWL AND WATER
Keeping your cat cool and well hydrated is of the greatest importance. Your cat will, even in the best of circumstances, be stressed. Drinking adequate amounts of fluid will help him cope with that stress better. Offer him water regularly, or leave a small amount in one of those bowls that snap on to the gate of a plastic carrier. Adding a little chicken or beef broth to the water helps encourage drinking.

Take a couple of bottles of your house water with you. New water can cause a tummy upset in some cats just as new food can. When you reach your destination, refill the bottle with a bit of new water after each use. After a few days of this, switch him over completely. You should have no problems.

ID Please!

A cat who travels, is boarded, or even stays at home with a sitter, should definitely have ID. There are several types of IDs available these days.

TAGS

Only use breakaway collars for tags, this could save your cat's life if he gets hung up on something. When traveling, make sure to list a phone number where someone is at home. Pros: Easy to use, inexpensive, anyone can read them. Cons: Easily removed or lost.

MICROCHIPS

These are inserted under the skin of your cat for a permanent ID. Pros: Can't be removed, give lots of information, positive proof of ownership. Cons: This type of ID is not well known yet. Few shelters or veterinarians have the scanners yet. There are several competing systems, and not all scanners read all chips. It's a promising technology, but as of this writing isn't perfected yet.

TATTOOS

Numbers are permanently tattooed on your cat's abdomen. Pros: Can't be removed, and is positive proof of ownership. Most laboratories won't use tattooed animals for experimentation. It only takes a minute or less to do and does not hurt the cat. Cons: Some cats don't like the process, since it involves being held down and touched with a somewhat noisy, vibrating tool. Proper restraint and an experienced person resolve this problem. Not every shelter looks for or knows what the tattoos mean, but more do all the time.

Groups to contact about tattooing are ID PET, 800-243-9147; National Dog Registry (they do cats as well), 800-637-3647, and Tattoo-A-Pet, 800-828-8667. All have twenty-four-hour-a-day switchboards and cooperate with one another if a call comes in about a number that isn't theirs.

Moving

Most cats are not fans of change. If the world were up to them to manage, I think all meals would come on time, few strangers would ever come to visit, all cat-chasing dogs would be banished, and moving would not be allowed.

More than one cat has caused their person a few gray hairs by bolting out the door while the moving men carry out one more box. A frightened cat may well choose to watch from afar, refusing to come home for days. This is dangerous for her, heartwrenching for you, and a possible catastrophe if you are on a tight schedule.

There are also all the box nesters. You wouldn't think a cat could get boxed and put on a truck but believe me it happens. They curl up for a nap, get frightened by the strange sounds, hunker down, and—quick as a wink—your cat is trapped in a box on the truck.

Protect all of you from these traumas by planning ahead. The best way to help your friend through the move is either to board her while the actual packing is going on or to set up a secure room just for her.

If you choose to set up a room an extra bathroom is a good choice. It's easy for you to pack up yourself and then make comfy for your cat. There she can go unbothered during the whole ordeal. Put in her bed, a sweatshirt or T-shirt that you have worn, her litter box, food and water, and a few toys. A radio left on a talk station will help block out some of the unusual noises that will be filling your home.

Be sure to put a "Do Not Enter" sign on the door and tell the moving men not to go in that room.

Once you arrive at your new home, set up a room for her again. If you have a cat who spends some of her time outside, confine her in your new home for at least a week. Once she knows where you are, where the food is, and where her favorite spot in the sun is, she'll be less likely to wander off.

Anytime you have to be going in and out frequently lugging boxes or emptying the car, confine her. You don't need her making a break for freedom at this juncture.

It's not a bad idea to feed rather gourmet fare for the first week or so. That will make a big impression in her head that this is a *fine* spot.

The following are some instructions *if* you decide to let your cat outside. Letting your cat outside is always a risk. These instructions are not meant as a guarantee. If you are worried about your cat's safety, keep her inside.

After a week or two of strict house arrest, you can start spending some supervised time outside. Before you step out the door, put her ID tag on her—the *new* ID tag you had made with your new address and phone number on it.

This is where your retractable lead and well-fitting harness come back into play. Let her explore the yard and general area. If you are worried about her going into a street, have a friend hide near the road. If your cat happens to wander near the pavement, have your friend jump out and run just a few steps at her shaking a couple of shake cans. Don't chase her! Your cat will hightail it away from the road, which, of course, is the idea.

vet saying it is not necessary for your cat to be fed. Get this letter if possible because you don't want people opening the crate door. If your cat is medicated in any way, you will need to notify the airline and comply with their requirements. And for heaven's sake, use a sturdy airline-approved crate! Cats have gotten loose in the cargo area and hidden for days in terror. Make sure your cat is secure! To that end, both the cat and your crate should have full ID on them at all times.

Here some of the airline counter-to-counter services. These are the next best thing to flying with your cat:

American Airlines: Priority Parcel (800-334-7400).
Delta Airlines: Delta Dash (800-638-7333).
Delta has some particularly nice features to their program. Your cat is hand-carried to and from the plane, not put onto any conveyor belts. They have a last-on, first-off pet policy, which we think is great.
Northwest Airlines: VIP (800-638-7337).
USAir: PDQ (800-428-4322).

Cat Sitting

Finding a wonderful, reliable cat sitter is a huge boon to any traveling cat owner. A good cat sitter either comes by your house a couple of times a day to take care of feeding, the litter box, and general loving, or stays at your home. Other things they can do for you is take in mail, tend household plants, turn lights on and off, and otherwise do light household maintenance. A good one is worth his or her weight in gold.

There are national organizations now for pet sitters; please see the Bibliography and Resources section for their numbers. Contacting them is an excellent way to find professionals near you.

If there aren't any near you, do not give up hope. Calling around to local veterinarians and groomers can be a great way to locate people. Once you get a few names, give Better Business Bureau and Consumer Affairs a call. Check to make sure they have a clean record. If these places have no record of the person, that is no guarantee they are good, but if they have had complaints filed, that certainly doesn't bode well.

When interviewing, note how the person interacts with your cat. Does the cat like her or not? Ask for references, especially professional ones like a vet or humane society. Just about anyone can find a person or two to use as a recommendation. How long have they been doing this? Are they bonded? What is their experience with cats? Make up a detailed list ahead of time of what exactly you

will want done. How many feedings a day, how often the litter should be changed, plants watered and so forth. Go over the list with the potential sitter item by item to make sure she can do everything you ask and that your desires are crystal clear.

Most people who do pet sitting are responsible animal lovers who'll treat your animal like one of their own. It makes sense though to be a little cautious about it, as you are leaving your heart and your home in their care.

Sarah Wilson

Orange Community Pet Hospital has an excellent boarding setup. Large cages with two perches, one with a comfy cover on it, a large litter pan, spotless bowls — we'd leave our cats here in a minute.

Boarding Your Cat

SEPARATE AREA FOR CATS

Boarding is a stressful experience for most cats. Being boarded in full view of strange dogs and people is a feline nightmare. The best boarding facilities have separate rooms specially suited for your beloved companion.

CLEAN SMELL

A building that houses only animals probably will have an animal odor to it, but it should be a clean one. A properly cleaned cattery with good ventilation has little odor.

VENTILATION

This is extremely important for cats, as many cat diseases are spread through the air. Any cat room should have a separate and adequate ventilation system.

SECURE

There should be *at least* two doors between your cat and the outside world.

INDIVIDUAL

Each cage should be fully separated from the neighboring ones. Not only will a solid wall provide more security but it lessens the spread of disease. Wire cages pressed one against another are not appropriate.

REQUIRED VACCINES

Any good boarding facility will require proof of vaccination (Rabies, Feline Infectious Peritonitis, Feline Leukemia Virus, Feline Panleukopenia Virus [Distemper] as well as protection from upper respiratory disease) as well as proof that your cat does not carry a contagious disease. Boarding facilities without these requirements are suspect.

Frequently Asked Questions

Can cats get heartworms, like my dog?

Yes. It is quite rare but does occasionally happen. Ask your vet if there is any reason to be concerned in your area.

I like to spoil my cat. Is it okay just to feed her canned tuna? She really likes it.

As most of us know from painful personal experience, what we like a lot may not be what is good for us. The same is true for your feline friend. Canned tuna, in and of itself, is not a balanced diet. We are assuming you are spoiling your cat because you love her. Part of loving her is doing what's right for her, even if she isn't wildly enthusiastic about the idea.

Your job as her caretaker is not just to indulge her whims, but to keep her healthy so you can spoil her in more productive ways for many years to come. You know that old saying "I just love you to death"? Make sure you don't.

Feed her a balanced, complete cat food. Try a tuna flavor. Or mix in a small amount of tuna to make it more palatable. She may argue with you about this at first, but stick to your guns. Please see pages 190–191 on curing finicky eating for more detailed assistance.

My cat drools when he is purring and kneading me with his paws, what's that all about?

The drooling, purring, kneading behavior that many cats do as adults is left over from the nursing behavior of kittenhood. Now, as an adult, when your cat is particularly happy and content, he reenacts this behavior from bygone days. Often seen in kittens who were weaned too early, it is a harmless and we think a sweet habit, albeit a damp one.

I feed my cat a good food, why does he want to eat grass?

As fine as many cat foods are, most cats feel the need to supplement it with some fresh greens on a regular basis. Grass clearly provides roughage, and probably other things not yet identified. Give him access to a pot of kitty greens or wheat grass year-round. He'll enjoy it.

Vomiting after eating grass is normally nothing to be concerned about. Some cats seem to make that a ritual, others just nibble and don't bring it up. Cats vomit rather easily, basically whenever they want to. If it happens a great deal and is a bother, skip the greens, or just offer them for a few minutes at a time.

My black cat's coat becomes reddish in the summertime. Why?

Just as human hair can bleach out in the sun, so can your cat's coat. Black cats who like to sun themselves may take on a reddish hue, especially when the light hits the hair just right. It is normal and natural and nothing to worry about. In the winter, the fur will shed out and your cat will be his old glossy midnight self again.

Is there any way to clean my cat well without bathing him?

Keeping your cat well combed out is the best way to maintain him in good condition. If your cat constantly has dandruff or oily fur despite routine grooming, ask your veterinarian what to do. You may need a change of diet.

There are dry shampoos you can use on your cat; most pet supply stores sell them. Foams, powders, and sometimes liquids, they all work without water. The foams and liquids are applied, allowed to dry, and then brushed out. The powders are shaken out into the coat, rubbed in well, and then brushed out thoroughly. These powders absorb oils, cleaning the coat and deodorizing at the same time.

Dry shampoos are great for cold weather, older, young, or sickly animals, when you are traveling, or anytime that it just isn't convenient to bathe your cat.

Mirror, Mirror on the wall ...

Tina McDermott

4 🐾
Solving Feline Behavior Problems

You love your cat. You love the way he curls up in your lap when you read, purrs in your ear while you watch TV, and runs to greet you as you come home. But you don't love a few things about him. It might be that he eats your houseplants, attacks your ankles, uses the tub for a litter box, or wakes you up every morning at 4:00 A.M.; whatever the problem, you are not amused. But you don't think much about it because *everyone* knows you can't train a cat—right?

Wrong. Cats are extremely trainable, it's just that you don't train them like a dog. To understand how to train a cat you must first understand that cats have certain predictable instinctual, inevitable behaviors. If you give these a positive outlet, the behavior will not annoy you. If you don't, prepare to be annoyed.

What do we mean? We mean, for example, that all cats need to scratch. It is an inborn behavior that serves many purposes such as exercising, marking territory, maintaining their claws. It is guaranteed that your cat will scratch things. If you give them something they enjoy scratching, they will scratch that. If you don't, they will find something else—normally something expensive like the door moldings or your couch.

To attempt to punish them for scratching is like scolding a bird for flying—scold all you want, but the animal will continue because it has to. The best way to handle inevitable behaviors is to supply your pet with an acceptable outlet, in this case, a scratching post. Do this and with a small amount of effort, attention, and praise on your part, your cat will soon be happily focused on that object.

What Motivates Your Cat

A cat's behavior is motivated by several predictable needs. These needs—to hunt, to eat, to establish and maintain territory, to play, to reproduce, to seek safety, and to interact—are the foundation of the vast majority of feline activities.

Once you understand which of the needs is involved, it is usually a fairly straightforward business redirecting your companion.

Let's go through them one by one:

HUNTING

Cats are predatory animals from the tips of their whiskers to the ends of their toes. Stalking, pouncing, and killing are great pleasures to most of them. There are cats who show little or no hunting instinct but they are exceptions. Punishing a cat for hunting is a useless activity. Instead think about how to prevent it—confinement, a bell, higher bird feeders—and how to redirect it—abundant play. Killing small animals, harassing smaller pets, ankle attacking all can be attributed to this predatory need.

EATING

Cats, being the unique individuals they are, are motivated by food to varying degrees. But many will take a free lunch when they find it. Once they learn that the countertop holds many delicious secrets—be prepared to cope. Begging, table walking, countertop raids, trash can tipping, early morning feed-me calls all fall under this category.

ESTABLISHING AND MAINTAINING TERRITORY

This is a particularly strong pressure for unneutered male cats. The more cats you have in your home or you have coming through your yard, the more likely it is that territorial pressures will take the lead. Spraying, inappropriate defecation, destructive scratching, cat fighting all belong here. As do, by the way, cats who assault dogs who enter their land. A small but feisty mackerel tabby named Little used to dispatch large dogs from her domain. She dealt with them swiftly using the coveted cat-attached-to-canine-nose hold—a method that has worked for cats for hundreds of years.

PLAYING

Well-fed predators, with few dangers and a lot of time on their hands, use play to keep their hunting skills sharp and to pass the time. Undirected play may include toe pouncing, knickknack hockey, Venetian blind cord swinging, paper shredding, and other basically silly, but at times trying, behaviors.

REPRODUCING

Unless they are neutered, all animals have an overriding urge to reproduce. This point will be undeniably driven home if you have a female cat in heat in your home. Cats know more about the sounds of desire than X-rated movie stars. Males, when confronted with a female in heat, become single-minded and aggressive.

Pets are best neutered. If you feel this is cruel or unnatural—get over it. What is cruel is the millions upon millions of cats killed *every year* because there aren't enough homes. If you love cats, you will neuter yours. He or she will live a longer, healthier, and more trouble-free life if you do.

SEEKING SAFETY

Cats make their own decisions about what is or isn't safe. Once they decide a situation is dangerous, it is best to stay well out of their way. Many cats won't take your word for it that they are safe and will do everything in their four-footed power to protect themselves.

INTERACTING

With Emily sitting on my lap, rubbing against my wrists as I type, I can't avoid this one. She is not hungry, thirsty, or in need of anything other than a little time with me. Cats have a desire to socialize to a greater or lesser degree. Some may never seek out your company, others will constantly.

These behavioral drives are the root of almost all feline behavior. Block these drives in some way and expect unwanted behaviors to develop. Certain fundamental feline truths are immutable. Scold a cat for scratching on furniture and he won't stop scratching. He'll just stop scratching in front of you. But scratch he must and scratch he will, for that is part of his nature.

Attempt to interfere with a frightened cat in retreat and watch out. His desire to seek a haven will override his trust of you, in most cases. Ninety-nine times out of a hundred you'll simply become an object in his path and you'll have the scratch marks to prove it.

Most problems between feline and human develop from a misunderstanding of the cat's basic nature and the silly human belief that a cat can stop being a cat. The decision to have a cat is not a decision to own a cat. Spiritually and morally, we share our lives with our animals. We do not own them like a piece of furniture. We watch over them and they watch over us, each in our own ways as to our natures. Our cats do not ask us to stop being human, although perhaps they would if they could. And you cannot ask them to cease being cats. The joy of cats as companions comes from accepting them as they are and finding pleasure in that. And pleasure there is, in huge quantities.

How Problems Develop

Cats are not static beings. They develop new behaviors for as long as they live. Problem behaviors can develop in several ways, and the ways they develop are telling. In general, the sudden onset of a new, undesirable behavior is a sign of an intense new pressure or stress in the animal's life.

Behaviors don't usually develop "out of the blue," but if they do, I

PATIENCE PLEASE!

Most of us, if we were to be brutally honest with ourselves, misbehave on a regular basis. As an excuse we offer up that we were under stress, bored, lonely, unhappy, or that our childhood was less than ideal. Armed with these reasons, much of our behavior is excusable, at least to ourselves.

Please, offer the same tolerance to your cat. Cats often misbehave for exactly the same reasons we do and deserve at least a small portion of the patience and understanding we expect for ourselves. Before you lose your temper too quickly, see if you can fix the problem by figuring out what is causing it. Yelling, chasing, and hitting are only going to increase his stress level, making matters worse.

Bored cat = mischievous cat.

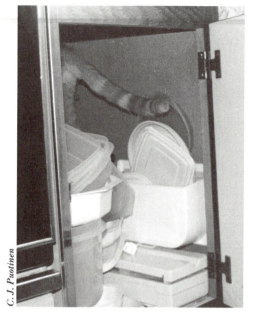

C.J. Puotinen

look for what is causing it. If a previously clean cat suddenly begins to urinate on the rug, I would run—not walk—to the vet. The behavior is the symptom, you need to find the cause. Fix the cause, the symptom will go away. Ignore the cause, and good luck getting rid of the symptom!

If your cat is physically healthy, look for some distinct environmental change that might have started the unwanted behavior ball rolling. Maybe a new brand of litter was tried, you redecorated, your spouse moved in or out, the litter box was moved. Did his world change in some way: new furniture, new cat, new schedule? Since animals can't tell you in words what has happened, some owner detective work from a cat's-eye view usually is what's needed.

Another reason a cat may develop a new, undesirable behavior is that he is

getting some pleasure out of it. Getting up on the counter is a good example. A cat who has never climbed a counter in his life may become a permanent fixture once he stumbles upon a chicken breast up there. Finding and eating something good is a great reward for counter climbing, sink raiding, and trash tipping. You can tell your cat that it is a moral weakness to do these things but he will not be impressed. Changing the situation so he gets something he doesn't want (like a spritz from a plant sprayer) instead of something he does want is the fastest way to change the behavior.

Boredom is another common key to problem behavior. While most cats handle solitude fairly well, it is boredom that gets them. Being locked in an apartment all day long with nothing going on is an invitation for a cat to make his own fun. Making his own fun can involve any number of feline activities, most of them not good from a human perspective.

These types of boredom-related problems are typically found in young cats under the age of two, and active cats like Siamese and Abyssinian.

If your cat has most of his troubles when you are not home, consider the following: get him a companion. Even if he never really becomes buddies with the other cat or the dog, they will occupy his day by keeping things interesting. We know cats who pined for their missing companions after they were gone, but seemed to pay no mind to them when they were alive.

Enrich his environment, offer him areas to climb on—the more levels are in a home, the more interesting for the cat. Leave surprises around the house, maybe a few tiny piles of catnip here and there or a new toy. Make a feline Easter egg hunt by hiding treats around the house. Get a timed feeder, and give him lunch while you're away. Rest a Ping-Pong ball in such a way that if he bumps a door a bit it will fall and bounce off. Be creative! Your cat will appreciate it, and when your cat is happy, you'll appreciate it.

Rotating favorite toys is an easy way to keep things perky. Divide his toys into three or more groups. Every few days, pick up one group and put down another. Variety is indeed the spice of life where toys are concerned.

Be sure to play with and teach your cat daily, as this will exercise both his mind and body, making him ever so much more likely to sleep when he is alone. Cats are bright, but not really programmed to concentrate for long periods. Encouraging them to do so tends to make them want to sleep.

Are You Part of the Problem?

Many of us owners unwittingly contribute to our cat's behavior problems. We think we are being loving, supportive, or clear when we are actually being overbearing, too emotional, or incoherently punitive. Do you recognize yourself in any of these scenarios?

HOUSE SOILING AND SPANKING

How many of you have gotten the advice to rub a cat's face in his mess? Or to spank him? Physical punishment of cats will *only* make things worse! Sure, you'll teach your cat something, you'll teach him to fear you. You'll teach him nothing, zero, zip, nada about using the litter box. Since many litter box problems are a result of stress on the animal, physically attacking the animal will increase his stress, and increasing his stress will increase the number of mistakes.

Most people resort to physical punishment when they are totally frustrated, at times when they do not

Tina McDermott

This cat trusts his person completely. Such trust is a precious thing.

know how to get their needs and desires across. But don't confuse frustration with training or teaching, it is neither. It is a loss of control that your cat easily recognizes as such. Cats are not above defending themselves. They will seek safety and if that safety exists somewhere away from you the cat will either flee or drive you off in an effort to find it.

CHANGING THE RULES

Here's a classic. Your beloved cat, who has slept on your pillow her whole life, is now scolded and swatted when she leaps onto the bed because your new friend doesn't like the cat in bed. Now, when you wake up in the morning the toilet paper is shredded for the first time in years. You scold the cat, but it doesn't do any good. You think she is jealous and spiteful because of your new friend, but think again. We promise you that your cat doesn't get up in the morning thinking, "Gee, I wonder how I can irritate my owner today and get scolded?"

She is stressed because her routine has been changed for no reason that she can see. She has been attacked in her own house by the person she adores most in her life for no understandable reason. If she were human, she might toss down a box of cookies, cry into her beer, or storm off in a huff. But she can't, she's a cat. She has a more limited array of behaviors to choose from when she wants to release stress. She can yowl, scratch, urinate or defecate, chew, or knock stuff over. She elected to scratch. She could just as well have left a wet spot on your favorite chair.

IGNORING YOUR CAT

She was your best, and frankly only, friend when you moved into town. You would come home from work, kick off your shoes, and roll the Ping-Pong ball for her. She slept on your pillow, licking your eyelids in the morning when the alarm went off. She dined with you, cried with you. Now your job has taken off, as has your social life. You're home off and on, spending as much time as you can with her but you're tired. All of a sudden, she is clawing on your favorite chair and knocking things off the shelves. She's always been so good, why is she making your life miserable now?

Funny, your cat is asking you exactly the same thing! Why are you making her life miserable? Don't expect to be able to radically withdraw interaction from a social cat without getting some reaction from your friend. She has no idea what is going on in your life. All she knows is you were here and now you're gone. Now might be a good time to get her a companion; an older cat who has been raised with other cats would be a nice choice. There are always older cats in need of good homes. If you are busy at work and at life, this is no time to add a kitten.

REWARDING UNWANTED BEHAVIOR

You are sprawled on the couch in front of the TV—exhausted. Then comes a meoyowl from the kitchen. Then another. You are trying to ignore it, but the cat is having none of that. Then another louder and more demanding call. You surrender. "You want a snack, big guy?" you say, pulling yourself up from the couch and heading for the kitchen. "Okay, there you go." And you pad back to the couch, hoping for some peace and quiet.

What just happened? In short, you are becoming well trained. But since your training isn't the focus here, let's turn it the other way and say the cat has just been rewarded for yowling. Likely result? He will yowl *more* in the future. Worse yet, you have just taught him to yowl repeatedly. Persistence is not something you want to build up in your cat, as it comes hard-wired in the species as it is.

So here are two rules of cat tending, although we've been told it applies to child rearing and spousal management as well: 1) Successful blackmail is always repeated. 2) If you are going to give in, give in early.

BEING INCONSISTENT

Allowing, even encouraging, misbehavior when *you* feel like it, then correcting when you don't is the quickest way to develop unwanted behavior in just about any species. Here's an example: She chased your fingers as a kitten and you thought it was adorable. You played spider walking across the floor with your hand. When she pounced, you'd laugh and tumble her on her back, tickling her tummy as she gave you kittenish bites. Now, as an adult cat, she pounces on your feet in bed when you turn over. When you shake your foot and tell her "No!" she bucks with her back feet and bites harder. You think maybe she is crazy and wonder why this is happening. After all, her behavior is unacceptable, isn't it?

In the immortal words of some wise person, "Be careful what you wish for—you just might get it!" You trained your cat to behave this way, so don't blame her when she does. Behaviors you need to be careful about rewarding in a kitten include pant leg climbing, finger chasing, hand biting, hair chewing, ear lobe nursing, foot pouncing, etc.

Cats are painfully logical beings whose behavior is rarely unfounded, regardless of how it may initially appear to us. Our job—as their guardians, guides, caretakers, and companions—is to see things from a cat's perspective and react accordingly. Most behaviors can be changed, once we understand what the behavior is motivated by. Cats aren't really all that mysterious, although their actions may seem so at first.

How to Change Behavior

There are many ways to change a behavior. In general, these fall into two large categories. On one side you can make the behavior you don't want unpleasant in some way. On the other side, you can make the behavior you do want pleasant. The best and most effective behavioral work comes from the judicious combination of these two general approaches.

You cannot force a cat to do any-

thing. If you get anything at all out of this chapter, remember that. Force can fall into several categories but they all generally entail trying to *make* a cat do something.

The most effective and humane methods of changing cat behavior have to do with making the cat think the behavior change you want is *his* idea. By enlisting your cat's cooperation in behavior change, virtually anything is possible.

Here's an example:

Your cat scratches your couch. You yell at him, swat at him, and generally force your ideas upon him. Your message: "I don't want you to scratch the couch." The cat's reply: "Get a life. I like the couch, so I'll scratch the couch. If you don't like it I will simply scratch it when you aren't around."

Score one for the cat.

Now, instead of scolding him, let's use some common sense and enlist his cooperation in this project. First, you clip his nails and keep them clipped. Next you purchase a sturdy scratching post covered in an acceptable material and about the same height as the couch or taller. Rub catnip into it if your cat is responsive to

Scolding a cat when you catch him only teaches him to get off the counter when you come in.

Wells Wilson

catnip. This will help him get used to the object and to think kindly of it. Praise and pet him whenever you see him near it. Put the post next to the couch where he likes to scratch.

Next, booby-trap the couch to prevent further damage. You have many ways to do this; you choose to cover the area with double-sided sticky tape. You give the wall a smack whenever you catch him scratching the couch. You say *nothing*.

Your message to the cat: "Here's a great object to scratch, feels good, smells good, conveniently located, and you get praised for using it. And that old place you used to scratch, no fun anymore. Your choice." Cat's reply: "I'm no dummy, I like that new thing you got me. Thanks." Score one for you, with no emotional wear and tear on anyone.

UNDERSTANDING THE FORCE OF HABIT

Cats are creatures of habit. The best way to handle a bad habit is to never allow it to develop, but, if you are reading this section, we assume that you are human and that a bad habit has already developed with your cat. While a cat's routine loving nature can be a pain around unwanted behaviors, it can be used to your advantage in developing new, acceptable behaviors.

Most animals, cats included, do things that give them pleasure in some way or that avoid unpleasantness. The pleasure can be easy to understand—like stealing a hamburger off the table—or a little more complex—like the humanly incompre-hensible joy some cats take in urinating on plastic. The avoidance of the unpleasant can be straightforward—like leaping away from a spritz of water—or more subtle, like protesting being picked up for a few hours after an unpleasant nail-clipping episode. Either way, a cat's motivations are always clear—to the cat.

Cats do not do things because they plan to destroy your possessions, annoy you, disrupt your life, or embarrass you with friends although certainly all those things may happen. Please keep in mind that a cat, no matter how wonderful, can only see the world through cat eyes and that their behavior is always limited by that perception.

Understand a cat's behavior through the cat's viewpoint and you'll have great success changing it. Try to see it through a human's gaze, and you are headed straight for conflict, frustration, misunderstanding, and failure.

If you've been arguing with your cat about a behavior for a long time and your cat persists—stop! Take a deep breath, relax, and reevaluate. When behavior is properly understood and approached, you will see almost immediate change from your cat. If you do not, do not continue what you are doing. It isn't working. It's like dialing the wrong number over and over, still expecting that one of these times the right person will pick up. Won't happen. If you are dialing the wrong number, stop, call directory assistance. If you're unsuccessful with your cat, stop and get help. Both you and your cat will be happier for it.

WHY NOT JUST SMACK THE CAT?

Hitting doesn't work well, especially with cats. Cats are just as likely to turn around and bite you, which, by the way, you richly deserve. You shouldn't be surprised by this; after all you just attacked the cat, why shouldn't the cat attack you back?

Anyway, do you really feel good about hitting him? There is an old horse-training axiom that violence begins where knowledge ends. Truer words have not been spoken. Violence is a loss of control usually due to frustration. Since most animal training is about asking the animal to show some control—like not jumping on the counter and only scratching his post—how can you ask them to control themselves when you can't control yourself? Skip the hitting, teach instead.

Your Behavior-Changing Arsenal

Environmental corrections, combined with praise and rewards, are *the* way to convince a cat to change his ways. To help you set up these environmental corrections, you need tools. Those listed below are some of the tried and true. Use them all, use a few, use what works. As long as you find them useful and your cat dislikes them, select as you wish. There is no best or worst in this group.

SPRAY BOTTLE

Often used for misting plants or holding cleaning agents, these are wonderful cat-training tools. Effective for most cats and, we confess, fun to use at the human end. No additives please, water is all that is needed. When you set the nozzle on stream you can squirt a cat who is six or more feet away. The sneakier you are, the more effective you'll be. The idea is for the cat to link the watery blast with the unwanted behavior, not with you being there. If you scold him or move toward him while squirting he'll quickly learn to correct himself in your presence but will probably continue the same behavior when you are not around.

MOUSETRAPS

Used upside down *only*. The mouse-traps we mean are the old-fashioned snap type, not the glue ones. Set the trap, then gently rest it upside down on objects you don't want the cat on or near. The surprise thwacking noise and the sudden movement are enough to spook most cats without any risk of harming them. These are best used in areas seldom frequented by humans, such as on the soil of the potted plant or on shelves you want the cat to stay off. These are not recommended in homes with small children, tiny kittens, pint-sized dogs, or any other small pets.

SHAKE CANS

An empty rinsed aluminum soda or beer can with twelve pennies inside it makes a terrific noise correction. Shaken at your side, or lobbed near to—not AT—the cat, it will startle most animals into stopping what they are doing. These can also be rigged as environmental booby-trap-style corrections quite easily. Nice tools, but not our first choice for a noise-sensitive cat or for a new addition who is already anxious enough. Otherwise, safe and effective.

COMPRESSED-AIR HORN

Small handheld compressed-air horns are available at many bicycle shops and boating supply stores. These little canisters let out a tremendous screech when you press down on the trigger, frightening most cats out of the vicinity instantaneously.

This is a serious tool for serious behaviors—such as aggression or spraying. Used correctly it is marvelous, which can be said of most tools. We would not use this tool with a sound-sensitive cat, a cat who's easily stressed, or a cat who was recently severely stressed.

Discretion is called for when used in apartment complexes. This noise is unlikely to endear you to your neighbors.

PRESSURIZED AIR

Purchased from a photography supply store, these canisters have a trigger on them that releases bursts of air. Used for blowing dust safely off slides and negatives, they are equally effective for correcting cats. A quick blast toward the face will discourage most felines, who recognize it as a giant hiss.

Although we've never had a problem with it and always found it to be a safe, effective tool, we wouldn't use it near a gritty substance that might irritate the cat's eyes.

DOUBLE-SIDED TAPE

Cats hate, we mean *hate*, sticky feet. Works well, though once applied, it can be hard to remove from some surfaces. Therefore, in areas where you want a temporary control, consider contact paper, or place a piece of paper under the tape, leaving room on either end to attach it to the surface. Then it works like contact paper.

CONTACT PAPER

Great stuff used upside down, as cats hate walking on it. Be sure to flip the ends down to tack it in place or you may come home to a cat wrapped up in a sheet. Meant to be unpleasant, not a torment. Can easily be cut to fit an area.

REPELLENT

Any number of repellents exist on the pet market these days. There are products made just for indoors. There are herbal products, non-herbal products—you have lots to choose from. Try one at a time until you find a smell your cat hates and that you can live with. Remember always that cats have sensitive noses. You don't have to soak the area to make it repellent to the average cat.

And there are always the age-old favorites: certain perfumes, citrus room deodorizers, or simply citrus peels. All of these have been repelling cats for many years.

WHAT IS AN ENVIRONMENTAL CORRECTION?

Example: You rest a shake can on the back edge of the waste paper basket. Your cat tips the basket. The can falls with a bang. The cat links tipping the basket with the frightening noise, making it less likely that he will tip the basket in the future.

The great thing about environmental corrections is that the cat gets corrected exactly as he's doing something, whether you are home or not. If the cat links correction with your presence he'll just wait for you to leave to get into trouble. If he links it with the basket itself, he'll stay away from it, no matter where you are. An environmental correction doesn't make a mistake. The shake can only falls if the cat tips the basket over. No confusion, no more problem.

Amica: A Lesson in the Inevitable

Amica was all white with blue eyes. She was one of the prettiest kittens we had ever seen. She came to live with us from a shelter right after my parents got divorced. She was sweet. She was playful. She was stone deaf. Because of her limitations though, she was a strictly indoor companion. Since she was unable to hear danger coming, we had to protect her because she could not protect herself.

Other than that, and not coming when called, life is uneventful. I can highly recommend a beam of light from a flashlight or a spot of light from a handheld mirror as toys for these guys. As with many animals deprived of one sense, they often compensate for that limitation with extra attentiveness to the other senses. Amica was a wonderful chaser and pouncer. Movement fascinated her and we amused ourselves for hours by amusing her.

One of the downsides of deafness in cats is that they cannot hear themselves. My mother misjudged her age a bit and Amica came into heat before we could spay her. She would sit by the window and howl the most sexually charged sounds my young ears had ever heard. They were positively embarrassing. They were so compelling that Captain, our older neutered male cat, leaped up in desperation, raced to her and mounted her—ineffectually. He did his best, but he wasn't really up for the task, so to speak. She squatted for a moment and then turned on him, fire in her eyes, and slapped him silly. He skulked off, defeated, and she returned to her windowsill to sing her lust. We spayed her as soon as we could.

Amica is a wonderful example of a cat being a cat. Her behavior was no problem to *her*. It was a problem to *us*. Most people have no real expectation of stopping a cat in the throes of hormones and instinct. It is important for us humans to remember that the urge to scratch is just as innate in most cats as the urge to merge—just not as noisy.

Litter Box Problems

Cats missing their litter boxes by an inch or a mile is one of the most common cat-owner complaints. While the problem itself is common, the causes of the problem can be quite complex.

The first thing you need to determine is whether the cat is simply eliminating or spraying, which is a part of marking territory. Here are a few simple ways to figure out what's going on at your house:

Urination against vertical surfaces: Spraying

Urination on horizontal surfaces: Elimination, usually

Urination accompanied by vertical tail twitching and treading of feet: Spraying

Backing up to objects or quick squat urination: Spraying

Scratches trying to cover urine or feces, even if just going through the motions: Elimination

Never uses the box anymore: Elimination

Urinating and defecating in the same area: Elimination—although this is being debated.

This section discusses cats who are not using the box when they need to go. Spraying is discussed on pages 153–157.

There are many patterns of litter box mistakes. The following are some of the most common:

OUT OF THE BLUE

Your previously impeccable cat has, all-of-a-sudden, become dirty. You have no idea what has started this behavior, but you are tired of stepping in the wet spots. What can cause this sudden change in behavior?

A cat may start urinating out of the box because of a urinary tract infection or other physical problem. Cats are usually good about letting you know when they need help—if you understand how they ask for it. It is not uncommon for cats who aren't feeling well to urinate directly in front of you or in an obvious spot in the house. Once your vet gives your cat a clean bill of health, it is time to put on your detective hat.

Cats normally start missing the box because of a stress of one kind or another, which can set more than one cat on the road to ruin:

A week of boarding, or staying at a friend's house who has a dog.

Adding or subtracting a cat or dog.

Household upheaval, ranging from fighting to preparing to move.

Renovations, with workmen in and out and the attendant noise.

Redecorating, adding new furniture or rearranging the old.

Having guests for a long period of time.

A new intimate friend who is sleeping over regularly.

Adding an infant or young child to the household.

HOW A PREFERENCE FOR NOT USING THE BOX DEVELOPS

There are cats who, after many years of faithful litter box use, suddenly start to use a smooth surface for their bathroom habits. Why is that?

Usually this is a cat who is an ardent post-elimination scratcher, who will stand in the box and scratch at the walls of the box or the back wall of the room in a ritualized effort to cover their mess. Surface preference develops from this. It's what she scratches *after* she goes that determines what she likes to go in. If she scratches the wall, she may develop a preference for smoothness. These cats start using the sink or tub when they feel the urge. If she reaches over the box and scratches at a rug, she may well start using the rug for a toilet.

Get the idea? When you upset your cat's routine, don't be surprised if the cat upsets yours in return.

Some cats do not take kindly to having changes made with their box. If you move the box. If you clean it with something new. (By the way, mild soap and water is ALL you should ever clean it with. A strong-smelling cleanser can put a cat off.) If you try a new brand of litter (*Beware* of scented litters, as not all cats appreciate the smell). If you add or subtract more litter than usual. Any of these can start an avalanche of mistakes. If you have recently made changes, change back to what he is used to.

Again and always, keep the box spotless. Change the litter every day if you have to. That's a small price to pay for a clean house. If the box stinks when you change it, change it *more* often, not less. If you must, train yourself. Reward yourself with something special after you clean the box. There's nothing wrong with positive reinforcement and it sure makes the job easier.

If you let that box pile up and then the cat starts using your bed as an alternative, ten points for your cat. I couldn't have said it better myself.

The only way to kill the smell of urine or feces to a feline nose is to use an odor neutralizer from a pet supply store or veterinarian. Even if you scrub a mistake area with soap and water till it is odorless to you, your cat will still be able to smell it. That scent is like a big "Go Here Now" sign for your cat.

BATHTUB BOMBERS

Captain would, on occasion, leave me a calling card in the bathtub. Why cats like to use the tub as an alternative litter box is quite beyond me, but they do. Actually, as places to go, that's not a bad one. Easy to clean up and disinfect, no stain. I never really minded.

There are many people though who find it repulsive and for them I offer this advice—leave an inch or so of water in your tub. That is a 100 percent effective method of keeping your cat from using your tub as an outhouse. HOWEVER, and this is a big however, there is no guarantee that your cat won't then march himself off to use some even less acceptable place as a toilet. Know your cat. If he makes this error because you inadvertently locked him out of his box, fine. Leave the water in the tub and the door(s) to the litter box open. But if he uses this area without any rhyme or reason you can see, then move ahead with caution. The devil you know is sometimes better than the devil you don't.

STRESS BOMBERS

One owner of a particularly spunky cat had a run-in with his companion over the destruction of a certain valued article of clothing. The irate owner chased the cat out of the house using much noise and intensity.

Two hours later, when he went to use the car, he found a large pile of cat poop on the hood. Never happened before or since. This is not a spite-filled act as many like to think it is. Rather, cats use feces to mark their territory, and after the tiff between the two adult males in this group, the four-legged member decided to redefine the territorial lines to include his attacker's territory—his car.

Such behaviors can be brought on by a new lover, a long-term guest, intense family fighting, or any other stressful encroachment on a cat's territory or lifestyle. The classic place to find these types of eliminatory releases is on the offender's side of the bed, in his or her closet, on some of their laundry, or on their favorite chair.

Coping with this involves eliminating the stress. If it is a person who has offended, have him spend some extra time giving attention to the cat, handing out treats, generally making peace, and giving your cat his due attention and worship. Eliminating fighting in the house will do everyone a lot of good! Take the cue from your cat—settle your differences some other way.

CAUGHT WITH HIS PANTS DOWN

More than one cat has been surprised or frightened when using his box. One good scare can put a cat off his box completely. A feline housemate bullying him when he is indisposed, a freak accident where something falls on or near him, or a sudden, frightening noise that occurs just as he settles into the litter can all be off-putting. If a human surprises or punishes him while in the box, he may learn exactly what you didn't want

him to learn—that the box is a dangerous place and the safer option is to pee behind the couch.

If this has happened, set up a couple of boxes in a few different areas of the house. This way your cat may choose to use an alternative spot where he feels safer. If he's getting sideswiped by another cat, confining the victim for a few days with his own private box will give him a chance to relieve himself in peace. Then set up another box away from the usual one.

When he is doing what he should where he should, then open the doors and see what happens. With

Sarah Wilson

Emily might feel ambushed, if the loop of string didn't keep our dogs from opening the door to her box area. But she's safe and she knows it.

any luck at all, the bully will claim the old box as his exclusively and leave your ambushed cat alone to use his new box in peace.

Canine ambush can be readily taken care of by setting up a cat room. Use a baby gate, sturdy hook and eye, or a cat door to keep the dog out of the cat's area. Everyone, even your cat, deserves some peace and quiet in the bathroom.

PAINFUL MEMORIES

There are certain medical conditions that cause cats a great deal of pain when they attempt to eliminate. Instead of blaming the pain on their physical problem, cats, with their unarguable logic, blame it on the box. Classically this type of box avoidance occurs after a bout of FUS (feline urologic syndrome) or constipation. Since the pain occurs only when the cat is in the box, it is not hard to see why they would come to avoid it.

To reiterate: FUS is signaled by frequent trips to the box, straining to urinate with limited or no success, blood in the urine, crying while urinating, crying in general around the house, urinating outside the box: RUN TO YOUR VET. This is a life-threatening condition. Do not wait. Put down the book and go right now!

Constipation is signaled by lethargy, depression, and frequent trips to the box where there is much straining to defecate but no results; not quite an emergency. You still should go to your vet ASAP for a general checkup and possible diet change.

HIDDEN TREASURES

You have a nice, clean box for your friend, and yet she finds behind the couch, or under the bed, more appealing. Why?

Some cats like to use an enclosed space for a bathroom. You can check out this theory by confining her to a room with nothing she can get behind or under. Set up two boxes. One out in the open. One with a large cardboard box with a door cut in it set over a litter tray so it is covered. See which one she selects.

If she shows a preference for the covered box, fine. That's an easy solution. Either continue with the cardboard box cover or purchase one of the many premade covered boxes available at most pet supply stores. If she wants privacy, she can have it.

At the same time, either block off or booby-trap the old areas using contact paper, cardboard boxes, double-sided tape, upside-down mousetraps, or a repellent. If she can't get back there, she can't go there. Simple, yet effective.

HEY, THAT'S MY SPOT!

Cats can develop a strong preference for one or two areas in your home, none of which will be the box, of course! Even when you clean them thoroughly with an odor neutralizer your cat returns to that spot. Even when you remove the rug you were sure was his favorite, he still returns to that spot. He's like the swallows of San Juan Capistrano, he always returns.

Here are a few tacks to take. If the

spot is at all convenient for this, move the box there. Why fight it? Once he gets on track again, you can slowly—inch by inch—move the box back to a more convenient area for you.

If the area isn't right for a box, try feeding him in that location. That should help. Covering the area with tinfoil may deter him. Using an indoor repellent may also send him elsewhere. Playing with him in that zone may make him rethink his dirty ways as well.

REFUSES THE BOX COMPLETELY

The cat will not use a litter box. Although this is extremely rare, it can be a real trial. If this is the case, you have to get serious immediately and stay serious until the problem is resolved.

First, have you changed anything about the box lately? A new litter, a new soap when cleaning the box, a new location—anything you can think of? If you have, change it back, right now. If that works, wonderful. They should all be this easy to resolve. But if there has been no change, you have to take a different approach.

Try using very little litter in the box for a while and confining him in a room away from his new favored areas. It may also be necessary to use a shallower pan for a while until the cat gets reconditioned to step into a box to eliminate.

You can try confining him to his room with his box, but if he errs in there as well, you'll need to take more direct measures. In these cases, we recommend confining him to a comfortable carrier. It should be large enough for him to stand up, turn around, and lie down in, but not so large he can use a corner as a toilet with enough room left to get away from it.

When you can't be with him, confine him to his crate. Supply water, preferably in the kind of dish that attaches to the crate itself to reduce spills. Every four to six hours take him to his box. Encourage him with warm words to use the facilities. Quietly observe. Read a magazine, relax. When he uses the box, praise him warmly. Immediately feed him after every successful trip to the box.

In close confinement, he will not want to dirty. By forcing him to hold it and then rewarding him for using the box, you are setting up a situation where he can be successful and where you can be present to cheer him on. A few weeks of this, and he should be back on track.

If you would like to spend time with him, but don't trust him for a minute, then put on his harness and lead and tether him to you. That way you two can spend quality time cuddling with no worries that he'll sneak off down the hall and anoint the guest bed—again.

Some cats develop a real love of some type of surface other than litter. If your cat likes to urinate on newspapers, why fight it? Rip up newspapers and put them in the box. Confine him to his room which should have not an ounce of his preferred surface in it—except, of course, in the box.

Once he starts using the box regu-

larly, start adding small amounts of an unscented litter to the newspaper. As he accepts this new material, continue to add more of it and use less of the newspaper. Over time, you can change his mind about litter.

Cats not only develop surface preferences, but they can also have strong ideas about the scratching quality of the object. For example, toweling that he can bunch up through scratching at it and then urinate on may become a favorite. You may actually have to put a towel in the box for a bit. Use expendable ones (obviously). As the cat accepts the box, you can start cutting the toweling down into smaller and smaller pieces. At the same time, add small amounts of litter to the box.

Don't be shy about telling him how pleased you are about his new-found clean habits. Warm praise and food rewards after a successful box experience won't hurt, and with some cats it helps a great deal.

Don't confuse success in the box with a giving up on his preference. Be it newspaper, plastic, towels, or carpeting, you will need to keep him away from his favorite surfaces. Old habits die hard for all of us; your cat is no exception.

Remove any temptation you can. Carefully booby-trap any area where he has access to his preferred surface. Use any method you like—contact paper, indoor repellent, inverted mousetraps. Use the one that suits you and your cat best.

From now on he gets zero unsupervised time in his danger zones. Keep a correction tool near you, be it a shake can, compressed-air horn, or sprayer. If he starts to sniff around an area, correct him. Do not say anything during the correction. Praise him after he scoots away. This will encourage him to dread the area, not you. Again, keeping him on lead near you is a great way to regulate his access to the forbidden zones.

NATURE LOVERS

You have the biggest, best cat box in the land. You keep it spotlessly clean. It's in a discreet but convenient spot. You've done everything right, but still, your cat likes to use your house plants as his litter pan. For details about handling this problem, refer to page 61.

CLIFF HANGERS

Your cat goes *to* his box religiously, but never seems to go *in* it. After much dancing around, he squats on the edge and drops his gifts over the side. As frustrating as this is, never scold a cat for this, as he is likely to connect the scolding with the box and you'll be worse off than you were.

Cliff hangers are often trying to tell you that they hate the litter that is being used. They avoid touching it. They shake their paws after being in it. They do not scratch in it, preferring to scratch at the air or the walls of the box. Do a little household field test. Get a few cat boxes and put an inch or so of different litter in each. Does the cat have a strong preference for one over another? If he does, use that one. No point arguing with your cat.

A covered box will solve the problem almost entirely, except if he hangs out the door. If your cat will use one, this is a great solution. Alternatively, there are boxes made now with edges that overhang the interior of the box making it awkward at best for the edge perchers to perch there. These are worth a try. Also, there are specially made boxes now with tall sides just for this type of cat. You can locate these advertised in the back of cat magazines, a few of which are listed in the Bibliography and Resources section. Or you can ask a local pet supply store if they can special-order one for you. Or, you can simply put the litter pan in a cardboard box of the same general floor size, then cut a door in the front. Not exactly high-decor, but works like a charm and costs nothing.

Some cats are forced to cliff hanging by a disgusting box filled with feces. Do your cat a favor, stop complaining about him and start scooping that box. If *you* think it's a gross job to clean it, imagine having to use it!

LITTER TOSSERS

If your cat were human, he could be a pitcher in the big leagues, but since he's a feline he occupies his time tossing litter vigorously in all directions. As above, do not scold him for this, that will only put him off the box entirely. Instead, try a few changes that have worked for many.

Putting less litter in the box in the first place will help limit the amount of litter he has to throw around. Less in, less out; or use one of the taller boxes just described.

The covered boxes discussed previously can lessen the problem although a cat with good aim will toss some litter out the door. The tall-sided box will improve the situation as well. The box with an overhanging edge is your best bet. Most cats scratch the litter vigorously against the sides of the box; if the sides are covered, the litter tossing will be controlled.

All in all it is more of a pain than a problem. The definitive solution is a handheld vacuum always on the ready.

Spraying

Spraying is normally a "this is mine" type of behavioral statement. This is why a cat may back up to a new couch or recently purchased item and leave his calling card. He may mark your bed, laundry, or shoes, maybe your favorite armchair. Why? Because it smells strongly like you. By marking your areas with his scent he claims you and your home as his. Anything new to his environment may be marked, including but not limited to, plastic bags, suitcases just brought out of storage, your Aunt Mabel's handbag—you get the idea.

What can you do?

The bad news is this can be a difficult problem to stop, so get ready to be consistent and persistent. The good news is there is lots you can do to help change this behavior.

Let's start with the basics:

NEUTER YOUR CAT!

Unneutered male cats almost all mark—inevitable and immutable. Just get the job done and he'll most likely (90 percent of the time) stop stinking up your house. The sooner you get him neutered the better, as once this becomes a strong habit, he may continue even after neutering. He's not going to grow out of this. Scolding and punishment isn't going to work. Until he is neutered, behavioral approaches aren't going to work either.

CONFINE HIM

Did you move? Redecorate? Move the furniture around? Any of these can lead to a spraying spree. Confinement when you can't supervise for the first few weeks, combined with supervised visits, are part of the overall plan here. Keep the spray bottle or compressed-air horn nearby and correct him if he is backing up to anything.

TETHER HIM

If you are home and you want your cat out with you, but you don't want him to be able to wander off, even for a minute, then put on his lead and harness. There is nothing wrong with keeping your cat on lead when he is out in the house with you and plenty of things that are right. This way the cat gets to spend some happy lap time with you without being able to get into any trouble.

Tina McDermott

Willy stays on harness and lead when he spends time out with his owner; otherwise Willy sprays.

ELIMINATE STRESS

This is not always easy or possible, but where you can make some changes, it will help your cat. Here are a few common stresses that lead to marking messes:

Adding a new member of any species to the family can set off marking. Even a new cat walking within eyesight can stimulate a cat to mark. If it's an outside animal that's stirring up your inside cat either figure out a way to keep the intruding cat out of your yard or your cat away from the window.

Keeping the intruder out can involve repellents, correcting him with a compressed-air horn blast, or a squirt from the hose, none of which we would expect to be completely effective. The most surefire way of handling this is to keep your cat from seeing the intruder. Confine him away from that window; move anything that he can use to sit on and stare out the window; booby-trap the sill with upside-down contact paper, double-sided tape, or upside-down mouse traps.

If it's a new family member who's started the commotion, see the section (57–60) on introducing a new member to the family for guidelines on how to do this with minimal stress and maximal success.

Proximity causes stress. If you're a cat enthusiast with ten or more cats, your probability of spraying among the housemates is high. Why? In general, the higher the population density in one area, the more territory is squabbled over, defined, and marked. In human terms, if everyone has a two-hundred-acre spread, why bother putting up a fence? But if you live in tiny plots, with tiny yards, which all your neighbors want to use as their own, how long would it take you to put up a fence? Cats are no different. Territory is important to them. The more competition there is for that territory, the more spraying—the feline version of fence building—you will have.

You can add some floor-to-ceiling cat climbers into your house. The more places there are to hang out unbothered, the fewer squabbles there will be. But still, be realistic—either accept spraying as a part of owning that many cats, or adopt out some of your group to good, loving homes.

Many cats are both sensitive to and frightened by loud, unexpected sounds. Construction close by? Your youngest having a sleepover? Lots of door slamming and yelling going on? If possible, set up a quiet room for your cat away from the commotion. Leave a radio on to help cover up the offending sounds.

Once you have gotten a handle on what is stressing your cat and causing this spraying, then you can start thinking about how to eliminate the behavior. But you must identify and take action of some kind on the stress, otherwise all the good work in the world isn't going to stop the behavior.

Sexual pressure is a huge stress on animals. I said it above, but just in case you're skimming the book—DO IT! This is not optional with this problem. Your male cat must be neutered!

ELIMINATE ODOR

Get an odor neutralizer from the pet store or vet's office made especially for feline urine. Use it. Use it repeatedly, if necessary. Cleaning up marked areas with soap and water will not do the trick. If the cat can smell urine, he will want to re-mark.

BOOBY-TRAP THE AREA

When you are home, you can carefully give him supervised access to the area. But even with careful supervision, a bit of booby-trapping never hurts. That way if your atten-

tion wanders for a moment he'll still get corrected for going into his old favorite haunts. An environmental correction, in which the place, not the person, corrects your cat, will teach him to keep out of those areas, not just out of your view.

Taping tinfoil on the walls he has marked, making a sticky moat around the area with contact paper or double-sided tape, or rigging up inverted mousetraps are all effective ways to teach your cat not to leave his calling card.

DINING IN THE MARKING AREA

Another approach to this problem is to set his table in the spot he dirties. By feeding him in those areas (only after they've been thoroughly cleaned please!), you will inhibit his desire to mark there. Of course, this is only going to work if he sprays in one or two spots. If he has many places he uses, he'll just move to marking another. However, it's worth a try.

KEEP HIM OUT OF THE AREA

Lovingly known as the "No go in, No go on" rule. No go in the room, no go on the bed. It's simple. It's humane. It's inexpensive. It's quick. It works. What more can you ask for?

Some folks resist this answer because they don't feel that they have taught their cat anything. And they are right. It's more like the cat has taught you. But who cares anyway? This isn't reform school, it's life.

Why take the long hard road when a short easy one will do just as well? If your cat likes to urinate on the guest bed, put a self-closing mechanism on the guest room door. Done, no pain, no stain.

Or keep a plastic drop cloth over the bed. Not helpful for plastic lovers, but many cats do not like to urinate if it means getting their feet wet. For the plastic aficionados out there, try taping several sheets of aluminum foil together to cover the bed. Tell your friends you're planning to bake a really big potato... yes, it looks pretty silly but it works in many cases.

EXERCISE HIM

Exercise, both mental and physical, impacts positively on almost all feline problems. While certainly not a cure-all, exercise is an integral part of any retraining process. Make sure your cat gets plenty of opportunity to stretch his legs and mind. Teach him new behaviors. Develop fun play routines. Not only will this help relieve boredom for him, but it helps keep the bond between the two of you strong. Enjoying each other's company is particularly important when the relationship is being stressed badly by unwanted behavior.

MEDICATE HIM

There are medications that help control spraying. As spraying can be a difficult problem to eliminate on its own, the use of medications should be considered early on. Discuss the available options with your vet. Medications to control spraying tend to fall into two general categories, either hormonal or anti-stress.

New medications are being developed all the time that are increasingly specific to the problems at hand. Many work well with few if any side effects even when used for long periods. Spraying is a make-or-break behavior in that if the cat doesn't stop it you may not be able to keep him. And don't think there is a long line of people waiting to adopt adult cats who spray, there isn't. Basically it's stop spraying or face euthanasia. With this reality in mind, side effects can seem to pale. But nonetheless, discuss the treatment thoroughly with your vet. You should know what you and your cat are getting into.

I'm supposed to do what? In where?

Toilet Training

Some cats can be trained to use the toilet instead of a litter box. This certainly is a neater option, and eliminates the odor and trouble of having a conventional box. The only downsides are if you fail to explain to guests about your cat's training before they use your facilities or if you have a toilet-drinking canine—most of us don't want our dogs bobbing for feces.

Teaching a cat to use the toilet is a fairly straightforward behavioral trick. The most difficult part of it is being patient. Expect to spend four to six weeks conditioning the cat. Some folks say you can do it faster but it pays to take your time. A few extra days spent teaching are never

wasted. If you proceed too quickly, you'll set your cat back more than if you had just taken your time in the first place.

Because of the time it takes, we advise that you use a bathroom that is expendable for a few weeks, if possible. That will make it easier for everyone. If you don't have an extra bathroom, so be it. Everyone will just have to work around it for a while.

Every complex behavior, like toilet training, can be broken down into individual steps. Teach the animal each step separately, then put it all together. Toilet training involves three basic steps and they are as follows:

Learning to balance on a toilet seat while eliminating.

Learning to jump up to eliminate.

Learning to use an area without litter.

Now, there are several different methods you can use to teach your cat to use the toilet. Most of these methods involve teaching the cat one of these things first and the rest later.

We'll start by teaching the cat to balance on the toilet seat while eliminating. This is not difficult in and of itself. The most difficult part of this whole process is attaching an old toilet seat to the litter box in such a way that it will not slip, wobble, or fall off. One unexpected tumble and your cat may not use the seat ever again.

You can go as far as to glue an old seat to an old box. Or you can use duct tape to attach it. But whatever you do, make it secure! Remove the lid of the seat you are training with so it doesn't unexpectedly close on him. That could throw a cat off for good.

Once you have attached the seat to the box, fill as usual and let the cat get used to the whole situation for a few days. Don't worry if he balances on it yet; when the time comes, he will. If he uses it as normal, praise him warmly. Tell him what a brilliant animal he is, as that's the absolute truth. If he is hesitant, you may need to help him out a bit by placing him in the box and praising him. He'll soon relax and get the idea. As soon as he is using it without concern, you can start step two in the process. This involves raising the litter box slowly till it is the same height as your toilet.

The most important elements of this training are to go slowly and to make sure the box is sturdy. Absolutely no wobbles or slip-offs allowed. Some people recommend magazines or newspapers to raise the box, we don't. These simply are not stable enough when piled high. Heavy-duty cardboard boxes are a better idea. The best are ones that are piled box inside of box making them extra strong. If the bathroom floor isn't carpeted, putting a layer of newspaper or an old towel underneath the boxes will stop them from slipping. Make sure the boxes are large enough to accommodate both the litter pan and a landing spot for the cat. Roll up some newspaper into small tubes and tape them onto the top of the box to form a frame into which you can place the pan. Even a small frame will keep the box from slipping when the cat leaps in and out.

Keep the litter pan at each height for four or five days at least. Even if the cat is using the pan, he may still be slightly stressed about it. Rush him too fast and that stress will eventually build up, popping out in the likely form of refusing to use the box altogether. Progress slowly if you want to make headway quickly.

Once he happily scales the heights to relieve himself, it is time to take the final steps. This is when things become truly inconvenient for the humans of the house if there is only one bathroom. Just think of it as a couple of weeks of annoyance, in exchange for more than a decade of litter-free living.

The final stage involves getting your cat actually onto your toilet seat. There are some readymade plastic pans just for this purpose sold in some pet supply stores and in the back of most cat magazines (several of which are listed in the Bibliography and Resources section). These are easy to lift in and out, making the use of the toilet possible, if not convenient. If you can't get a hold of one of these, improvise. Rig up some heavy-duty plastic wrap or a piece of a plastic drop cloth taped into place onto the rim of the bowl of the toilet. It should be set up to form a shallow bowl in the middle. It shouldn't sag down tremendously, nor should you be able to bounce a quarter off it. Depending on the strength of the plastic, some may sag a bit once some litter is added, so experiment.

Into this pour a small amount of *flushable* kitty litter. As accidents can and do happen, use a product that won't clog your pipes if the whole rig collapses into the bowl.

If the plastic wrap is too flimsy, collapsing when the cat touches it, the cat may become spooked. Make it sturdy at first, while your friend is getting the hang of things. The fact that the plastic moves when stepped on will discourage him from putting his full weight on it. As he gets the hang of the process, you do not have to be as concerned with the strength of the plastic.

Once you have discreetly observed your friend balancing consistently on the seat, then it is time to start slowly removing the litter and poking a small hole in the center of the plastic. Not only will the hole allow urine to escape, but it will begin to get the cat used to the tinkling sound of liquid hitting liquid.

As your cat becomes comfortable with the situation, slowly widen the hole until there is no litter underneath him. You've done it. Now all you have to do is leave the door open and the seat up. Happy flushing!

Destructive Scratching

In this section we will deal with destructive scratching of objects. If you are having a problem with your cat scratching people, please see the section "Aggression" on pages 164-171.

Remember that scratching is a natural behavior, a behavior you only find annoying because it involves objects you value. If your cat only scratched his post or a tree outside, you would never think about it at all. Begin this section by understanding it is *what* he scratches not *that* he scratches that is the problem.

The three most common reasons for destructive scratching are nail maintenance, marking territory, and stress release.

Nail maintenance is pretty much a side benefit to most scratching. From the look on cats' faces when they scratch, we suspect it is pleasurable for them to sink their claws in and pull. Probably gives a wonderful stretch to all the retractor muscles in the paw.

Scratching cleans the nails up, removing the scaling outer shell. It also sharpens the claws. *You can greatly limit the damage done by a scratching cat by keeping his nails trimmed short.* Only do this if your cat is an exclusively indoor animal.

Marking territory is the usual motivation for this behavior. As all cats have a number of zones they are aware of, cats in general, males in particular, tend these territories carefully. As they can't post signs saying "mine" or build fences, they leave

(Left) Ben marks his territory for all to see
by scratching the bench.
(Right) Ben's favorite scratching post,
sleeping area, and lookout spot.

calling cards by scratching. Scratching leaves both visual (the marks left by the claws) and olfactory (the scent left by the glands in the feet) marks for all other cats to see and smell.

One reason cats often reach up and scratch downward is to leave a clue of how big they are. The higher the marks, the bigger the cat. The bigger the cat, the tougher the competitor. Having some idea how big your opponent is before you meet him saves on fighting.

Cats scratch in predictable places: the entrance to their home turf, a favorite sleeping area, a challenged boundary, commonly used entrances and exits.

The other reason cats scratch, and it's tied to the territorial one, is stress.

If your cat is sitting at a window and sees a strange cat wander through "his" yard it is going to frustrate him. That frustration may well show itself by your cat turning and scratching the sill of the window. He is marking his territory, but that marking is being motivated by stress.

GUIDELINES FOR A GOOD POST

Before we get into how to handle specific destructive scratching, let's go over again what makes a scratching post desirable to a cat. For a cat to be taught to use a post consistently, it must be the right kind of post. The best, most cat-acceptable posts have several common qualities.

STURDY

Your cat isn't going to use a wobbly post. A cat wants to brace himself and really tear at the surface he scratches. This desire is one reason heavy pieces of furniture are so feline-friendly. A large, strong base can make a post stable, as can attaching it firmly to the wall, floor, or ceiling.

TALL

Most cats like to reach upward, grab ahold, and rake their claws downward. This means that the ideal post needs to be a decent height, the taller the better. A good guideline is to get a post at least as high as his favorite scratching spot.

GOOD SURFACE

Studies have shown most cats prefer material with a vertical grain, which they can easily pull their claws down and through. Both sisal and carpeted posts are widely accepted. If making your own post, consider attaching the carpet wrong side out, as the coarse burlap backing is favored by many cats.

LOCATION, LOCATION, LOCATION

You can have the best darn scratching post on the block, but it won't be used if it's in the wrong place. How often would you use a bathroom in the basement, no matter how pretty, if you had a more convenient one on the floor with you? So thinks the cat. Why march myself to the back bedroom to use the post when a perfectly good couch is sitting right here?

And for cats it's not just a matter of convenience. Since cats use scratch-

ing as a message, why post a sign in a place where no one goes?

STOPPING DESTRUCTIVE SCRATCHING

The easiest time to direct scratching behavior is in kittenhood when you can develop the behavior you want, instead of trying to eliminate an established behavior you don't want.

MATERIAL

Before any behavioral control or direction can be started, you must first figure out what your cat likes to scratch. While some cats are horizontal-oriented—enjoying rugs, carpeting, seats of chairs or couches, or doormats, most like vertical posts—the corners of furniture, backs of chairs, side moldings, or such.

Whatever your cat's preference,

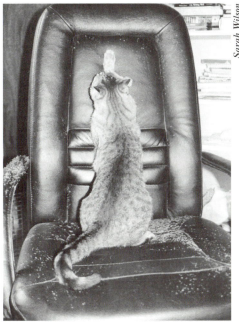

Sarah Wilson

It doesn't take long for real damage to be done.

you need to indulge it if you want to be successful. That said, most kittens develop their preference early in life and if you are starting off young, you can dictate the material to some extent.

CONFINEMENT

Confinement is the key to both developing good behavior in kittens and redirecting unwanted behavior in older cats. Confining your cat in a room with no favorable scratching surfaces except the post is a sure way to focus him on the post for his scratching needs. Placing the post next to his bed further weights things in your favor.

You can even gently take your cat to the post and drag his feet down it. This distributes some of his scent on it, which can help give him the idea. But only do this if your cat is relaxed about this handling. If he is tense, it will only forge a bad association with the post.

PRAISE, PRAISE, PRAISE

Cats respond well to being praised. Praise is readily available at all times, is inexpensive and easy to apply—*heap* it on! If you catch your cat in the act of scratching his post—*praise him!* Whisper sweet nothings in his ear, cuddle him, cheer him on—whatever tickles his fancy!

STACK THE DECK

It is perfectly legal, acceptable, and moral to stack the deck in your favor.

Rub catnip or treats into the post. While this may not encourage him to scratch right away, he will be putting his scent all over it when he rubs his face against it in ecstasy. Once his scent is on it, he'll be more likely to return later.

Dragging toys up the post seductively encourages him to sink his claws in. Be creative! Have fun! The more contact he has with the post, the more successful your efforts will be.

BOOBY-TRAP THE OLD AREAS

Cat lovers are a creative group. They have developed all kinds of ways to deter a cat from a once favorite scratching area. These include: taping tinfoil over the area, hanging inverted mousetraps or balloons in the area, covering it with inverted contact paper or double-sided tape, spraying it with an indoor repellent, attaching citrus peels to the area, using Plexiglas as a shield—the list goes on. Try these, make up your own. If it is humane and it works, then it is a fine method whether you read about it in a book, or came up with the great idea on your own.

Always remember though that nature abhors a vacuum. Never try to remove one behavior without offering a better, acceptable one in its place. Cats must and will scratch. Instead of fighting that, use it to your advantage.

The Great Declaw Debate

Few things will cause more fur to fly in the cat community than declawing and with good reason. Declawing is nothing to take lightly. It is a serious operation that amputates the nails and the nail beds. It is painful. It is permanent.

Here are our thoughts on declawing:

Kittens scratch things, that's part of being a kitten. To expect them not to is unreasonable. Most kittens can be taught to scratch a post, if the time is taken early to teach them. Confinement, praise, consistency, and nail trimming are keys to surviving this stage. We do not understand people who think confining a kitten is cruel, then declaw to prevent a problem.

Older cats can be retrained to focus their scratching energies on a post with the same techniques used for teaching a kitten. An older cat, with established habits, may take a little longer to train, but it is possible. Patience, prevention, persistence, and praise are the keys here.

If you have tried everything, and your older cat still destroys things at a level you cannot tolerate, and if it is now a choice between keeping a cat you otherwise love and surgery—then, and only then, do we think declawing is an option.

The cold facts are that older cats in shelters often do not find homes, and it is not likely there are many people who will be more tolerant of your cat than you are. Given a choice between likely death and declawing, we vote declawing.

But never do it lightly. It is mutilation. It leaves the cat vulnerable to attack, unable to climb as easily or effectively, and limited in his play. Just because something can be done, doesn't mean it necessarily should be done. Instead of complaining about your cat's destructive scratching, take the time to teach your cat what you want.

There are many beliefs floating around about declawing, ranging from declawed cats bite more to declawed cats show no ill effects. We suspect that your cat's reaction to the surgery depends on your cat. Some easygoing felines will take it all in stride, while others will have an extreme reaction. Not surprising really, given what individuals cats are.

Aggression

Feline aggression can be frightening to live with. It ranges from a playful pounce from behind the couch to a full-blown assault. Fortunately, once you know a few things about feline aggression, it is largely preventable.

Aggression, although undesirable in a human household, has many important functions in a wild feline's life. It is the sine qua non of hunting. Aggression is used to protect territory, young, a kill, and the cat himself. It is a part of most feline play, and is integral in the cat's sexual practices. Given this, being aggressive is part of being a cat. Most feline aggression falls into these general categories:

DEFENSIVE AGGRESSION

A frightened cat is a cat who needs to be left alone. No discussions. Unless your cat is in a life-threatening situation, do not try to calm, carry, or contact your friend. The cat who loves

you is not present when frightened. You are facing an animal whose only interest is her own preservation. Any attempt to comfort her will only be seen as a further threat. Allow her to hide. Allow her to retreat. Allow her to calm down.

If the cat is about to endanger herself in some way, you can contain her by putting a sturdy box or wastepaper basket over her. But be aware that it may scare her as well, causing her to run away if she sees the box coming near her. Speak soothingly, move slowly, and keep the box out of sight as much as possible, but by far, it is just better to leave her alone.

How can you tell if a cat is terrified? Her body will be flattened against the ground, ears will be flattened against her head, her pupils will be dilated, she may be growling or hissing. She may even roll on her back, in what looks like a submissive posture. Wrong, stay clear.

Time is the best medicine for the frightened cat. At the moment of fright, time to calm down. Depending on the event, object, or animal causing the fear, time to get used to it. Give her all the time she needs. You'll know when she's back to her old self when she gives herself a bath, indulges in a snack, or approaches you for some attention.

If the fear is severe, you cannot remove the cause of the fear, and she doesn't seem to be getting used to it at all, speak to your veterinarian. There are drugs available that can help a cat over this. Drugs are never to be used casually, or as an easy answer, and they certainly should never be used without a veterinarian's in-

Punk, an ankle biter, needs a good predatory release every day to control his aggressive urges. This game of attack-the-rolled-up-newspaper works well for him.

Marsha Wilson

structions, but they have their use. Better to have a cat medicated for a few weeks or months until she can learn to handle a new situation than to have her live in terror for that time period or longer.

IRRITABLE AGGRESSION

Irritable aggression is exactly what it sounds like—your cat gets irritated, then bites or scratches you. The good news, if it can be called that, is normally this is inhibited aggression. The claws are kept sheathed, or mostly sheathed, and the bite, if there is one, does not normally break the skin.

The best way to handle this is to remain absolutely passive, holding still while the cat is wrapped on your hand. Complete passivity is a signal of submission, which most cats will respect almost immediately by releasing. If you struggle, the cat figures you aren't getting the "submit to me now" message, and may intensify the aggression. Now you're headed for some skin damage.

A loud, sudden noise can work to distract the cat and back him off. Slapping the wall, table, or any available hard surface with the flat of your hand will startle most cats away from you. A quick blast from a pressurized-air canister will put most cats in retreat as well.

Some cats rarely, if ever, show this behavior. Others display it anytime you push them the least bit too far. And pushing them too far can be easy to do. The classic irritable aggression situation is petting. You are petting your cat, all is well, then he turns and

bites you. That fast. That surprisingly. What happened? Basically, like the rest of us, your cat likes contact up to a point and then doesn't want it anymore. Only, we tend to miss his signals. A key sign to look for is tail lashing. If it starts to lash, you'd better stop.

Such aggression has nothing to do with your animal liking you or being attached. Think of it this way; a very good friend sits next to you and, in a friendly way, pats your arm. Only, she keeps patting your arm—for five, maybe ten minutes. Some days that might be okay. Other days you might say, "Hey, knock it off!" That's your cat. Nothing personal, he's still your buddy, but... knock it off!

One of the big red "I'm going to bite you now" buttons is your cat's belly. Some cats even roll over to expose their tummy, appearing to the owner like an invitation to pet that soft wonderful spot. Proceed with caution. Stomach petting is a trigger for many cats to wrap their front paws around your hand, bite at your wrist, and rabbit kick with their hind legs against your arm. None of this is pleasant. But again, if you stay calm and relaxed, the cat is more likely to release than if you struggle.

Cats' tolerance for petting varies widely. Some enjoy it. Some demand it, for long periods of time. A few cats just want to be next to you or on you but not be stroked. If that's the deal, accept it. Your job is to watch, learn, and then do what your cat enjoys. The more you accept and respect his desires, the better your chances are of him becoming more tolerant. If you would like him to be more toler-

ABSCESSES

Puncture wounds, the type that cats often get when they fight, are prone to abscessing. This is because dirt from a bite or scratch gets deep into the wound. The wound then heals over at skin level, first forming a germ-filled pocket that grows more infected and swollen by the day.

If your cat comes home looking like he's been in a battle, wash his wounds twice a day with Betadine mixed with warm water. It is critical that the top of the wound stays open, healing from the inside out. If the wound looks deep, see your vet. If a swelling starts to develop, see your vet. If the wound gets hot, red, or angry looking, see your vet.

ant, see Hates to Be Handled on pages 171–172.

PLAY AGGRESSION

Ankle hockey, hand batting, overhead ambushes all fall into this category. These types of games normally have a surprise aspect to them. You're carrying the laundry into the bedroom and your cat leaps out from behind the door. He may run sideways at you, slightly arched, then spin and race away. Or he may latch on to your closest moving limb, usually a foot, and give it a couple of bites. These bites range in intensity, depending on your cat and his level of excitement. This type of aggression is made worse by struggling and squealing. Again, become passive. A motionless prey is less fun. A loud, sudden noise—as described above—can help you here as well.

If you know you have this type of cat, carry a small compressed-air horn in your pocket at all times. This will set him back a bit. If you're an apartment dweller, where such loud noises are likely to earn you complaints from the neighbors, use the plant sprayer, shake can, or pressurized air to break his train of thought.

Correcting this behavior is not enough. The aggression is a symptom, it is not the real problem. The real problem, the cause of these outbursts, is his frustrated hunting urges. To really solve this problem, spend time interacting with your friend. Aerobic play, basic training, and rotating toys can all help entertain without pain. The best toys for this type of cat are chase-pounce toys and bite-rip toys. Chase-pounce toys can be any variation of the thing-on-a-string or fishing pole type of toy. Bite-rip toys need to be larger so the cat can really wrap himself around it and "kill" it. Often a stuffed animal on a string works well for releasing this kind of energy.

One of the best ways to deal with play aggression is to get your bored cat a feline friend. Let them entertain each other, and keep your ankles out of it.

AGGRESSION TOWARD A NEW CAT

A certain amount of aggression is expected when a new cat is added to a household. As territories are being worked out and acceptance being developed, you can expect hissing, arching of the back, puffing of the hair, laying back of the ears, and the like. Normally, this is all more hiss than hurt, and the animals have little actual contact with each other, at the most a brief scuffle followed by rapid retreat. No blood is shed and only feelings are hurt.

On the other hand, on rare occasions, cats take strong offense to an addition into their lives. In these cases, you will need to take steps to help them accept each other. Those steps are outlined on pages 57–58.

TERRITORIAL AGGRESSION

Cats fight over territory. For unneutered males it's a way of life, a main concern, and a favorite hobby. As has been mentioned, all companion cats should be neutered, and for males it is as much for their own safety as for your olfactory convenience.

If you have an indoor-outdoor hard-core fighter on your hands, you have a few options. You can make him an indoor cat. This is a 100 percent successful cure for this problem. If he can't meet Ole One Eye behind the shrubs, he won't get into fight No. 920 with him.

If keeping him indoors all the time is not an option, then only let him out during the day. Most territorial disputes are settled at night. If you only feed him in the evening, you can ensure he comes home on time.

Consider building a large, outdoor area for him that he can't get out of and other cats can't get in. This allows him outdoor time without risking more damage to him.

SEXUAL AGGRESSION

Cats are feisty lovers. The male bites the female on the neck as they mate, a behavior that may be triggered by stroking his belly. This type of stroking can trigger more than one type of aggression, but all types have the same cure: don't stroke the belly area. But you don't have to take our word for it. Do what you want, your cat will teach you.

FELINE FRIENDS
FIGHTING

Most cats who live together settle in, given time. Some become fast friends, sleeping curled against each other, grooming each other tenderly. Others live at a polite distance in a generally agreed upon truce.

In most multi-cat households there are occasional spats, as there are in any group of friends, but they don't usually amount to much. Generally, they are over with quickly and no blood is drawn. But occasionally a major battle breaks out. Normally this occurs after some kind of scare that one cat blames the other for. An example: A book falls off the shelf, narrowly missing one cat. She leaps back with a yowl and runs out of the way. In the process she careens into the other cat. He thinks he is being attacked and retaliates in kind. The frightened cat, pumped up with fear, defends herself intensely. And now you have a problem.

A similar trouble can develop after a sick cat comes home from a stay at the vet's, or a longhaired cat returns, shaved, from the groomer's. In both cases, the returning cat may smell and look substantially different. The cat who stayed at home may genuinely not recognize her. If this is the case, follow the instructions in the sections on how to introduce a new cat to the household.

Odd as it may seem, you'll have to go through those motions. Often it takes substantially less time, but you will have to be patient. There's no way to explain what the problem is to them. As tempting as it is, do not lavish tons of extra attention on the confused, returning cat. This will only set up more tension between the two animals. Be attentive to both, treat them both normally.

Sometimes with a fear-stimulated

problem, giving everyone a few hours to cool off is all that is needed. Occasionally, both cats stay on the defensive, looking at the other to suddenly attack out of the blue. In this case, set up separate areas, one for each cat. Each area should have all the amenities—litter box, food, water, bed, toys. Every day, switch the cats. Then after two to three days of this, start feeding them in the same room. Start at opposite ends and slowly, each meal, move the bowls a few inches closer. If at any time you think you see either cat getting tense or nervous, move the bowls back a foot or so and leave them at that distance for three to four meals. After that, continue bringing them closer.

DISPLACEMENT AGGRESSION

Displacement aggression happens when a cat is highly stimulated by

Photos by Sarah Wilson

Cats are hunters. Here Ben plays with a mouse he caught. Why? Because he's a cat!

someone or something, and then turns that excitement on the nearest breathing thing, which unfortunately may be you. An example, your cat is looking out his living room window into his backyard. He sees a neighboring, much hated cat crossing your yard. Your cat starts to growl. He is not amused. You come over to see what's going on. You reach forward to lean against the sill just next to your cat. He turns, biting you hard. You scream and shake your arm. He bites again and runs off.

You are shook up as well as bleeding. Why did your beloved friend do this to you? Take heart. Although you were the recipient of this misfortune, it was not directed at you personally. When some cats get to a certain level of excitement/stimulation they fire on anyone close by. The vast majority of cats never do this. Neutered animals are much less likely to do this. Of all the cats we've shared our lives with over the years, we've never had a cat do this to us. But we've had clients who have, and if you are having this problem you should know about it.

Controlling this includes: neutering is *not* optional. If the aggression is window-related, as it often is, make that window inaccessible to him. Confine him in a room away from that window. Booby-trap the sill area with contact paper or inverted mousetraps. Block the window so he cannot see out. Be creative, but be effective. This is too frightening a behavior to take half measures with. Discourage intruders from crossing your yard. Use repellents outdoors. Install a fence, although some cats can get over most any fence. Turn the hose on the in-truder, toss shake cans down near him from a window in your house. Don't hurt him, but do harass him anytime he sets a paw in your yard. Leave your cat alone when he is upset. Go the other way when you see your cat focused on something, growling.

Keep a small compressed-air horn handy. An air horn is a strong correction for both your cat and anyone in the vicinity, but this is serious stuff. Keep it handy and use it without hesitation if your cat looks like he's headed your way in an aggressive manner. Stop the instant he turns away. He must understand that stopping his assault stops yours.

If the problem continues, seek professional assistance immediately. Ask your veterinarian if he can refer a behaviorist or behavioral counselor in your area.

PAIN-INDUCED AGGRESSION

Cats will often attack if attacked. This is not hard to understand, but people can still miss the point. They complain that their cat scratched or bit them, but if pressed will admit that they were angry when they reached for the cat. If you hit a cat, you will hurt him. If you hurt a cat, the cat is likely to return the favor. If he has been hurt in the past by you or any other person and he sees that you're coming at him in an angry way, he may well try to defend himself before he is hurt again. This is a sensible plan on the cat's part.

Control this aggression by controlling yourself. Do not frighten or hurt your cat and this behavior will immediately be completely controlled.

SUDDEN, UNEXPLAINED AGGRESSION

If your cat is suddenly becoming aggressive for reasons you cannot figure out, go to your veterinarian. Pain resulting from a hidden disease or illness can be causing the problem. Unpredictable behavior can be caused by a chemical or physiological disorder. It's certainly worth checking out that possibility, if you can't make any sense out of your cat's behavior. If your vet gives him a clean bill of health, seek out a qualified cat behavioral counselor. Something is definitely amiss.

PREDATORY AGGRESSION

Cats are hunters. If your cat's killing of small animals bothers you, then keep him indoors. There is nothing you can do to discourage his hunting that won't actually simply discourage him from being around you. Of course, warning the little critters that death is stalking them is fair, and using a cat-safe collar with a bell attached is somewhat effective for that purpose.

MEDICAL SOLUTIONS TO AGGRESSION

There are some wonderful new drugs available for handling aggression in cats. These new drugs are more specific to the problems they are administered for, with fewer side effects, even with long-term use, and more effectiveness than any previous medications. If we had an animal who failed to respond to behavioral approaches, we would not hesitate to medicate him.

It is not within the scope of this book to describe the most commonly used drugs and, with all the new ones coming out, it is not even productive to do so. Just know that they are available, that they work well, that they cause few, if any, problems for your cat, and that they can be a lifesaver. If you are envisioning your cat drugged and disoriented from the medication, don't. That's not the way it is these days.

If you are having problems, ask your vet. If he doesn't have the answers, and he might not since behavioral pharmacology is its own specialty, call Tufts University School of Veterinary Medicine in Grafton, Massachusetts, at 508-839-5395. Ask to speak to their Behavior Department. They are a wonderful group of people with much experience in this area.

EUTHANIZING THE AGGRESSIVE CAT

It is a rare thing to have to euthanize a cat for aggression, but it is a choice that occasionally has to be made. Please give your animal every benefit of the doubt. Seek help from your veterinarian in regards to medication that you can try. Locate a qualified behaviorist or behavioral counselor to assist you in teaching your cat better manners. But if you have tried everything, and you still are having serious aggressive incidents with your cat, then a decision has to be made.

This decision is never easy. No matter how many things you have tried, there is almost always a small voice in the back of your mind whispering, "What if...?" What if you tried another doctor? What if the cat lived in a different home? It is natural to want to find a positive solution for your cat's problem. It is natural not to want to euthanize. But at times it is the best and kindest option.

Passing him off to another home can be tempting. It seems like an easy way to "fix" your problem so that you don't have to make the decision that you dread. But don't do it. You are by far the most loving, tolerant home your cat can hope to find. If you are taking the time to read this book, you are doing more than many people would in an effort to help your cat. Giving him to someone else is wrong for a variety of reasons. First, you have no guarantee that these new people are going to be as tolerant or loving as you. Leaving your cat to be hit or worse by an angry human being is not acceptable. Secondly, what if he really hurts someone, especially a child? Not only would this make you feel horrible, but you could possibly be liable for it. And lastly, if he gets dropped by these new owners at a shelter or passed on to yet another home, he may well end up in a cage somewhere, isolated and confused, to be euthanized by strangers.

As hard as it is, helping your animal leave this life in as gentle and loving a way as possible can be the last act of kindness you offer to your companion. He will go, in loving hands, hearing a loving voice in his ears.

Expect to feel miserable for a while. How long you grieve is individual. Some people are distraught for days, others get depressed off and on for weeks. Try not to judge yourself. However you deal with it, it is your way and it is fine. The guilt and sadness that come with having to make this kind of decision can be intense. Fortunately, there are groups around the country that deal with just these situations. It is a wonderful thing to have understanding people to talk to. If you are not sure how to find such groups locally, give a grief counselor at the Animal Medical Center in New York City a call at 212-838-8100. They have a wonderful program and can assist you in finding the support you need.

Hates to Be Handled

There are cats who want the world strictly on their terms. These are animals who generally fall into one of three groups: either they have been mishandled, making them leery of all handling; not handled, making handling foreign to them; or just aren't the cuddly type. If you have reason to believe he has never been handled before, please see the section for taming the feral cat on pages 193–194 for what to do.

If your cat has been mishandled start off by immediately stopping any mishandling that may be going on. If you cannot stop this in your household, do not attempt to recondition your cat. Rather, find him a loving home outside of yours. If this is go-

HANDLING THE UNHANDLEABLE

How do you approach handling a cat you know doesn't want to be brushed, medicated, or have his nails clipped? We approach it with a thick bath towel in hand. Do not call the cat to you. Instead, walk up casually. Take a few seconds to scratch him lovingly while speaking to him kindly, then carefully drape the towel under his chin like you were putting on a bib. Wrap the ends of the towel snugly over his shoulders and scoop him up. Now you have a cat papoose.

Carefully do what needs to be done. When you are through, take a minute to speak to him softly. Stroke him lovingly, then slowly unwrap him. If you are rough with him, you just set the stage for a bigger battle next time.

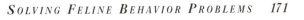

Brian Kilcommons

Emily is no fan of the out-of-doors and demonstrates well how hard it is to hold on to a cat who wants to be somewhere else. Much to her sweet-tempered credit, she did not hurt Sarah.

ing on in your household, and you can't stop it, you've got other things to worry about.

If he just isn't all that cuddly or came to your loving home previously abused, here are a few things you can try:

RESPECT THE CAT

If he wants to move away from you—allow it. By respecting his wishes you are teaching him to trust you. Accept whatever he is willing to offer. Maybe you want a lap cuddler and you have a sit-near-you type. Start there.

TEACH HIM TO BE FRIENDLY

Offer him treats whenever he sits near you. As he gets enthusiastic about this idea, hold the treat closer to you, so he has to reach out to get it. When he gets tired of reaching out, he'll move closer.

If you want to move this along quicker, stop feeding him from his bowl and only feed him from your hand. As he accepts this, move the hand closer and closer to you. You'll know you can bring it even closer when he eats readily from wherever it is.

If he resists treats, and you know that ordinarily he loves them, fine. Quit for that session. Try again in eight to twelve hours. When he gets hungry, your lap won't seem like the worst place on earth.

Once he is happily sitting next to you or on your lap, start adding one light stroke before each treat. One stroke while eating one treat. One stroke, one treat.

If, at any point in this training, he gets positively friendly or makes some big breakthrough, give him a big bonus—a handful of treats and quit for the day! Let him learn that extra effort on his part reaps large rewards.

As he adjusts to these sessions, add more general stroking over his whole body. But limit yourself to one new thing at a time. If you want to try two strokes for the first time do so, but don't add handling his tail also. One thing at a time.

Stuck in Tree

Most of the time if a cat manages to get himself up in a tree, he'll manage to get himself down—eventually. Cats come down on their time schedule, not yours.

One time Sarah's old wonderful cat Captain got himself into a real jam. He climbed up a large old oak. Whether intentional or not, he ended up near a bluejays' nest. Poor Captain huddled in the first crotch of the tree hoping to be left alone. Crouched there, his magnificent black tail hanging out the back, the perfect target for aerial assault. As one jay dove at his head, the other would swoop in grabbing his tail. He'd spin around to defend himself but by that time that bird was gone and the other one was grabbing his tail from behind. We did our best to help him, but he was high up and the birds were on a mission. After half an hour or so of this torment, he decided that retreat was the better part of valor and came down out of the tree.

Most normally fit adult cats will come down. But kittens, obese cats, frightened cats, and even declawed cats who managed to go up okay can't always come down. Here's how you can assist them:

GIVE HIM TIME

Often he will figure things out on his own. This is not true for declaws, who should *never* have been let outside in the first place.

What goes up, must come down... usually.

GET A LADDER

Only use a ladder if you know how and have someone to spot you. If you aren't confident about how to use one safely, you may end up needing some help yourself.

GET HELP

Call your local animal control officer who'll probably be able to help or will know someone who can. Others to consider are tree surgeons, firemen, roofers, chimney sweeps, construction workers, and other professions that require working at heights—all can be of help. Call around, many people love cats.

Kids and Cats

INFANTS

Although most cats adjust to a new baby in the house with ease, there are only a couple of things you need to be aware of regarding cats and infants.

After the baby arrives, if your cat starts acting out—making litter box mistakes, scratching new places, crying at odd hours—chances are the amount of attention she's been getting has changed. If your cat has been the recipient of all your parental urges during the pregnancy and then is suddenly put aside for the real infant, expect some behavioral fireworks. Here are a few things you can do *before* your baby arrives to help smooth the way after.

ESTABLISH A ROUTINE

Cats adore routine. Setting up mealtimes and a play-attention time during the day that you believe will work once the baby has arrived will set the stage for a smooth transition for all.

LIMIT HER ATTENTION

Don't heap attention onto your cat before the baby arrives in the misguided attempt to make up for the attention she will not receive in future months. This will make it difficult for your cat when she goes from feast—tons of attention—to famine—little or none. Instead, plan ahead for the limited amount of time you will have as a new parent and wean your cat back before the birth. This way her routine will stay the same, her stress

The father here is doing things just right. He's there paying close attention to the interaction, the cat can escape anytime he wants, and the child is having a ball. Perfect!

Tina McDermott

will be minimal, and you won't have to deal with any behavior problems—well, at least not from your cat.

CONTROL ACCESS TO THE INFANT

Another thing you may want to do is install a screen door on your baby's room. This will allow you to hear your baby easily but the cat won't be able to go in. Most cats adore infants, the only worry is that your cat, in friendliness, will curl up next to, or on, your infant for a shared nap, inadvertently suffocating the baby.

TODDLERS

The key to surviving toddlerhood in general is supervision. This truism extends to cat-toddler interactions as well. Just the other day, a client called that his cat was hissing at the toddler. The history? Well, seems that the cat adored the child and would "allow the child to do anything to him." Please do not make the mistake of thinking that because a cat tolerates certain abuse from a child that he either likes it or intends to continue to tolerate it. General rule to go by: supervise your toddler with your cat the way you would supervise your toddler with an infant. Behavior inappropriate with an infant is inappropriate with a cat.

Never, ever, allow a toddler to be with a cat, or any pet, unsupervised. Toddlers don't really mean harm, they just don't have a lot of physical or psychological self-control. Impulse rules and animals get hurt. Make it clear to your toddler that hurting the cat will not be allowed, and you'll have much less of a risk of your cat hurting your toddler.

Here is another time your cat may benefit from a room set up just for her with a baby gate across the front. Having a safe haven from your two-year-old may be just what she needs.

SMALL CHILDREN

Now is the fun time for the child, the parent, and the cat. The child is developed enough—in body and in mind—to act responsibly with a cat. This is the age of sharing, playtime, and constant companionship.

This is also the age children love doing chores. There is no reason that your child can't start taking some small responsibilities for the pet. Rinsing and filling the water bowl is possible for even the youngest cat lovers. Dishing out dinner, putting toys away, basic brushing are all possible as the child matures. A word of caution here though: no child is responsible enough to care for a pet completely. Cat care can be a challenge for an adult, and is way too much for a child. Instead, share the chores, rotating them among yourselves. In that way you will teach your child about sharing, responsibility, and teamwork. These things are better learned through demonstration than through lecture.

Let us also add one more word, on a serious note. Childhood animal abuse can indicate serious emotional problems in a child. Most every child will make a mistake, but if you have reason to believe that your child is repeatedly and intentionally hurting animals, please seek help for him immediately.

KEEP IT S.A.F.E.

Keeping a child and cat safe together is not so hard.

SUPERVISE
When together, cats and young children must always be supervised. Even a wonderful cat may lash out if frightened. Even a wonderful child may squeeze too hard or lose their balance.

ANTICIPATE
Cats are cats, kids are kids. If you anticipate that they will act true to their natures, you will have few problems.

FOLLOW THROUGH
If you say no to your child about picking the cat up by the tail, make sure he stops doing so.

ENFORCE
Dwell on the positive whenever your child is gentle but brook no nonsense about him hurting the cat.

Butler Please!

One big old lazy neutered male cat we know yowls at the front door until he's let in, then saunters down the hall to the back door, where he proceeds to yowl to go out. He's just too darn lazy to walk around the house.

Most of us are well trained by our feline companions to open doors for them on command. And since cats do not give up, you need to take evasive maneuvers. Eliminating the yowling is covered thoroughly on pages 182–183. Making an outdoor cat an indoor one is covered on pages 178–179. In this section, we devote ourselves to avoiding the problem by installing a cat door.

The upside to a cat door is that the cat can go in and out at will, taking you off the hook completely. The downsides are that he can come and go at will even when he is carrying in a half-dead rodent, or is soaking wet from a rainstorm, and it can let in another cat, who was, presumably, uninvited by you. These potential hazards can be completely eliminated by having the cat door go out to a screened-in, cat-safe area.

Many cats get the idea immediately, using the door virtually from the first day. Others need a little help figuring it all out. For these felines, we offer the following:

TEACHING A CAT TO USE A CAT DOOR

To start, give him a few days after installation to accept it before trying to enlighten him about its use. Moving his bowl right next to it helps to build a positive association.

Next, put a favorite delicacy on the other side and rub some of the food against the door itself. As he licks the food, the door will move. As it moves, he'll get more of the food scent outside. Hopefully, he'll stick his head out to get a better sniff.

If he resists this, prop or tape the door securely open. Make sure it is sturdy so if the cat bumps it, the door won't slap down on him, which may scare him away from going near it again. Then tempt him with treats to go through. Drag a toy through the opening. A fishing pole type toy is perfect for this. Play this game for a few minutes, several times a day, and he'll catch on.

C. J. Puotinen

We speak from experience here; a cat on a keyboard can create computer chaos. This is a definite OFF LIMITS to our cats.

Climbing Misdeeds

Most of us cat owners have encountered minor household disasters caused by the feline habit of climbing onto any and every available surface. Teaching your cat to stay out of, or off of, certain areas is as simple as making these areas unattractive to your cat. To state the obvious, if your cat doesn't want to go someplace, then he won't go there.

How do you make an area unattractive to a cat? The two best ways are to surprise him or disgust him. Cats don't like either of these things much and when faced with them will almost always retreat. If they meet either of these repeatedly, they will retreat permanently from the area.

Surprise is created with either shake cans or upside-down mouse-traps. Resting shake cans precariously on the edge of the surface so they tumble when bumped may scare some cats off the surface. You can tape a few cans together and set a trigger can on the edge and the rest all over the shelf so when the trigger can tumbles, it pulls the rest behind it. This makes a real racket.

Setting some old-fashioned snap-type mousetraps face down on the surface will deter most cats. Any touch will cause them to snap surprisingly and harmlessly.

Disgust him with an odor he considers foul. Certain odors a cat just can't stomach. Repellent products, indoor ones only please, can work extremely well. Other less-than-favorite smells include citrus deodorizers and certain perfumes. Reapplication may be necessary every couple of days un-

til your cat stops attempting to get to that surface.

Alternatively, make it disgust him by making it sticky with contact paper or double-sided tape. Cut a piece of contact paper the correct width and a few inches too long for the area. Peel an inch or two of the backing away from both ends, then lay the contact paper bottom side up, folding the sticky ends down adhering to the surface. Now peel off the rest of the backing.

Using tape, lay out a strip along the surface. If you do not want it to adhere to the whole area, lay some newspaper underneath the tape except under the ends. It can still be affixed, but that makes it easier to remove.

Making an Outdoor Cat an Indoor One

Convincing an outdoor cat to become an indoor cat is normally a simple, though often tedious, matter of you being more strong-willed, prepared, and observant than he is.

Cats are creatures of habit, something you will learn the full meaning of when you make this change. He has a daily routine outside involving a check of his territorial boundaries, a visit to his favorite scratching and napping places, a saunter through the best chipmunk-chasing areas. In fact, most of the truly interesting things in his life happen outside. So, when you bring him in for good, he will no doubt have much to say about the matter.

First off, make sure he has everything he needs in your home. A litter box of the size and shape he likes with litter he'll use. Access to fresh water and food, an acceptable scratching area, and someplace private where he won't be bothered. He will also need ample outlet for his hunting urges; if he has been a successful hunter in the past this will be especially important. That means daily play, sometimes twice-daily play, with you. Careful, watch your fingers! Some of these cats get mighty excited by a hunting-type game, taking it quite seriously. Once all his needs are supplied to him, then it's time to go cold turkey.

Pick a day when he's to become an indoor cat, then that's it. No more time outside, period. Weaning him off of the outside isn't going to work. Just end it and be done with it. Once done, the cat, like anyone else trying to break a habit, is not going to be amused. He is going to howl at the door, look at you longingly, pine, complain, bemoan, and otherwise cuss you out good. So what? If you let him out, even once, all you have taught him is that nagging works and next time he'll cry even longer and louder!

Do not give in. Expect unwanted behavior for the first week or so. He will be stressed by the change and stressed cats develop behaviors you are not always happy to see. Exercise will help, but don't hesitate to confine him to a safe room if he becomes destructive or starts missing the litter box in his frustration. This will pass, once he gets used to his new routine.

Here are a few things you can do to make the transition easier.

USE POSITIVE REINFORCEMENT

By making it as pleasant as possible for him when he is indoors, you are encouraging him to be content there. A few seconds after he has left the door area, go to him. Reward him with whatever he enjoys—praise, a treat, some play.

CORRECT HIM

Making the doorway a slightly unpleasant place to be helps keep the noise level down in your home. Give him a squirt from the spray bottle to quiet him. Give the shake can a shake at your side. If that is ineffective, toss it near the door (not at the cat, please!); that should do the trick. Combine this with rewarding him for leaving the doorway area, and things will progress smoothly.

KEEP HIS MIND ACTIVE

Not only does play help him to adjust, but so does training. Teach him anything you like, tricks, simple behaviors—whatever. This will build the bond between the two of you, and give him plenty to think about.

He'll change his ways, as long as you are committed to him doing so.

Once he has adjusted to being indoors, the occasional outing is possible. Building a large screened cage off a window can give your cat the outdoor time he craves without putting him at risk; always make such a cage fully enclosed. Put a large tree limb in for climbing, plant some catnip, have fun! Your cat will adore his own private oasis of feline pleasures.

Or take your cat for a stroll. It takes a little bit for your cat to get used to a harness and lead, but after he adapts, he'll get a kick out of strolling his old haunts with you. See pages 113–114 for teaching your cat how to walk on a lead. The only rule I would apply to this is do not take him out if he is demanding to go out. That will only reinforce demanding behavior and put you back where you started. Instead, put on the harness and go when he is being quiet in some other part of the house. That way he'll never know when it's going to happen.

Never tie a cat outside on a rope. He'll be easy prey for a passing dog and if you tie him near a tree thinking he can retreat if threatened, you have also put him at risk of hanging himself.

Door Dashing

Cats are agile, have excellent timing, and are mighty quick. Those traits, in combination, can lead to a first-class door dasher who sprints for freedom the moment he hears the keys in the lock.

This is a dangerous habit, not only for the cat, but for any poor soul standing outside with bags in their arms. Fortunately, door dashing is easily rectified with a bit of forethought on your part. Take the time to set up the situation when you aren't in a hurry or overburdened with bags of groceries. A couple of well-timed and well-executed corrections may save your cat's life one day.

If your cat hates water squirted at him, then use a plant sprayer set on stream to correct this. If he hates loud, surprising noise—use a shake can or compressed-air horn to change his mind. Whatever the tool you select, use it like this:

Carry the tool with you or set it outside by the door.

When you come home, get the tool ready and then carefully open the door just a bit.

If the cat is there, blast him. Say nothing, as you want him to associate the unpleasantness with the door opening—not with your presence.

If he isn't there, open the door slowly so you have plenty of time to react if he makes a break for it.

If you are caught unprepared, use your keys. Throw them down right in front of you. This will startle your cat without harming him in the least. It's not a perfect tool, but it's one you will almost always have when you come through the door.

If he gets through this blockade—*do not* turn and correct him as he runs off; that only teaches him to run away from the house very fast. Once the cat has run out the door, it is too late to teach him not to run out the door. Just chalk the experience up to learning and either open the door more slowly next time, or try a different tool that the cat is more frightened of.

For cats, two or three experiences like this and they'll stay well away from the door when you open it.

Dinner Plate Encroachment

Just about every cat has to be taught that food on your plate isn't an open invitation to dine.

The easiest way to deal with this is to never allow it to develop into a problem. Don't feed your cat when he is on the table. Do not feed your cat from your plate, period. Do not allow your cat to lick the dishes after the meal. If you want to share the wealth, put a tidbit in his bowl, so he thinks all good things come from his bowl and only his bowl. Do not allow your cat to snack from plates on the counter.

If you already have a dinner plate licker, set up the following situation. Get your tool of choice, make yourself a plate of food, and sit down for a pretend meal. Make cat training your priority here. A few sessions spent educating your cat and you'll have pleasant meals for years to come.

If he heads for your plate, tell him clearly and firmly, "Off." If he complies, great! Praise him because he really deserves it. If he doesn't move, a quick squirt will put him someplace else in an instant. A plant sprayer set on stream and filled with water is certainly an effective and easy technique for feline management with the dinnertime advantage of being minimally disruptive. If nothing is close by, a quick, flat hand whomp on the table or a blast from a can of pressurized air will send most cats elsewhere.

Sarah Wilson

Unless corrected quickly, this type of behavior can become a habit fast.

Regardless of how you get your cat to remove himself, follow his retreat with praise. As always, make sure all correction stops the moment he complies. The second all four feet leave the table, the water squirting or loud noise must end. He needs to connect jumping off the table with safety if he is to get the message you want him to get.

Yowling and Other Demanding Behaviors

Cats vocalize for a wide variety of reasons, at least three quarters of them seem to involve giving instructions to owners. Cats are wonderful teachers of focus, persistence, and patience. Once they have committed themselves to a project, say training you to open the door on command or teaching you to get up early and feed them, they are wholeheartedly committed.

They do not get distracted. They do not give up. They do not say you are stupid, spiteful, stubborn, or difficult. They just sit and cry... and cry... and cry. Unwittingly, perhaps, you have given in to this training process, by opening the door or getting up and getting him breakfast. When that happens, your cat says to himself, "Ah, a little slow, but she is getting the hang of it. I'll work with her more tomorrow."

Here are the rules of changing a cat's habit of yowling to get what she wants.

From this moment forward, you will not respond to a yowling cat. Or, at least, you will try not to. If you decide to sit this yowling business out, sit it out. Correct the cat, ignore the cat. Wear headphones. Do not give in to the cat. The worst thing you can do is wait ten minutes or so and then buckle under the pressure. If you do that, you have just *trained* the cat to yowl for ten or more minutes at a time. Bad lesson.

Decide that if you are going to give in, give in quickly. Realistically, if it's been a long day, you're not in the mood, you're down with the flu—or for whatever reason—you know that today of all days you will not be able to tolerate this, then for heaven's sake give in *immediately*. At least then you have not reinforced persistence in this behavior. Thirty seconds of yowling is much more easily lived with than several minutes.

CORRECTING YOWLING

There are several ways to correct a noisy cat, the easiest, time-proven techniques are using water or sound to break their train of thought. For example, your cat is staring at you, yowling. Immediately, and as discreetly as you can, toss a shake can in the general direction. Aim carefully to *avoid* the cat. Yowling is annoying, it's not a capital crime. She'll spook when it lands.

After a few seconds of silence, call her over to you. Praise her and give a treat. In this way you are rewarding silence, reassuring her that all is well and demonstrating that you had nothing to do with the noise thing falling from the sky, which just happens around noisy cats.

DISTRACT THE CAT

Sometimes a strong offense really is the best defense. Starting a rollicking game when you see your cat getting into the yowling position gives him the mental and physical exercise he needs as well as taking his mind completely off his troubles.

REWARD DESIRED BEHAVIOR

Not only can you praise her after a correction but you should also strive to notice when she is being quiet and reward her then. This takes a sharp eye and a patient spirit, but a few well-timed rewards for a quiet cat plants an interesting seed in her head.

It is not always easy to notice quiet, undemanding behavior. In a busy day, it is often the squeaky wheel that gets the grease. But if you are tired of the squeaky wheel, you will have to motivate yourself to watch for the easily missed in order to reward the basically normal and wait for the miracle of learning to take place.

CORRECTING THE DEMANDING CAT

Your cat is in your face twenty-four hours a day. He lies on your head when you sleep, he lounges on your newspaper when you try to read, he helps you make the bed, bats at the shower curtain while you bathe, licks at the drips when you brush your teeth, and in general participates with your day totally.

Most of the time you adore this, but there are times when you would like to do something without getting cat hair in it. Here's how you achieve this without alienating your friend.

TEACH HIM

The good news is you have an extremely intelligent cat. The bad news is you have an extremely intelligent cat. He wants desperately to communicate with you, spending a great deal of time attempting to do so. Developing a vocabulary between the two of you will be wonderful fun, a great way to develop his brain, and a foundation for directing him to more positive, desired behaviors.

Think up tricks to teach him and work on them. The great thing about training your cat is that if it takes two days to teach him something or two weeks, what does it matter? This isn't a race. Have fun, go easy, enjoy yourselves.

ENTERTAIN HIM

Up that exercise. Cats, especially energetic cats, exercise themselves. But it's not always the type of exercise you want him to be doing. So to prevent unwanted behaviors, and release the pent-up tension, break out the Ping-Pong balls and have some fun. Divide his toys into three groups and put a different set down every few days. Take special care to play for at least fifteen minutes in the morning and evening.

GET HIM A FRIEND

Two cats tend to amuse each other. Two kittens raised together are virtually inseparable. And a kitten raised

with a sibling rarely develops into the intensely demanding type of cat that a cat raised alone will be.

ACCEPT THE INEVITABLE

If you got yourself a Siamese or Abyssinian, don't come crying to us about his energy level. That's like complaining that a Ferrari goes fast. If you don't want a fast car, don't buy one built for speed. If you don't want a cat who needs and demands complete integration into your life, don't get a breed that is famous for just that.

SET DOWN HOUSE RULES

Understanding of boundaries is natural to a cat. The boundary just has to be presented in a way that makes sense to them. Telling them not to go somewhere because it will make you happy if they don't isn't going to work well for a cat. You will have to give them a better reason than that.

Making the area seemingly dangerous to them is much more effective. Areas can be made to seem dangerous, but not really be, by booby-trapping them or by correcting your cat when he enters those areas. If your cat is a pest when you have a snack in front of the TV, don't allow him on the couch with you at those times. Tell him "Off" and use a spray of water, air, or sound to correct him each and every time he does not comply. The moment he hops off, praise him. After all, that is what you want, isn't it?

If you are inconsistent about this, you will create a bigger monster than you had before. So if you take a stand, take it. Don't start waffling.

It's hard enough for your cat to understand humans without you being indecisive on top of it. Basically, if you can't enforce house rules, how can you expect your cat to abide by them?

STAY CALM

For heaven's sake, stay calm! Just because you have decided it is high time your cat changed his ways doesn't mean that your cat agrees with you! Since you have probably lived with these behaviors for a while now, take a deep breath and relax. Behaviors that have been established for months don't go away overnight. There is no magic to training an animal. It is largely heavy doses of consistency, persistence, and reward that get the job done. This does not mean the behavior won't be manageable in a short period of time, just that you can't expect a cat to immediately and completely stop attempting a behavior that was effective for so long.

Chewing and Suckling Behaviors

DESTRUCTIVE CHEWING

Destructive chewing can be controlled. The first step is to prevent it. This may mean confining her to a safe room. If such a room isn't available, a large crate that holds all her basic needs will work. Preventing the behavior from recurring is half the battle in breaking a behavior cycle.

Chewing behavior is most often a

stress reaction. By removing whatever the stress is, you'll be removing the trigger of the behavior. The sooner you take action the better, as the longer any animal does something, the more that behavior becomes an independent, freestanding behavior separate from any stress.

Do *not* punish your cat for chewing. Rather booby-trap her favorite spots, control her access, supervise her, exercise her daily, and offer plenty of acceptable toys she can chew on. Simply praising her whenever she is playing with a toy is a great way to relax her as well as encourage the good behavior.

SELF-CHEWING

Emily arrived at our home with large patches of hair missing from her belly. The veterinarian confirmed that nothing was wrong with her physically, but it is always a good idea to double-check, as fleas, allergies, fungus, and infections are just a few reasons a cat may chew at herself.

But in Emily's case it was stress. Many cases of hair loss are due to a sensitive cat's reaction to stress. Emily had been found in a dumpster in an alley, lived several months in a cage at the vet's, and then ended up with us, among several dogs and another cat. Her stress level was off the charts.

Add to this Emily's sensitive nature. She is prone to hissing at and worrying over the little things in life. She reacts strongly to sudden noises or movements and it is obvious from her actions that she was hit by people

prior to her rescue from the streets.

Given all this, Emily chewed herself, vigorously, when she first arrived. She would be grooming herself normally, and then dive at her belly with sudden intensity. We are happy to report that now, just a few months later, she is much improved. Her coat is not perfect, but it is improving. Here are a few of the things we did to help her.

DON'T WORRY ABOUT IT

She wasn't hurting herself. A little hair loss was not a real problem, so we all took a deep breath and decided to view it as a behavioral thermometer, a symptom of her stress, not as *the* problem.

If your cat is ripping herself bloody, see your vet. She may need some short-term medication to help her through this period. Start the behavioral routines while she is medicated. There are many new drugs being used for feline anxiety and stress that are both effective and safe. Don't hesitate to use them if your cat needs some help and your veterinarian feels they are warranted.

GIVE HER A GOOD RETREAT

We set up my office, where I am typing at this minute, as Emily's room. We installed a baby gate across the door. It is a dog-free zone. With this safe harbor, she could relax.

PUT HER ON A ROUTINE

The more predictability there is in a cat's life, the less stress there is. For this reason, Emily's meals were regulated, her play times predictable, and her cuddle times consistent.

Give Her "Free Time"

To give her a break, we put all the other animals away for a couple of hours in the early evening so that Emily could spend time with us uninterrupted and unconcerned. She adored this. Giving her that free time not only strengthened her bond with us, but made her more daring around the house, venturing from her safe room to our bedroom and back several times a day.

Tend to Her Diet

Because she was showing signs of stress and because I knew she had been under stress for months, I made sure she was getting everything she needed nutritionally and then some. I put her on a high-quality, easily digestible food with little artificial anything. I offered her lots of fresh water. She gets a coat supplement and a multi-vitamin daily.

Release Stress

Play and exercise are the best stress releasers around for all of us. Cats are no exception. Emily's repertoire of games is pretty limited, but she is not above chasing a ball. Do what your cat is interested in, there is no point going uphill with a cat.

Give Her Something Else to Think About

Teaching her a few basics like "Come" and "Sit" always helps. Its fun for both of you, and has a stabilizing effect. You'd be surprised how much it impacts on your cat.

All of the above makes for a good start. It can be a tricky problem to get under control. Think of success in terms of weeks and months, not days. Like any stress-triggered habit—biting nails, picking cuticles, or overeating in people—it is not going to go away instantly. Emily will still do it, but we take that as a cue that she is overwhelmed and as soon as we lessen the stress, the chewing stops again.

SUCKLING AND WOOL CHEWING

Suckling behavior, where your cat nurses on your clothing, another pet, or a blanket is responded to in many ways by owners. Some find it sweet—a throwback to kittenhood and generally endearing. Others find it disgusting, annoying, and obnoxious. The cat sees it neither way. It is an urge for the cat, an urge he neither understands nor can control. It is thought to be related to weaning too early, before the urge to nurse has extinguished naturally. In the wild, feral cats can nurse for many months. Most domestic kittens are weaned much earlier than that and separated from their mother soon after.

Some cats even develop the habit of sucking their own sides or paws. This seems to be a stress release as well, and increases in frequency and intensity with stress.

Wool chewing is another kettle of fish entirely. If you have a wool chewer, you know the problem well. If you don't, let me explain: these are cats who chew on wool, sometimes putting holes in a perfectly good blanket in a matter of minutes.

To get a handle on this behavior

you will have to approach it on a few levels.

SUPPLY ROUGHAGE
This seems to have something to do with the quest for fiber. Leaving out dry food for your cat round the clock helps. Grow greens for your cat. Reward the cat with praise and petting whenever your cat nibbles on his plants. We want to encourage him to focus his energies on a renewable resource like cat grass, and not on the brand-new virgin wool blanket in your guest bedroom.

SUPPLY AN ACCEPTABLE REPLACEMENT
Giving the cat a toy that you encourage her to suckle or chew is only fair. As always, you can hardly expect a cat to completely give up a favorite behavior unless you supply him with an acceptable outlet for those urges. There are many artificial lambskin dog toys that work well for this purpose. Or make a wool toy for the cat to use. Whenever you see her start on something inappropriate correct her with a loud noise—a wall slap or clap—then direct her to her toy. Go over to it while saying, "Where's your toy?," then point to it. Encourage her to go to it. Praise her if she does. Otherwise, bring the toy to her, coax her to play with it, then praise her. Over time, she'll get the message.

REMOVE TEMPTATION
Until you condition your cat to chew on appropriate things, remove his favorite objects. Store blankets, keep him out of certain rooms—prevention, as always, is the easiest cure. If you cannot remove everything, then supervision will be critical.

BOOBY-TRAP OBJECTS YOU CAN'T PUT AWAY
Use an anti-chew spray from the pet supply store to make favored objects unappealing to her. You may have to reapply daily for a while. Always use a small amount on a discreet corner before dousing the whole blanket, that way you can discover any fading or staining problems before you have a major mishap. You can also apply an indoor repellent.

Hyperactivity

Your cat is crazy! He's stampeding up and over everything in your home, leaping at you from under furniture, batting at you from the top of the refrigerator, tearing around the house in the middle of the night knocking things over. What's wrong with him?

Maybe, nothing. How old is your cat? For any cat less than a year old, this is perfectly normal behavior, even for some cats a bit over a year. Certain breeds have a naturally high energy level—Siamese and Abyssinians springing immediately to mind. Expect them to behave this way for many years.

Now, normal behavior does not mean acceptable behavior, so it is up to you to redirect or prevent the unwanted portions of this activity level. Here's how you can:

Energy like this must be released. You can't ask him not to run around at all, because he won't be able to be still and you won't be able to make

him be still. The best answer is to give him a positive outlet. Think of him as needing a hobby. Maybe Ping-Pong ball chasing or drag toy pursuit would be of interest to our young athlete. Whatever you decide, you will have to do it routinely, religiously, and rigorously. Don't expect one halfhearted game of chase a day to level off your young thing for the next twenty-four hours.

Consider getting your acrobat a companion, preferably one with a bit less enthusiasm for life than your troublemaker. Two companionable cats can have a great time exercising each other, making your life significantly easier. Of course, if you get two speed demons you have our sympathies.

Get him climbing structures that he can happily romp on. If you don't want him using your furniture as a gymnasium, than give him someplace he can climb on. A floor-to-ceiling cat climber is a wonderful, and in the long run a less expensive, option than your living room set.

Feed him his major meal late in the evening. A well-fed cat is often a sleepy cat. Timing meals is one way of influencing your cat's active hours.

Set up a room of his own. Although not meant as a place of banishment, bedding your roadrunner down there at night is a good way to get some rest without a midnight crash, thump, or pounce. As he matures, he'll have the run of the house, but not until he stops running in the house.

Trash Tipping

Trash cans are the fast-food windows of the cat world. If your cat is an all-you-can-eat kind of guy, then you probably have a trash can raider in your midst.

There are two basic ways of approaching this problem. One is to remove the can from the cat, the other is to remove the cat from the can. We'll take this one way at a time.

REMOVING THE CAN FROM THE CAT

Just what it sounds like. Put the trash under the sink, in a closet, or otherwise out of harm's way. Getting a can with a lid is also a painless solution. Why fight it when moving your present can or buying a new type eliminates the problem?

REMOVING THE CAT FROM THE CAN

If the can becomes less fun to go into, your cat will go into it less. If you are fortunate enough to catch your cat neck deep in a trash can, sneak up on him and give the can a good whack. The sudden noise will startle the heck out of him. If you can manage to be standing up, looking the other way instantaneously, there is a chance your cat will blame the can and not you for the surprise.

BOOBY-TRAP THE CAN

If your cat is a trash tipper, rig up three to four shake cans. Set them on the edge of a countertop or nearby surface. Tape thread to them and then tape that thread to the lip of the

C.J. Puotinen

Trash tipping is a hobby of many cats. Pumpkin here is no exception.

can. Make sure it's pretty taut. Also attach the thread to the back side of the can, running it along the wall. This will make accidental can crashing less likely. Then, let nature take its course. When the cat tips the can, the shake cans tumble down, spooking the malefactor. Alternatively, you can rest a few cans on the rear edge of the trash can, leaning against the wall. Any tipping will tumble them.

If your cat is not a trash tipper but a trash raider, try this. Put some contact paper, sticky side up, across the top of the trash, or along the rim—either way it'll deter your cat.

Finicky Eating

Let's begin with the basics. If your cat isn't losing weight, if he is passing stool on a daily basis, and your vet is unconcerned, then your cat doesn't have an eating problem. You may have a problem with his eating, but your cat is fine. I recommend buying a good book, taking up a hobby, or learning to skydive, but give the cat a break. If he looks normal, acts normal, and behaves normally—guess what? He's normal. Leave him alone. But if he is losing weight, isn't defecating regularly, and your vet is concerned, then you are right, your cat has a problem.

Of all the beings that have sought a holy grail, it is the cat who has found it—usually in a resealable pouch. Some cats, many cats, get very particular about what they even consider to be a food item, never mind edible, often limiting their options to one flavor of one brand of food. This should not be a concern to you unless that food is hard to come by or your vet does not feel it is a complete diet. If it's easy to get and vet-okayed, buy a few cases and count yourself lucky.

But what if you have to change the diet of a feline who is finicky, or how about just getting a finicky cat to eat at all?

Let's start by taking a deep breath and relaxing. No healthy animal has ever voluntarily starved herself to death. Anorexia is not chic among cats, although they may make you think it is for a few days.

Next, realize that cats, being predators, are biologically equipped to fast for a day or two with no harm done to anything. As long as they have access to clean, fresh water, a few skipped meals won't hurt. Armed with this information, you can begin.

The easiest place to start is to cut back on the regular food for a day or two. Only give one or two teaspoons of food at each meal and remove the bowl twenty minutes after it is set down. This should get your cat's appetite piqued and condition her to hit the food bowl running.

On the third day, mix a tiny amount of the new diet in. Leave a teaspoonful down for twenty minutes and remove. If the cat eats, wonderful. That was easy! If she seems hungry, give her another teaspoon or so. But, don't fill her up—yet.

If she doesn't eat, don't worry. Offer the same combination again the next meal. (Fresh food please, but same mixture.) Keep telling yourself, she won't starve herself. Once she has happily consumed this combination for a day or two, up the amount of new food you add. Now it should be about 25 percent of the meal. Again, if she eats well, give her another serving.

Once she is happily consuming that, make it a 50/50 mixture. You're almost home free. Once a cat is eating half and half, the success of your venture is ensured. Keep it at half and half for a day or two. At this point you can increase the quantity to her normal meal amounts.

Slowly, over the next week or so, decrease her regular food and increase the new diet. Some cats adjust easily at this point. Others balk at a certain amount or proportion. Never mind. Just keep it at an acceptable level to your cat for a few more days. She'll adjust.

Now you are done and the whole thing didn't take long. A slow changeover is not only easier for most cats mentally but allows their system to adjust to the new diet, thereby avoiding diarrhea and stomach upsets.

A word of warning here: A hungry cat is a resourceful cat. Keep everything off your counter and put dishes in the dishwasher right away. We don't need her supplementing her diet with stolen leftovers and sabotaging the whole process.

Plant Eating

Cats need and crave greens. Some cats like them more than others, but most will indulge at some point. Cats, with no other supply of green matter, may eat house plants, many of which are toxic. For a partial list, see page 36.

The best way to deal with this problem is to both supply your cat with acceptable greens to eat and to move the unacceptable ones out of harm's way.

Moving the house plants out of the way can be done by hanging them from the ceiling, putting them in a room that can be closed off to your cat, spraying them down with Bitter Apple plant spray, or creating a sticky moat around them.

Cats eat more than meat in the wild. Here, Ben indulges in a bit of grass.

Sarah Wilson

The Bitter Apple spray is made specially for plants and will not harm them. You may need to respray them every few days, as it tends to lose its effectiveness over time. As long as you offer your cat something he is supposed to nibble on, he should soon forget his plant-destroying ways.

Creating a sticky moat around a large potted plant with double-sided tape or inverted contact paper discourages most cats from approaching the plant. But again, unless you give him a good alternative, he has little choice but to figure out a way around your setup.

Growing your own cat salad is easy, and a necessary part of any house-plant-eating cat rehabilitation program.

HOW TO GROW CAT SALAD

Growing greens is easy once you realize one thing—plants want to grow. Given half a chance, seeds grow into plants. And half a chance for plants means food, light, and water.

Here's a no-frills, never-fail way to grow greens. I start a pot every month so I have a steady supply of fresh greens for my animals.

1. Put potting soil into a hard-to-tip plastic pot that has a bottom drainage hole and a saucer. Water well and allow it to drain for half an hour.

2. Spread the seeds (wheat, alfalfa, plain grass seed) across the soil, then run your fingers back and forth, burying the seeds shallowly in the soil. Press the soil down lightly.

3. Put plastic wrap over the top and stick the pot in a warm, dark spot. Check it daily for sprouting. If the soil looks dry around the edges, mist it a couple of times. If there is lots of condensation on the plastic, let the pot air for an hour before re-covering.

4. Once you see sprouts, put the pot on a bright windowsill and mist as needed. Avoid direct sunlight, a bright window is better. When the plants are well up, remove the plastic wrap, and water via the saucer.

5. Keep the soil moist, but not wet, and let your cat enjoy. It's that simple!

Taming the Feral Cat

Cats that raise themselves outside of human contact cannot be called domesticated. If they don't learn to enjoy human company as kittens, teaching them these skills later on is difficult and rarely completely effective.

Cats that were raised with people but for whatever reason were forced to fend for themselves for a period of time are easier to resocialize. But since cats don't wear tags saying, "I was kicked out at an early age," you will have to approach both in the same manner and take it from there.

You will need two things when you begin this process. The first is patience and the second is leverage. Patience is critical, as taming anything takes as long as it takes. Trusting you is completely up to the cat. You cannot force trust, and attempting to do so will set you back, possibly irretrievably, in the process.

Understand something here. The reason most cats survive in the wild is that they are shy, run rather than fight, retreat rather than explore, and generally take an extremely conservative view toward life. They will arrive in your home nocturnal, fearful, and predatory—otherwise, they would have never lasted a week on their own. Rehabilitating them is going to take time, probably a lot of time, and probably the best you will achieve is a rather tame feral cat, not a normal house pet. Knowing that, let's continue.

By leverage, we mean you have to have something the cat wants so you can influence his behavior. Food is normally that leverage. A reliable source of delicious food is a pretty irresistible force for an animal who's been toughing it out on his own for a while.

Feed him meals, twice a day. By becoming the meal bringer, you have already become an important person in his eyes. Do not attempt to approach him and do not look at him at first. Just enter the room, put down the food, and leave. Speak to him warmly and calmly as you do this. Try to say the same things every time, this will become part of the soothing routine for him.

Continue at this level until the cat stays relaxed when you enter. If he comes toward you anticipating dinner, great! That's marvelous. But even just sitting there, not hiding or cowering, should be considered a victory. Turning his head to watch you go about your business is an excellent sign that he is at least not terrified into motionlessness anymore. His eyes will clue you in to his internal state. If the pupils are dilated, he is still frightened. If they are a normal size for the light condition, then he is truly calming down. Once that is accomplished, move a bit closer to the cat to put down dinner. Keep up your dinnertime conversation, the familiar sound of your voice and words will help to relax him.

Spend as much time in the room as possible, doing as little as possible. Take to reading in his area. Don't look at or attempt to touch him during these visits. Even if he makes contact with you let it all be on his

**MAXIMUM
SECURITY PLEASE!**

Frightened cats,
newly acquired cats,
anxious cats—may
try to run off. Check
that all windows are
tightly shut and that
they have excellent
screens on them
strong enough to
withstand the weight
of your animal.

Make sure there
are always two or
more doors between
your new pet and the
outdoors. Cats are
astonishingly quick
when they want
to be.

terms. Allow him to explore, without moving toward or looking at him. Having a snack plate of yummy treats with you never hurts. Toss one in his general direction if he comes near. Even if he eats it later, that's okay. Over time he'll relax and eat it when you are there. Regardless, he'll still be associating your smell with a small pleasure.

Leave a radio or TV on with the volume set low to get him used to the sounds of humans. Make a tape of your voice and play that when you are away. Read quietly out loud. Every little bit helps.

If all your efforts go unrewarded and your feline friend is just as frightened after a couple of weeks as he was at the beginning, speak to your veterinarian. There are several effective and safe drugs available that may help him to calm down enough so that he can learn to enjoy your presence.

If medication doesn't work, you can try setting up an area where he can live undisturbed and in peace. A large cage built outside, or in the garage with plenty of climbing and hiding places, can become a safe haven for him.

But if a safe haven isn't possible and nothing is working, you have a tough choice. Asking an animal to live in terror is inhumane. Returning him to the wild to take his chances with weather, poisons, dogs, disease, and other cats is not humane either. The kindest choice, and the hardest choice, is to have him euthanized, an alternative we hate, but better than dying a slower, more agonizing death on his own.

Fearfulness

It is quite normal for a cat to be shy of new places, people, and things. It is predictable that a stray, abused, or newly acquired cat will be particularly shy. No one likes seeing an animal frightened, and although shyness is natural, there are things you can do to help your cat be more confident.

SOCIALIZING A YOUNGSTER

The more pleasant experiences your kitten has with people early in her life, the more relaxed and trusting she will be as she matures. Of course, if you have an adult cat, you can still work on expanding her horizons, it may just take a little longer.

If you have a bold kitten your job will be saving your guests from her intrusive curiosity. But if you don't, try the following.

As with all things, allow your kitten or cat to set her own pace. Your job is to make the interaction with strangers pleasant, if she decides to attempt it. Instruct your friends not to pursue the kitten, rather to allow the kitten to come to them. If the kitten does approach, allow the kitten to investigate first, before the person acknowledges the kitten's presence. Then have your friend offer a favored treat. Allow the kitten to eat it without interruption. Repeat three to four times. If the kitten seems relaxed or even eager, have the person start stroking the kitten a bit as the treat is given.

Another approach is to have the friend invite the kitten to play a game. A drag toy, casually drawn back and forth in the cat's view, is often all that is needed to elicit a rollicking romp. Play will relax the cat and give him pleasure, linking both those things with the stranger's presence.

MAKING A HIDING PLACE

Any frightened cat needs a place to hide, where they feel safe. It is much more convenient to give them a spot that is easy to get to than to allow them to select their own, which is inevitably out of the way.

Putting a box with an old sweater in it in the back of a closet often fits the bill nicely. But whether your cat uses the one you provide or selects his own, respect it. Do not ever reach in and haul him out, unless you have no other option. Like, the house is on fire, he escaped midbath, he ate something poisonous, or the vet appointment is in twenty minutes and it's a thirty-minute drive. Other than those things, leave him alone! If he can trust his sanctuary, he is much more likely to venture out.

REWARDING COURAGE

For a kitten or cat, getting a special treat from a stranger is a tremendous reward for courage. But if they can't manage that yet, try fasting them for a day or so. Then, when the guest is visiting, lay a trail of treats from your cat's hiding place to the door of the room where you will be entertaining. Use small, infrequent treats at the

beginning. As the trail gets closer to the doorway, put down bigger and better teats, with a small jackpot at the end. Then allow nature to take its course.

Pay absolutely no attention to whether the cat comes out or not. When your visit is over, wander over to the trail picking up any leftovers and see how far your cat managed to get. Over time, your cat will become bolder with this, eventually making it all the way to the doorway. Great! Next time put the jackpot a bit further into the room. Once the cat regularly gets to the jackpot, move it again, a foot or so forward.

Will this take a while? Sure, but what's the rush? It doesn't really matter, does it? If your cat wants to hide in his safe house, that's his business. Try not to get too invested in it. He's probably not nearly as upset about the situation as you are.

IGNORING FEAR

One mistake that almost every animal-loving person makes is they inadvertently reward fear. The cat begins to look frightened, you stroke her, saying in a soothing tone "It's okay, baby. Don't worry." Congratulations, you have just praised your cat for acting fearful.

It is universally true that none of us ever say "Don't worry" unless there is something real to worry about. "Don't worry" and "It's okay" become cue words for animals that something bad is happening or is about to happen. This is often established by the owner being concerned about the cat's reaction, not the situa-

tion itself. For example: You take your new kitten to the vet. The kitten is cautious, but not terrified. You are anxious about the shots and worried the cat will become frightened. You start stroking her rapidly while saying, "It's okay, it's okay." The kitten becomes tense because you are tense. When the shots do come, they reinforce the kitten's fears. Now the phrase "It's okay" and that tone of your voice instantly puts the kitten on alert. Something is up, something bad.

When we are nervous, we all tend to increase the speed and intensity of our breathing, talking, and petting. Your cat will pick right up on your tension as signs that danger is approaching. Help your cat by slowing your speech, hands, and breathing. Take a deep breath, exhale slowly, and relax. Work on sounding and act-ing casual. Your calm demeanor will comfort your cat.

NEVER FORCE

Forcing a fearful cat is a bad idea. Frightened cats will do just about anything to get away from this situation. At those moments, you are not their best friend, you are in their way. They will go through, around, or over you as necessary to escape.

Not only is it often painful to attempt to force a fearful cat but it is counterproductive. It costs you your animal's trust, without which no progress in this area can be made. It will probably increase your animal's phobia about whatever he is frightened of, because now he knows he is helpless to avoid it. All in all, force is a supreme waste of time when working with a cat.

Helping the Adopted Cat Adapt

A previously normal cat can be sent into hiding when she changes homes, especially if it's from one kind of lifestyle to another. Emily, coming from the street and then the vet's, was shocked beyond belief by our rambunctious household. She just took to the closet. She came out and joined us in her own time.

Usually, your cat will get her behavioral bearings and rejoin the family. Keep a good eye on her during this time, as stress can trigger illness and an illness can go undetected if your cat is nowhere to be seen.

If the hiding persists for more than a week, start getting sneaky. Cut her meals in half. Then, at night, when all is quiet, lay a trail of her food around the apartment and go to bed. If you feed wet food, use small paper plates. Leave larger portions in distant corners of her new domain. Keep the rest of the offerings tiny, so her appetite stays good. Her rumbling stomach may spur on her courage.

If you have other animal family members, confine them at night as well. Keep them in the bedroom with you and close the door. Let her have some privacy in which to explore.

Of course, none of the above applies if she is missing her box at this time. If that's going on, fix that first as instructed earlier in this section and then move on to fighting her fearfulness.

And, as with all frightened cats, be extra polite when you attempt to handle her. As long as she is relaxed, slowly extend your hand to within a foot or so of her face and stop. Look at her briefly, then look away. Don't stare at her. Speak to her calmly, say her name. Tell her how wonderful she is and how great this new place is.

If she withdraws at any point of the approach, *stop*. If she shows no interest, go no further. Either go away or sit quietly near her. Read a book, draw a picture, write a letter, but whatever you do, be calm and quiet and leave her alone. If she sniffs your hand and shows some curiosity, slowly reach in and stroke her under her jaw and neck. The quickest way to gain your cat's trust is to take things slow.

Separation Anxiety

Cats who have trouble with being alone are stressed. They may cry, be destructive, or eliminate outside the litter box. There are several ways to handle this.

CONFINE YOUR CAT WHEN YOU ARE AWAY
Every time your cat does a certain unwanted behavior, it becomes a more deeply ingrained habit. Preventing him from making the mistake in the first place goes a long way to breaking the unwanted cycle.

GIVE HIM PHYSICAL EXERCISE
A bored cat is often a naughty cat. Make sure you are giving him a good ten-minute aerobic workout twice a day, once in the morning and once at night. With one of the many available drag or fishing pole type toys, you can exercise your cat as you drink your coffee and watch the morning news.

GIVE HIM MENTAL EXERCISE
Playing with him will stimulate him mentally, but teaching him behaviors will make him work mentally. Mental work is almost as calming as physical work, so don't overlook it.

DO NOT PUNISH HIM
Punishing a stressed cat only makes him more stressed. More stress means more unwanted behavior. No matter what you come home to, stay calm. If you want to scold anyone, scold yourself. He should have been confined, shouldn't he?

CONSIDER GETTING HIM A COMPANION
Most cats like company, or at least grow to like company. Having company during the day certainly makes the day go faster, and takes the pressure off of you. Think about it. Having two cats is little more work than one, unless you have soft-coated, longhaired cats that require daily grooming.

Keeping Cats out of the Sandbox or Garden

Many cats seek out loose, easy-to-dig-in soil in which to relieve themselves. Unfortunately for all of us gardeners and sandbox users, our favorite places to relax are often cats' favorite places to dirty. How can a cat be discouraged from using these areas?

SANDBOXES
Sometimes the simplest answers are the best, so in short—keep a lid on it. There are sandboxes available that come with a cover. Or, you can build an easy-to-use lid. Tarps are lightweight and inexpensive, but they tend to hold water in the center, which can be a pain. The best option is a wooden lid in one or two sections depending on the size of the box. Not only will a lid keep your cat out of the box, but it keeps the sand dry, which is nice for your kids.

GARDENS

A good fence around your garden can keep a cat out, depending on the cat. Spot liked to climb the chain link fence. She did so regularly, walking along the top rail. Ben, although he saw Spot do this many times, never picked up the habit.

If your cat is not a fence climber, then a good fence should work fine. If he is, or if a fence is not something you want, here are a few other ideas: Cover your rows or seed beds with plastic. Not only will this discourage most cats from digging but it improves growing conditions for most plants. Other options include spreading a nontoxic repellent around the outside of your garden, or installing a low electric fence.

When You Can't Keep Your Cat

Adding a cat to your household is a long-term commitment, one that you hopefully considered fully before you acquired your feline friend, but there are rare times when you just can't keep your cat.

I have heard many reasons for having to give up a cat and many of them are ridiculous. "He doesn't match my new decor" is one of the stupidest reasons we ever heard. A cat is a living, feeling being—not a decorative item. If, for whatever reason, you cannot keep your cat there is a right way and a wrong way to find him a new home.

PLAN AHEAD

The most important step to finding a good home for your friend is time: taking the time to interview potential owners carefully, and having the time to turn a few people down if need be before you find the right home.

GET THE WORD OUT

There always seem to be nice people looking for nice animals, but they won't find you if you don't get the word out. Make up flyers, then post them in local vet's, pet supply stores, groomers, and supermarkets. Put an ad in your local paper. Tell people you meet, friends, co-workers, people at the stores you commonly use. A friend of a friend of the waitress at the diner may just be a wonderful home!

GET REFERENCES

We don't mean to scare you but there is a booming business in this country selling healthy unwanted pets to laboratories for research purposes. It is our belief that no home-raised companion animal should ever be used in experimentation. People who do this know they are unpopular and will not tell you the truth. They are salesmen, selling you on their interest in your cat. They are experts at sounding like wonderful folks. Fortunately, protecting yourself and your friend from this fate is not too complicated.

If the prospective new owners have had pets before, their veterinarian is the ideal reference. But other references are okay, too. This is not foolproof, but it's a good start.

DO NOT ABANDON

It seems to be a widely held belief, judging from the number of cats dumped in wooded areas and along lonely highways every year, that house pets can survive on their own. They CANNOT.

You are not "giving them a chance." You are sentencing them to death. It's just a death you don't have to deal with.

Abandoned animals usually die horribly. Mauled by dogs or wild animals, struck by cars but not killed immediately, starving, eating poison, or swallowing bones causing long suffering—the list is not pretty, but it is real.

If you cannot keep your animal, take it to a shelter. At least there, if a home cannot be found, your cat's death will be quick and painless. It's the least you can do for the animal who relies on you.

Make Them Wait

Do not give the cat to anyone on the first visit. Beware people who press you too hard on this issue. If they are leaving town, live a great distance, etc.—pass. People who are really interested won't mind waiting a day or two.

Check Them Out

Get an address and phone number, then call the number. Call information in their town and check that the listing matches. If the address is local, go there. This is a bit paranoid, but more than one owner has handed over their cat to a person who gave an address that didn't exist and a phone number that wasn't working.

If things check out, they are probably just anxious, wonderful, soon-to-be cat owners. Most people are honest, but because selling animals is big business, it pays to be a little cautious on your friend's behalf.

Taking the Cat to a Shelter

Public shelters do the best they can for the animals in their care, but the sheer numbers of animals abandoned is overwhelming in many areas. The majority of cats nationwide never find homes and have to be humanely destroyed. Older cats, in particular, are hard for shelters to place. If your cat is over a certain age, many shelters will not even attempt to adopt him out. He will simply be euthanized. This may seem harsh but shelters are driven by harsh realities. They would love to adopt out every animal they get, but there simply aren't enough homes. For every cage

taken up by an older, less adoptable cat, younger, more adoptable kittens will have to be killed. In the time the older cat waits, not being adopted, perhaps two to four kittens could have found homes. Only about one out of every ten animals dropped off at a shelter ever finds a permanent home.

Unfair? You bet. Spay and neuter your cats! Tell other people to spay and neuter their cats. Then no one would have to make such gruesome decisions ever again. But until that happens, do not blame the shelters for doing what they must. It is our fault, all cat owners' fault, that it has to be done at all.

There are many private no-kill shelters. There are often long waiting lists for animals coming into these places, so call ahead. Because they are no-kill, spots don't open up as often, and they have limited space. They may also be more selective about the type of animal they elect to take in. Animals that are hard to place for behavioral or health reasons may be turned away. Call and find out the details; all local shelters should be listed in the Yellow Pages under "Humane Society" or "Animal Shelter."

Beware of places that promise, for a small donation, to care for your cat for life regardless of behavioral or health problems. If something sounds too good to be true, it probably is. We've seen too many such places turn from good intentions into animal concentration camps where beloved family pets are packed into filthy cages with little food or water. The details are too horrible to print but never leave your cat anywhere unless you have seen where the animals are kept with your own eyes. If the staff won't let you see the facilities, take your cat elsewhere.

Living with an Older Cat

As cats age, they become even more focused on their creature comforts. Warmth, ease, and convenience become the priorities. If you have never gotten one before, your aging cat may enjoy an easy-to-reach perch situated in a sunny window.

Food bowls and litter boxes should be close at hand. Any leaping that has been a requirement in years past may now just be one leap too far for your aging friend.

A woman called us quite upset because her sixteen-year-old cat, who had never had a house-soiling problem before, was now dirtying in the house on a regular basis. My first concern was his health but she assured me the vet had checked the cat out carefully, found nothing wrong, and referred her to us.

That being the case we continued. As the Christmas season was approaching, I asked if her schedule had changed recently, if she was out more or entertaining guests. No, was the reply to all those questions. Well then, had she moved the box or changed brands of litter? No, she answered, it's on the fire escape where it's always been. The fire escape? In December! The case was solved.

For her aging cat, hopping out the window in subzero temperatures was not as much fun as it used to be. He had decided that a cat of his advancing years and experience could surely find a better solution than squatting out in the cold. And he did—squatting below the open window. When she brought the box inside, the problem disappeared. Cats are so eloquent.

Cats (and humans for that matter) slow down with age. The body gets achy, nerves and brain cells die off forever, leaving the messages sent from the brain to the body and back having to take the long road. And once the message is received, the body may not want to do what has been requested anyway.

As the nerves and brain cells die, the senses dull. Vision blurs, hearing lessens, smell depletes—not that any of this normally bothers the animal. Cats cope. They have to, they have no other options. They don't have dreams that some drug or potion will renew their youth. They don't have regrets for things undone or harsh words spoken. They accept age with the same grace as they accept the rest of their lives.

Older, slower does not mean dead however. And this is no time to stop playing his favorite games or taking a favorite walk. Older cats adore your company, seeming to appreciate the pleasures of a warm lap and a loving touch more than ever.

WHAT YOU CAN DO

You can make this time in your cat's life easier and safer if you do a few easy things.

COMMON OLD-AGE HEALTH PROBLEMS

TUMORS

Watch for any kind of lump on your cat's body. These are pretty common with some older cats and many are harmless, but all should be watched carefully and brought to your vet's attention. If you spayed your female late in her life or never spayed her at all, be on the lookout for any unusual mammary swelling.

URINARY PROBLEMS

Here's a common problem in older cat. Watch his water intake. Keep his box extremely clean. Put boxes near his favorite sleeping areas. Expect the occasional accident as your cat ages. But if they become frequent, if your cat is drinking a lot more water, if he is urinating frequently and profusely—get to your vet.

(continued)

Nancy Gush

Older cats crave warmth. Shotzie's no fool, he's napping in front of the heat duct. I guess that makes him a Hot Shotz.

PROVIDE WATER

Make sure he has plenty of fresh water in an easy-to-reach place. As cats get older, they are particularly susceptible to kidney and urinary problems. Drinking adequate amounts of water helps to combat these.

WATCH HIS WEIGHT

Weigh your cat once a month. Any drastic weight change—up or down more than 15 percent—is worth a call to the vet. Weight loss without a diet change can point to dental, kidney, thyroid, or other problems.

Excess weight puts a strain on the whole system. Obesity makes diabetes, surgical complications, and heart problems more likely. I know it is hard to resist a hungry cat, but love

him enough to do so. He can't watch his weight, you have to.

As he ages, his diet may need to be changed or limited. This is especially true if your cat becomes more sedentary. When he gets older, discuss food concerns with your vet before you make any change. Follow your veterinarian's recommendation.

GET A HEALTH WORKUP

Once your cat hits the double digits, it's not a bad idea to get a good general checkup for him as well as some baseline blood workups. Not only will this tell you if something is brewing but it gives you numbers to refer back to if a problem develops later.

Catching problems early is one of the best ways to insure your cat's long-term health. It's a good idea as your cat ages to see your veterinarian twice a year. Cats age more quickly than we do. Waiting a year between checkups is a little like only seeing your doctor once between the ages of sixty and sixty-six. Not a good plan, is it?

CHECK HIS BREATH

No, this is not to detect late-night carousing, it is to watch for signs of dental disease. Poor oral health and infections can take a real toll on your cat's general health. Anyone who has ever had a severe toothache knows what misery that is. Your cat gets gum disease and oral infections just like we do, so his mouth needs to be checked at least twice a month. Carefully look for swollen, inflamed gums or a foul odor. A sore mouth can cause a cat to stop eating. This is serious in an older cat, and could be a sign of more trouble than just a problem in his mouth! Any of these conditions warrants an immediate trip to the vet.

MAKE THINGS EASY

Set food and water bowls on the floor near his favorite sleeping spot. Litter boxes should not be too high-sided as the cat slows down. Put a litter box on every floor. An aging cat's bladder control may not be what it used to be. If he has a favorite perch but is having a hard time reaching it, consider moving your furniture around a bit to provide a step up. A trunk slid under a window perch may be just the thing for an arthritic older cat.

GIVE HIM A PRIVATE SPOT

For all cats, sleep is their national pastime. For older cats it is a fundamental requirement. If you have a busy household, or if your cat just likes his privacy, set up a special place for him that is warm and cozy. A bed near a radiator, a box with a blanket under a light, a window perch in the sun—nothing fancy, just a comfortable spot where the dreaming is good.

BOARDING

Even if you have successfully boarded your cat in the past, consider finding a pet sitter for him as he ages. Boarding, even in the best of circumstances, is stressful for a cat and stress can bring on illness. Don't blame a good boarding facility if your older animal gets sick or passes away while staying there. It probably isn't their fault. The stress of it all brought out underlying problems or lowered his resistance to disease. Whenever possible, don't board elderly animals.

A pet sitter who comes to your home is a far better option for an older cat. That way he can curl up on your bed and not be frightened of new noises, strange people, or the barking of many dogs.

Information on professional pet sitting is in the Bibliography and Resources section. Other resources include neighbors, your local vet, groomer, and your local pet supply store. Asking around and putting up signs are good ways of locating people.

There are many reasons for these problems, things can be done—just don't wait.

CONSTIPATION
Older cats often get constipated occasionally. This is not unusual. But persistent constipation is cause for alarm and you should speak to your vet about it. For occasional trouble, consider giving a bit of milk if that's not something your cat gets regularly. Milk loosens up many cats quite naturally. Don't give him a huge amount, though—you don't want to go from one problem straight to another.

HEART PROBLEMS
If your cat suddenly seems lethargic, sleeps constantly, maybe has a cough, ask your vet about possible heart trouble. It isn't all that common but it does occur.

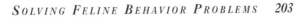

Photos by Eileen Nixon

Tina has grown up with Larue by her side. At the time of this writing, Larue is twenty-four plus or minus a year or two and Tina is married, expecting her first child. These two have truly been lifetime companions.

GROOMING

Ah, to be young again—to gracefully reach around and groom the base of your tail or to spryly toss your rear leg over your head to get to the areas that need your attention. Such feats of limberness may not be as simple as they used to be. Your cat may need more brushing to remove loose hair, or combing to control tangles. His nails, once points of pride, may need your attention. The extra care he needs now has its benefits. Brushing and combing him several times a week guarantees you will be touching him all over, noticing any new bumps or lumps as well as hair loss and scabs.

GENTLE PLEASE!

As your cat ages, his skin becomes more delicate, his coat thins, he may lose weight—all of which add up to a sensitivity to grooming. Put away your wire slicker brush, use a comb or a natural-bristle brush instead. Brush gently and carefully, in slow strokes, carefully watching your cat's reactions. A good grooming should still make him purr with bliss.

EXERCISE

My grandmother practiced yoga every morning for decades, and as a woman in her sixties and seventies she was more limber than I was in my twenties. There is no reason an older cat can't maintain strength and flexibility, as long as he takes it slow. There is much you can do with your cat to encourage him to stay active.

PULL YOURSELF UP

Supporting your cat under the chest and rear, put him in front of the edge of your bed. Slowly lower him. Chances are he will reach up and grab hold, attempting to pull himself up. Support him as he does this, then slowly lower him again. This is a good basic chin-up with you helping at every step.

REACH FOR THE FLOOR

Supporting your cat under his chest and rear, lower him toward the ground. Tilt him so his front is lower than his rear. As he approaches the floor, chances are he'll reach out for it. Good! Allow him to stretch, then lift him back up and repeat.

ARCH YOUR BACK

Often, by simply scratching at the base of your cat's tail or on the top of the spine your cat will arch their back. This is a good overall stretch. Do a couple in a row.

GENTLE STRETCHING EXERCISES

When your cat is relaxed and lying down, sit down and start stroking him. Speak to him affectionately. Gently take his front legs and stretch them forward. Most cats will enjoy the stretch. You can feel them stretch and then relax. When he relaxes, slowly release. Do the same thing to the rear legs. You can also give him a nice body stretch by gently stretching the front legs and rear legs at once. One hand behind his elbows, one by his hind legs. Always release gently when the stretch is over or if the cat does not seem to enjoy it. The key to these exercises is to be sensitive to the animal's limits, never forcing anything. Once the cat understands that you will release and you are gentle, he'll adore these little sessions.

MINI-MARATHONS

Putting her down away from her food bowl or favorite sleeping place forces her to hustle a bit to reach them. Feel free to be a bit fiendish—moving her bowl a few times during a meal so she has to walk more each time, holding her in your lap as an ac-

complice shows her the bowl and then goes to the other end of the house. Do what is necessary to get her moving. The more she moves, the better.

Make up your own exercises. As long as they are gentle, slow, and your cat enjoys them, go ahead. Be creative. Cats are rugged individuals who develop a routine to suit yours.

ADDING A KITTEN

For some cats, adding a kitten to the house can be just what they needed to up their exercise, bring interest back into their lives, and generally add to the quality of their life. For other cats, it is a nightmare, an invasion of their territory just when they are most vulnerable to invasion. A new kitten to them is about as amusing as dental work without anesthesia. You have to know your cat before you add a kitten.

If you think that it would brighten your cat's day to bring youth into your home, do it calmly and give everyone plenty of time to adjust. Make sure you spend as much time, if not more, fussing over your oldster. This extra attention will help him through the adjustment period.

Saying Goodbye

The only two downsides to sharing your life with an animal are that they don't live as long as we do and that we can choose to end their suffering. Being able to end suffering is a mixed blessing. On the one hand you get to love your companion one last time, in a profound and selfless way. You can decide that you love them too much to let the inevitable come with pain and torment. When the inevitable becomes inevitable, you can ease them out of life with as much gentleness and love as you strived to have them live it.

On the other hand, you bear the burden of that decision. When is enough enough? The cat who cries when he stretches in the morning may be the same cat that lies purring contentedly next to you at night. When do you know when it is time? Is there some other medical miracle that can be performed? If you had more money, could the cat be saved? Hard questions, real questions. Questions you will have to make your peace with.

Do your best. That has always been plenty for your cat in the past and it will serve him well now. Trust yourself and your knowledge of your companion. Some cats bear pain well, some do not. At these times, I think of my animals' lives on a scale—pleasure and contentment on one side, suffering and pain on the other. When the suffering side weighs down the pleasure side, it's probably time.

For those of you who have never

seen an animal euthanized, let me tell you something about the experience so you will be better prepared when the time comes.

You can either be with your cat when it is done or not. That is your choice. There is no right or wrong here—do what feels right for you and what is best for your friend.

If you choose to stay with your cat, strive to be as calm and happy as possible until the deed is done. That way your cat will not become worried or frightened. It is a terrible choice to have to make, but once made, I want my animal to be as relaxed and content as possible. I want the last thing they hear in the world to be my voice full of love and my hand stroking them tenderly as it has a million times before. When they are gone, I break down but I try not to beforehand.

Death comes very quickly. It is a single shot. The only pain involved is the needle itself. In the seconds it takes for the plunger to be depressed and the needle withdrawn, your friend will already be asleep and unconscious. Seconds later, it is all over.

With as many times as I have had to do this in shelters, working at a vet's and for my own animals, I am seldom prepared. I always feel as if it happened too fast, that I wasn't ready. Savor your last few moments with your cat well before the needle goes in. After that—it is over.

Most vets are extremely thoughtful and sensitive to your loss. They will give you whatever time you need with your friend. Stay for a few minutes if you want, or go, whatever feels right.

I ask when I set up the appointment for the clinic to bill me or I send the money ahead of time because I am always a wreck afterward. It never makes a difference how right it is to my head, it is never right to my heart.

Eulogy for Spot

Something in our home had to be named Spot, and this little bit of a Manx kitten fit the bill. She was pure white with gray-black splotches around her ears, and one by the base of her nonexistent tail. She was everything we had hoped for, sweet, and people-oriented beyond belief, she lived for shoulder riding. When we bent over in our garden she leaped from the fence onto our backs. She was born purring and seldom stopped. Her love of humanity extended to children, whom she adored.

But she had a physical problem that turns out to be a Manx genetic defect that comes from breeding for no tail. What happens when you get no tail is you sometimes don't get enough spinal column at the same time. Not enough spinal column can lead to, and did in Spot's case, not being able to control her bowels.

This was heartbreaking for all of us, especially for her, since she wanted to be close to a human at all times. She developed an ongoing rash, was dirty most of the time, and couldn't understand why no one wanted her to sit on their shoulder anymore.

It was a terrible situation and a terrible decision to have to make. Her problem caused her no pain, just confusion and heartbreak as the things she valued most in her life, humans, shunned her. We did everything we could think of to alleviate the situation but without success. After much soul searching and discussions with our vet, we all felt that euthanasia was the kindest option in an unkind situation.

It was the hardest euthanasia we have ever done. Spotty was loving to the end, trusting every step. Purring, rubbing against us, rubbing against the vet, not fighting the handling we had to do, not fighting the needle, not fighting her own death. We wept for a long time then. We weep now as we write this. It is the one time that we are sorry we are cat lovers, although we are never sorry that we knew Spot. She was a great gift and we will not dishonor her life by regretting her death.

Goodbye, Spotty.

Sarah Wilson

Spot loved children. Spot was a good soul who will always be missed.

Frequently Asked Questions

My cat Ruby is thirteen years old. Since I moved into a new apartment a few months back she has been waking me up several times a week, by yowling in the living room. I can call her in to comfort her, but it seems to be getting worse. I have several other cats, none of whom are having any trouble. What is going on?

In short, what started out as a normal reaction to a move has now become a learned behavior. Without being able to ask you more, I am betting that of all your cats this one is the most reserved. She is easy to miss day to day, your other more outgoing cats getting most of the attention.

The first night she did this, she probably was a bit confused by the new surroundings. But when you called her in to you and comforted her, she realized she was onto something good here. For once she had your undivided attention, with all her competition being sound asleep. By petting her and comforting her, you effectively rewarded her for waking you up. Now, months later, she is simply doing what you trained her to do, wake you up at 3:00 A.M.

Oops!

Changing this behavior requires a two-pronged approach. One, you have to make sure her needs are met during more convenient hours. And two, you need to discourage this behavior.

Give her extra attention in the evening. Establish a playtime where she gets to release some of this pent-up energy and stress. Groom her, stroke her—make sure she gets plenty of attention. This should help her relax.

Then at night, when she starts yowling, don't call her in to you. Giving her any attention will only reward her obnoxious behavior. Either shut her in your bedroom with you so she can't go out wandering, or shut her out so she can't wake you up. Any way you work it out, simply ignore the noise.

If you can't ignore it, give her a silent correction with a couple of long-distance squirts from a plant mister, then go back to bed. She's no dummy, she'll put two and two together.

Why does my cat make scratching motions around her food dish?

She is burying it. It doesn't seem to matter to the cat that she isn't really burying anything, it's motion that's important.

In the wild, a cat may cover a partially eaten kill to save it for later. It also appears to be a feline version of sending it back to the kitchen. If your cat finds something distasteful, she may well go through the motions of burying it.

My cat sleeps all day long. Is this okay?

Okay, normal, and not to be worried about—usually. Most cats sleep most of the day. Animals that survive by hunting carefully conserve their energy when they are not out looking for food. This is a sensible thing to do when you don't know when you'll be able to catch your next meal. The behavior continues, even in our pampered domestic cats who have

Sarah Wilson

Cats sleep a great deal of the time. Here Ben nods off for an afternoon snooze.

plasmosis to become infectious in feces, so if the box is cleaned daily there is little chance of a problem developing.

Nonetheless, your spouse should clean the box and wash thoroughly after doing so. If you have to clean the box, wear rubber gloves, use a clean long-handled scoop, and wash thoroughly afterward. Your cat(s) should be tested and kept inside for the duration of your pregnancy. Then you should relax, you've got more of a worry from eating or handling raw and undercooked meat than from your feline friend purring on your ever-growing belly.

Can cats tell time?

That's an excellent question. On one hand, we say no, not in the sense we humans mean it, although cats can become extremely attuned to routines and certainly know full well when it's 7:00 A.M. We've had too many cats wake us up on the dot to doubt that skill. But if they have an internal sense of time or are working off some subtle external cues, like some sound the alarm clock makes just before it goes off, we cannot say.

In a larger sense, cats can have an astounding sense of something, maybe it's time. Growing up, when Sarah went off to camp, Captain would take off too. For eight weeks he would not be seen, but the day of Sarah's arrival home he would be sitting on the steps or spotted in a back field. He was always on time, summer after summer, though none of us ever knew how he did it. It is nice to know that there are still a few mysteries left in the world.

never skipped a meal in their lives.

Certain breeds are more prone to napping than others—Persians and Himalayans spring to mind. But if your normally active cat all of a sudden can't seem to stay awake for more than a few minutes, a call to your vet is warranted.

I'm pregnant and my mother-in-law says I shouldn't keep my cats, that they can damage my baby somehow. Is this true?

There is a disease called toxoplasmosis that you can get from your cat *if* your cat has it. You can also get it from undercooked meat, which is the way most people get it. If you have had cats your whole life, there's a good chance you've had it. When Sarah was tested, she found out she had it long ago. Most people don't even know they've been infected, since its symptoms are similar to the flu.

The story for cats is that they get it from eating birds and rodents. If you have an indoor cat, chances are your cat doesn't have it. You can have your cat tested, then keep it inside until after you give birth.

It takes one to five days for toxo-

A Final Word

We hope that you have enjoyed this book, we certainly enjoyed writing it. We have remembered, laughed, struggled, and learned. It's been a journey, a good journey.

Cats have always been and will always be a big part of our lives. They greet us each morning and curl up with us each night. They work with us daily, although they were especially interested in this book for some reason.

We hope that this book helps you include cats in your life in the easiest way possible, bringing joy to both your cats and yourself.

May there always be a cat to comfort you when you are sad, to amuse you when you are bored, to keep you company when you are lonely, to remind you that a nap in the sun is a fine thing, and to show you that the natural world is always just a purr and a pounce away.

All our best and a caress to your cat—

Brian and Sarah

Brian Kilcommons

Bibliography and Resources

BOOKS

Caras, Roger.
A Cat Is Watching.
New York: Fireside Books, 1990.
Always entertaining, Roger Caras has a wealth of experience with animals of all sorts. He is a prolific writer, and any of his works are well worth reading.

Clark, Ross D., ed.
Medical, Genetic & Behavioral Aspects of Purebred Cats.
Georgia: Forum Publications, 1992.
This book is a must if you are looking into owning or breeding purebred cats. Contains an in-depth listing of genetic problems, if any, associated with each breed and much more. It's a bit expensive but not compared to a purebred kitten!

Cohen, Barbara and Louise Taylor.
Cats and Their Women.
New York: Little, Brown, 1992.
Pictures of women and their cats with stories. Wonderful fun, highly recommended. It is a book we return to again and again.

Comfort, David.
The First Pet History of the World.
New York: Fireside Books, 1994.
What a riot! This man has sought out the true, if bizarre, history of man and animal together. Amusing, appalling—we are glad we stumbled on this.

Fleming, Bill and Judy Petersen-Fleming.
The Tiger on Your Couch.
New York: Quill, 1992.
A thorough, sensible book with incredible pictures and tales of tigers and tiger training.

Jankowski, Connie.
Adopting Cats and Kittens.
New York: Howell Books, 1993.
A short, useful book for anyone adopting a cat or kitten. Ms. Jankowski is pragmatic and sensible—her experience shows.

Ryden, Hope.
Your Cat's Wild Cousins.
New York: Lodestar Books, 1991.
A children's book with fantastic pictures of a variety of wild cats by the author. Some of these cats we had never seen. A pleasure for cat lovers of all ages.

Siegal, Mordecai, ed.
The Cornell Book of Cats.
New York: Villard Books, 1991.
This is a tome! While not light reading it is a thorough medical reference on cats. All serious cat lovers need this on their shelf.

MAGAZINES

Cat Fancy
P.O. Box 52864, Boulder, CO 80322-2864; Phone: 303-786-7306.
Monthly. General Interest.

Cats Magazine
P.O. Box 420240, Palm Coast, FL 32142-0240; Phone: 904-788-2770.
Monthly. General Interest.

Cats USA
P.O. Box 55811, Boulder, CO 80322-5811; Phone: 303-786-7652.
Annual. Its focus is purebred cats and it is an excellent resource for people interested in them.

Popular Cats
Harris Publications, Inc., 1115 Broadway, New York, NY 10010; Phone: 212-807-7100.
Monthly. General Interest.

Tiger Tribe
1407 East College Street, Iowa City, IA 52245-4410; Phone: 319-351-6698.
Monthly. A holistic health care magazine for cats.

NEWSLETTERS

CATNIP : A Newsletter for Caring
  Cat Owners
Tufts University School of Veterinary Medicine
An excellent publication that gives valuable information on the medical and behavioral aspects of cats. Well worth getting.
P.O. Box 420014, Palm Court, FL 32142-0014; Phone: 800-829-0926.

Animal Health
Cornell University College of Veterinary Medicine
Unlike the Tufts newsletter, which is exclusively about cats, Cornell's covers dogs and horses as well. So if these animals interest you, this newsletter will. If they don't, you'll get less information on cats per issue than the Tufts publication.
P.O. Box 52816, Boulder, CO 80322-2816; Phone: 800-873-2808.

PET SITTING AND BOARDING

National Association of Pet Sitters
1200 G Street
Washington, DC 20005
800-296-PETS or 202-393-3312.

Pet Sitters International
418 East King Street
King, NC 27021
910-983-9222.

POISON HOTLINE

National Animal Poison Control
Center: 800-548-2423.
This service charges a fee, which
goes to support its twenty-four-
hour staffing. We are all lucky to have
this available. We are happy to pay
them for always being available with
the knowledge that might save our
cat's life.

DOG-TRAINING RESOURCES

Kilcommons, Brian and Sarah
Wilson. *Good Owners, Great Dogs.*
New York: Warner Books, 1992.
Kilcommons, Brian and Sarah
Wilson. *Childproofing Your Dog.*
New York: Warner Books, 1994.
Kilcommons, Brian and Sarah
Wilson. *Good Owners, Great Dogs*
video. New York: Family Dog
Distribution, Inc., 1990.

All of the above can be purchased
through 800-457-PETS. The books
are readily available through local
bookstores.

Index